PLAYERS' WORK TIME

Manchester University Press

WITHDRAWN
UTSA LIBRARIES

PLAYERS' WORK TIME

A history of the British Musicians' Union, 1893–2013

JOHN WILLIAMSON AND
MARTIN CLOONAN

Manchester University Press

Published by Manchester University Press
Altrincham Street, Manchester M1 7JA
www.manchesteruniversitypress.co.uk

British Library Cataloguing-in-Publication Data
A catalogue record for this book is available from the British Library

Library of Congress Cataloguing-in-Publication Data applied for

ISBN 978 1 5261 1394 8 paperback
ISBN 978 1 7849 9132 6 hardback

First published 2016

Typeset by Out of House Publishing
Printed in Great Britain
by Bell & Bain Ltd, Glasgow

For Dixie

Contents

Figures

Acknowledgements

This book would not have been possible without the support and encouragement of a number of people to whom we are indebted. We would like particularly to thank the following: the Arts and Humanities Research Council and the Economic and Social Research Council, who supplied funding for the project on which the book is based; the Musicians' Union, which supported our work in the full knowledge that we did not always support their policies; Karl Magee from the University of Stirling Archives; and Louise North at the BBC Written Archives Centre. We would also like to thank all those working in other archives that supported our work, and especially staff at Phonographic Performance Ltd and Society of London Theatre/Theatre UK for allowing access to their private archives. All of our interviewees are thanked for their time and patience and for helping to make this a much livelier account than might otherwise have been the case. In particular, Bill Sweeney was a constant source of help and advice. Alison Eales provided excellent support. The Steering Group for the project gave their time and expertise willingly and so provided invaluable support. Our sincere thanks to all. Of course, any errors and oversights are our own and we take full responsibility.

As we say in the Notes on archives and other sources, a lot of the work here derives from the Musicians' Union Archive. This was saved for posterity by Kate McBain and Neil Blain. We, and future historians, are in their debt.

At one stage we planned to call this *Dear Diary*, an in-joke that some MU members will understand. So, finally, thanks are due to the thousands of MU members who helped the Union make history. We hope that the results of our endeavours do you all justice.

Personal thanks

John would like to thank Susan Hansen, Jim Gillan, and his parents.

Martin would like to thank Claire for helping in more ways than she'll ever know, and John for going well beyond the call of duty.

In memoriam

During the work for this book, we were saddened to hear of the passing of two of our interviewees, Gary Hyde and Tony Lucas. Both were stalwarts of the MU and offered great assistance to our work. We would like to pay tribute to their generosity of spirit.

Notes on archives and other sources

This work drew on a number of archives, and here we list the main ones used and explain how they are referenced. All our references are based on the box/catalogue system used by the different archives unless stated otherwise.

Musicians' Union Archive (MU)

Based at the University of Stirling, the archive contains materials such as minutes of national executive meetings, agendas for conferences, the Union's journal, its Bulletin to Branches, correspondence, press cuttings, and financial records on both a national and local level. Where materials are used that are not otherwise available we have referenced them here, in the manner adopted at Stirling, according to which box they are in: e.g. MU, 2/1/5. The full catalogue can be found at www.calmview.eu/stirling/CalmView/Record.aspx?src=CalmView.Catalog&id=MU&pos=1.

BBC Written Archive Centre (WAC)

The other main archive used was the BBC Written Archive Centre in Caversham, www.bbc.co.uk/historyofthebbc/research/wac. This contains written records going back to the BBC's formation in 1923, with researchers able to access documents up to 1980. It proved invaluable for unpacking the complex relationships between the BBC and the Union, and especially the key period between 1946 and the mid-1960s.

The National Archives (TNA)

The National Archives, www.nationalarchives.gov.uk, is the official archive of the UK Government. This was used primarily for materials relating to the

Union's campaigns around 'alien' musicians and the Security Services' monitoring of CPGB activity within the Union.

Modern Records Centre (MRC)

The Modern Records Centre at the University of Warwick, www2.warwick.ac.uk/services/library/mrc/, contains a number of materials relating to trade unions. It was drawn on primarily for materials relating to the MU's relationships with the broader labour movement.

Farmer Collection (Farmer)

George Henry Farmer was a musicologist, musical director, and MU activist who edited the *Musicians' Journal and Monthly Report* from April 1929 to January 1933. His papers are held in the University of Glasgow's Special Collections, www.gla.ac.uk/services/specialcollections/collectionsa-z/farmercollection/.

Theatrical Managers' Association (TMA)/Society of West End Theatre Managers (SWETM)

UK Theatre and the Society of London Theatre (SOLT) – the successors of TMA and SWETM – share offices in Covent Garden. They hold various ad hoc minute books from their previous incarnations, not generally available to the public. We used them to contextualise employment arrangements in theatre orchestras.

Phonographic Performance Ltd (PPL)

Phonographic Performance Ltd is a licensing company that collects royalties on behalf of its members for the use of their music in public. We were granted access to its minute books, which were used to provide greater insight for this work. As these files remain confidential they are not cited directly here.

Orchestral Employers' Association (OEA)/Association of British Orchestras (ABO)

The OEA Archive is at the University of York: http://discovery.nationalarchives.gov.uk/details/rd/N13918123. It contains materials from the OEA's early days. The ABO has an incomplete archive of minutes and correspondence to which we were granted access and which has also been used to provide greater context.

Trades Union Congress (TUC) Archive

The TUC archive is housed at London Metropolitan University: https://metranet.londonmet.ac.uk/services/sas/library-services/tuc/geninfo.cfm and contains materials relating both to the TUC and individual unions. Materials from this archive are referenced by their original publication.

Communist Party of Great Britain (CPGB) archive

Housed at the People's History Museum in Manchester, www.phm.org.uk/archive-study-centre/, this contains a wealth of Party materials and was drawn on to flesh out its involvement in the MU. Materials from this archive are referenced by their original publication.

Jack Hylton Archive

The jazz musician's archive is located at the University of Lancaster, www.lancaster.ac.uk/library/resources/special-collections/archives/jack-hylton-archive/. This was used for details of his involvement in the MU, especially around issues of 'alien' workers. Materials from this archive are referenced by their original publication.

British Library Sound Archive

This contains a number of recorded interviews with jazz musicians and record industry personnel that we used for background. Dave Laing's (2011) interview with John Morton is not currently publicly available, but will hopefully be so by the time this book is published.

Newspaper and magazine archives

We have endeavoured to provide full details for all our sources, although it has proved impossible to reference some articles fully. As many articles, newspapers, and magazines from the period before the 1960s were not attributed to individual journalists, we have cited the source in the text but have not included them in the references.

Internet sources

Where we have only been able to use online sources, URLs are correct as of October 2015.

Abbreviations

ABO	Association of British Orchestras
ACAS	Advisory Conciliation and Arbitration Service
ACGB	Arts Council of Great Britain
AFL	American Federation of Labor
AFM	American Federation of Musicians
AGS	Assistant General Secretary
AIM	Association of Independent Music
AIRC	Association of Independent Radio Contractors
AMU	Amalgamated Musicians' Union
AURA	Association of United Recording Artists
BARD	British Association of Record Dealers
BASCA	British Association of Songwriters, Composers and Authors
BBC	British Broadcasting Corporation
BBCNSO	BBC Northern Symphony Orchestra
BBCSO	BBC Symphony Orchestra
BBCSSO	BBC Scottish Symphony Orchestra
BIP	British International Pictures
BMR	British Music Rights
BNOC	British National Opera Company
BPI	British Phonographic Industry
CALM	Campaign for the Advance of Live Music
CAS	Contract Advisory Scheme
CEA	Cinema Exhibitors' Association
CEMA	Committee for the Encouragement of Music and the Arts
CMA	Circuits Management Association
CMG	Concerned Musicians' Group
CPGB	Communist Party of Great Britain
DBDA	Dance Band Directors' Association
DCMS	Department of Culture, Media and Sport

DGS	Deputy General Secretary
DJ	disc jockey
DMPPA	Dramatic and Musical Performers' Protection Act
EC	Executive Committee
ENSC	Entertainments National Service Committee
Farmer	Farmer Collection
FIM	Fédération Internationale des Musiciens
GS	General Secretary
IBA	Independent Broadcasting Authority
ICA	Institute for Contemporary Arts
ICM	International Confederation of Musicians
IEA	Institute of Economic Affairs
IFPI	International Federation of Phonographic Industries
ILO	International Labour Organization
ILR	Independent Local Radio
IMF	International Managers' Forum
ISM	Incorporated Society of Musicians
ITV	Independent Television
JCC	Joint Consultative Committee
LDC	London District Committee
LFM	London Fellowship of Musicians
LMF	Live Music Forum
LPO	London Philharmonic Orchestra
LOA	London Orchestral Association
MBF	Music Business Forum
MCPS	Mechanical-Copyright Protection Society
MDC	Music Development Committee
MMAPA	Manchester Musical Artistes' Protection Association
MMC	Monopolies and Mergers Commission
MMF	Music Managers' Forum
MPC	Music Promotion Committee
MMRJ	*Musicians' Monthly Report and Journal*
MNSC	Music National Service Committee
MPA	Music Publishers' Association
MPPA	Musical Performers' Protection Association
MRC	Modern Records Centre, University of Warwick
MU	Musicians' Union
MUC	Music Users' Council
NCMU	National Council of Music Users
NDfM	New Deal for Musicians
NDLP	National Democratic and Labour Party

NDO	Northern Dance Orchestra
NFJO	National Federation of Jazz Organisations
NFPM	National Federation of Professional Musicians
NIMA	Northern Ireland Music Association
NME	*New Musical Express*
NOA	National Orchestral Association
NOUPM	National Orchestral Union of Professional Musicians
OA	Orchestral Association
OEA	Orchestral Employers' Association
P2P	peer-to-peer
PAMRA	Performing Artists Media Rights Association
PEL	Public Entertainment Licence
PKF	Pannell Kerr Forster
PPL	Phonographic Performance Ltd
PRS	Performing Right Society
PRT	Performing Right Tribunal
RCM	Royal College of Music
RPO	Royal Philharmonic Orchestra
RSAMD	Royal Scottish Academy of Music and Drama
RSM	Royal Society of Musicians
SOLT	Society of London Theatre
SRO	Scottish Radio Orchestra
SWETM	Society of West End Theatre Managers
TMA	Theatrical Management Association (now Theatre UK)
TNA	The National Archives
TUC	Trades Union Congress
TUCO	Trade Union Certification Officer
UGM	Union of Graduates in Music
VAF	Variety Artistes' Federation
VOC	Voluntary Organising Committee
VOCA	Visiting Orchestras Consultative Association
WAC	BBC Written Archive Centre
WIPO	World Intellectual Property Organization
WMA	Workers' Music Association

Introduction

Prologue

Towards the end of writing this book during the summer of 2015 we attended the Musicians' Union's (MU's) thirty-sixth Biennial Conference in Brighton. By this point, having pored through conference reports dating back to 1943,[1] we were all too familiar with the nature and concerns of such gatherings and our attendance presented an obvious opportunity to reflect on the differences and similarities between the current machinations of the Union and those evident throughout the history we had just written.

The conferences are arguably the most visible representation of the Union's concerns at any given point, as its Executive Committee (EC) reports on the organisation's work and delegates put forward motions supporting or critiquing this work, while also having the opportunity to change Union policy.

We observed that of the many changes the most apparent are in the demographics and dynamics of the conference. This is visible amongst both the delegates on the conference floor and the EC and Secretariat on the podium. Conference pictures from the 1950s are notable for the almost complete lack of women amid the smoke-filled rooms of the colleges within which they traditionally took place. By 2015, although there were still a number of conference veterans in attendance, this was generally a younger, more diverse event.[2] For the second time, the conference was chaired by the Union's first female Chair, Kathy Dyson.

Our second observation was that while the composition of Conference (see below, page 109) had changed, in many ways its agenda represented 'Business as Usual'. The more seasoned conference attendees would have soon

1 This was the year in which the Union began to hold such conferences regularly.

2 According to the conference report, there were thirty-eight male and eighteen female delegates (MU 2015: xi). The EC had thirteen men and six women (viii) and the three-person Secretariat was all male.

recognised that many of the issues at stake and campaigns under discussion were relatively immutable. It came as little surprise to see matters relating to pay and conditions, copyright, and public-sector support for music – all hardy annuals and major themes in this history – remaining at the top of the Union's agenda in 2015.

As we show below, by its very nature the Union is a campaigning organisation and such campaigns are duly reported to Conference. While some of these are now conducted entirely under the auspices of the MU,[3] others take place in conjunction with other trade unions[4] or as part of broader initiatives by music industries' groups. For example, as part of UK Music – the sector's lobbying group – the Union was successful in getting a High Court ruling against the UK Government over a proposed private copying exception in July 2015,[5] and was also behind one of a number of petitions[6] to protect the British Broadcasting Corporation's (BBC's) music services when they came under review as part of the Corporation's charter renewal process.[7]

Our third observation was that, in line with other contemporary trade union and party political conferences, there was an almost complete lack of dissent. Historically these conferences were often fractious affairs, but in 2015, only a last-minute emergency motion calling on the Union to support the candidacy of Jeremy Corbyn for the Labour Party leadership caused any serious debate. This was defeated, but only after criticism from some delegates of the Executive's decision, taken on the eve of the conference, to back Andy Burnham. This appeared to be based more on pragmatism than ideology. Burnham had been more supportive to the Union in its previous campaigns, particularly when, in his role as Culture Secretary under Gordon Brown's premiership, he had instigated a change in Government policy on the issue of copyright term extension (Burnham 2008).

The Executive's decision to back Burnham as a 'friend of the music industry' rather than Corbyn reflects some of the tensions that have characterised attempts to build organisations that represent musicians' interests. It can also be seen as illustrating in microcosm the considerable change in the Union's orientation – from being largely a workers' organisation towards becoming a music industries' one – that we outline in this history.

What follows traces this development. This book is about the working lives of musicians in the UK since 1893 as viewed via the evolution of an

3 For example, the Work Not Play campaign, www.worknotplay.co.uk.

4 For example, the Lost Arts campaign, www.lost-arts.org/.

5 Details of this and an explanation of the issues can be found at www.musiciansunion.org.uk/Home/News/2015/Jul/Private-Copying-Exception-FAQ.

6 This came under the banner/hash-tag '#LetItBeeb': https://petition.parliament.uk/petitions/106091.

7 The BBC's Royal Charter is granted for a ten-year period and is due to expire in 2016.

organisation that was founded in that year to protect and promote their interests. That organisation was the Amalgamated Musicians' Union (AMU), which became the MU in 1921. The MU has been at the centre of all the major collective agreements covering the UK's musicians for over 120 years. It has negotiated with all the major employers of musicians and has also represented individual musicians who have come into conflict with an almost bewildering array of organisations, and individuals who have been involved in hiring musicians. As the *only* organisation at the centre of all these collective agreements and individual cases, the MU's story is unique. Its history is one of triumph and failure, of good times and bad, but above all of endurance. It is a history that has hitherto been largely neglected, but that needs to be told in order to understand musicians' working lives, the industries they work in, and wider British musical life.

Our aim here is twofold – to use the prism of the MU to provide insight into musicians' working lives and, via this, to provide further understanding of the music – and broader creative – industries. We begin this Introduction with some reflections on the approach, methods, and sources adopted in our research before turning to our underpinning thesis – that musicians are best conceived of as particular sorts of workers seeking remuneration within a complex matrix of industries clustered in and around music. Finally, we look at a number of recurring themes in the Union's history.

Approach, methods, and sources

The book emerges from a research project that was funded by the UK's Arts and Humanities Research Council (AHRC) and Economic Research Council (ESRC) and that ran between April 2012 and March 2016. At the outset, we billed it as a 'social history' of the Union, but as the work developed we realised that such a designation was somewhat limiting and did not cover the full extent of the history that we were writing. We did, however, use the work of prominent social historians as a starting point, inspired by the importance they attached to trade unions, class, and the study of industry (for example Cole and Postgate 1948; Hobsbawm 1968; Thompson 1963; Webb and Webb 1920). Of equal interest was that their histories of modern British society were constructed 'from the bottom', with the emphasis on those workers whose stories had been marginalised in previous historical accounts that emphasised great men and institutions.

This history of the MU therefore contains a hybrid of approaches and is something of a combination of an institutional history, a history of particular types of workers, and a wider social and cultural history of (popular) music and its attendant industries during the period of the Union's existence. As this became evident during the course of our research, we felt that it would be impossible to do full justice to story of the MU without also paying close attention to the other organisations with which it was closely connected. In particular, the story of the Union is closely intertwined with those of Phonographic Performance Ltd (PPL) and the BBC.

Realising the previously unrecognised importance of the MU's role in the development of the post-war music industries, we found ourselves faced with many of the same research dilemmas detailed by Sarah Thornton (1990) when attempting to 'reconstruct the popular past'. In writing a history of British dance halls and discothèques, she found her work obfuscated by the presence of abundant histories that were 'heterogeneous, unofficial and informal' (87), of the type found in the press and individual biographies. This was also the case with the MU, which, as we discuss below, appears mainly as a footnote in both informal and academic histories. Moreover, we also encountered issues of bias,[8] and the scant attention and scrutiny the Union enjoyed were perhaps a reflection of the fact that its members were not generally associated with the top end of the music profession, but were rather seen as being jobbing musicians of little interest to historians. We, of course, would beg to differ.

To unpack the importance of the Union, we employed a three-part methodology. The first of these was a review of the existing literature, the second archival work, and the third detailed interviews with a number of key important figures in the Union's story. Each of those came with its own problems – the limited bibliography, the disappearing paper trails within incomplete archives, and the sometimes conflicting and contradictory recollections of interviewees – but when combined, we trust that they have produced a detailed and revealing history of the Union. We will now look at each of these methods in turn.

Precedents

Like any project, this history builds on a range of existent literature and we stand on the shoulders of giants. Our work necessitated drawing on a wide range of sources including work on the Union itself, musicians' working lives, and the labour movement. We wanted to investigate the working lives of musicians in the UK since 1893 via an organisation that was founded in that year to protect and promote their interests.

8 The Union's own publications were largely uncritical of its activities, whereas at various points in its history, the music press pursued either pro- or anti-Union agendas.

Prior to our research there was comparatively little academic work on the MU's overall history. What existed were articles that examined either particular eras (David-Guillou 2009) or aspects of the Union's work (Cloonan and Brennan 2013) with passing references to it in works on music and politics (e.g. Frith 1978; Street 1986). In sum, existing academic literature on the Union is somewhat scant, especially when comparisons are made to the work that has been done on musicians' unions in the USA (e.g. Anderson 2004; Countryman 1948; Gorman 1983; Leiter 1953; Roberts 2014; Seltzer 1989) and Australia (Arthur 1997, 2003; Dreyfus 2009; Michelson 1997).

Despite being involved in negotiating musicians' working conditions since 1893, the MU has generally been either neglected or completely overlooked in most of the substantial accounts of the UK's music industries (e.g. Jones 2012; Martland 2013; Negus 1992). If music industries' literature has marginalised the Union, things are little better within trade union studies. Major accounts of British trade unionism (e.g. Clegg *et al.* 1964; Flanders 1968; Pelling 1992; Reid 2004; Wrigley 2002) barely mention it. It has fared better in jazz studies (McKay 2005; Nott 2002; Parsonage 2005) and in histories of broadcasting (Baade 2012; Briggs 1979, 1995; Doctor 1999). While both fields limit themselves to particular facets of the Union's work, they provide greater prominence to the MU's role than the trade union histories do.

Outside the academy there are two important accounts originating from within the Union itself.[9] In 1929 its second General Secretary (GS), E. S. Teale, wrote an account covering the early years of the AMU (Teale 1929a, 1929b). This contains interesting detail, but remains largely descriptive and anecdotal. A more recent history was written by Mike Jempson (1993) to commemorate the Union's centenary. This is invaluable to historians, but is inevitably partial and constrained by both scope and its official nature.

The Union's work has also regularly been reported in the pages of music and entertainment trade magazines like *The Stage*, *Era*, and *Music Week*. These have, at various times, detailed aspects of the Union's work, including negotiations with employers or campaigns to improve the working musician's lot. Broadsheet newspapers, notably the *Daily Telegraph*, *Guardian*, and *The Times*, have also periodically reported on aspects of the Union's work. These have generally provided snippets for us to follow up.

Beyond the specificities of the Union's work, there is more work on the music profession as a whole and some accounts of UK musicians' working lives. By far the most important of these for our work is Ehrlich's *The Music*

[9] There is also a brief account on the Union's first sixty years written by Bertram Newton Brooke in 1954, which can be found in Farmer, 67/3.

Profession in Britain since the Eighteenth Century (1985). This contains several references to the AMU and its early battles with employers as well as outlining the subsequent development of the MU, but has little on the recording era. Nott's *Music for the People* (2002) also provides some insight into the Union's problems in the 1920s and 1930s. Cottrell's *Professional Music-Making in London* (2004) is a useful ethnographic study of orchestral musicians and the challenges they face. Within popular music, Thompson (2008) examines working practices in the 1960s with some recognition of the MU's work, while in accounts such as Finnegan's *The Hidden Musicians* (1989) and Cohen's *Rock Culture in Liverpool* (1991) insights are provided in to the working patterns and aspirations of certain types of musicians.

The working conditions of orchestral players in the UK have also been documented in histories of the major orchestras (e.g. Davies 2012; Kennedy 1960; Kenyon 1981; King-Smith 1995; Morrison 2004; Russell 1945, 1952, 1953). However, once again, these generally offer little more than passing reference to the MU and none subjects it to sustained analysis. Helpfully, former MU activist Basil 'Nick' Tschaikov (2009) has written an autobiography covering his work in orchestras and the Union during a period spanning almost sixty years.

Perhaps the most systematic overview of attempts to organise musicians comes in an unpublished Ph.D. by Abram Loft (1950) that examines attempts by a range of guilds, protective societies, and trade unions across Europe, the UK, and the USA to do so. This is a fascinating account of how musicians have constantly sought to build organisations that represent their interests, often seeking to limit competition by trying to ensure that musical employment is open only to members – and that membership is strictly controlled. Attali (1985) provides a compelling account of how musicians' working lives were transformed by the onset of industrial capitalism, while Kraft (1996) provides an excellent study of US musicians' early encounters with the recording industry and Stahl (2013) offers a similarly impressive account of more recent developments.

There have also been growing numbers of accounts of work within the creative industries. At the forefront of this in the UK has been David Hesmondhalgh (see Hesmondhalgh and Baker 2010, 2011a, 2011b; and Hesmondhalgh and Percival, 2014). This work has highlighted the notoriously perilous state of much employment in the creative industries and lamented the inability of trade unions to remedy matters. Mulder (2009) offers some arguments as to how orchestral musicians might do this, and suggests that the structural position of Broadway musicians leaves them ideally placed to implement a 'communist workplace' (99). Recently Baade *et al.* (2014) have led research into musical labour across the Atlantic. More broadly Heery *et al.* (2004)

have illustrated how trade unions in the creative industries with memberships containing large numbers of freelance workers have become providers of 'industrial services' (31) and 'labour market intermediaries' (27).

While such accounts have much to offer, the comparative lack of literature specifically on the MU is a major lacuna in a context where, as noted above, it can lay claim to be the *only* organisation to have an involvement in and/or influence on all of the major agreements that have often underpinned musicians' working lives. This book aims to rescue its history from its current marginalisation and to bring previously neglected materials forward.

The second part of our methodology involved analysing documents held in various archives. Prime amongst these was the Union's own archive, housed at the University of Stirling. A survey of this content provided the basis for the formation of a chronology of the Union.[10] These materials provided a rich source of data through which to compile a history of the Union and develop an overview of its work. However, they are inevitably partial – minute books can hide as much as they reveal – and are, of their very nature, biased towards the Union's own viewpoint. In addition, while wide-ranging, the MU Archive is by no means complete. There was thus a need to supplement its materials. One way of doing this was via further archival research, especially among those of musicians' employers.

The most important of these was the BBC Written Archive Centre (WAC) in Caversham. We have also drawn on a range of other archives for both wider context and details of specific aspects of the Union's work. These include The National Archives at Kew (TNA), the Modern Records Centre at the University of Warwick (MRC), the Farmer Collection at the University of Glasgow (Farmer), the Jack Hylton Archive at the University of Lancaster, the Trades Union Congress (TUC) Archive based at London Metropolitan University, the Communist Party of Great Britain (CPGB) archive at the People's History Museum in Manchester, and the Orchestral Employers' Association (OEA) Archive at the University of York.

While these are all open to the public, access to three other archives was provided to us by kind permission of their owners. The first of these was PPL[11] minute books covering the periods 1933–36 and 1962–91. The years in between appear to have been lost and the more recent ones were deemed, understandably, to be (commercially) confidential. The second was various minute books held at the offices of UK Theatre/the Society of London Theatre (SOLT) – an ad hoc collection largely covering predecessor organisations'

10 See www.muhistory.com.

11 PPL licenses the public use of recordings and collects royalties on behalf of its members for such usage.

activities. The last was the minute books of the OEA's successor organisation, the Association of British Orchestras (ABO). These collections all served to supplement the MU Archive, often offering different perspectives on key events and giving a sense of the underlying atmosphere. Overall the archival work helped to give a fuller picture of the Union and its work than has previously existed. However, it seldom provided details of the lived experience of those either working on behalf of the Union or interacting with it. For this a separate strand of research was necessary.

This entailed a series of interviews with MU activists, officials, and those who had interacted with the Union over the years. Those from the Union included three General Secretaries[12] and a number of other employees, including regional organisers and those officials responsible for particular aspects of the Union's work, such as recording and orchestras. Activists interviewed included current and former members of the EC and Branch Secretaries. For an outside view we interviewed employers, broadcasters, record company employees, DJs, and commentators.[13] All this provided greater depth to our understanding of the Union and its work – something we approached from a particular perspective.

Musicians as workers

Our approach is to treat musicians as workers or, more accurately, as particular sorts of workers seeking paid employment.[14] They may also be creators, performers, celebrities, and stars, but what matters to us is that they are people seeking to do jobs. The term 'musician' incorporates a wide range of people playing a diverse range of instruments (and/or singing) across a wide variety of musical genres. They may be more or less skilled; play solo or in ensembles; compose or not; and be further demarcated by age, class, gender, sexuality, ethnicity, and race. But what unites those who join the MU is their status as workers seeking employment within music. Our orientation is not an original one, as writers such as Attali (1985), Ehrlich (1985), Kraft (1996), Loft (1950), and Mulder (2009) have all placed emphasis on musicians as people undertaking work. What subsequently becomes important is the sort of work they undertake, the places in which it takes place, and who is funding and controlling such places.

12 John Morton, Dennis Scard, and John Smith. Various attempts to interview the other surviving General Secretary, Derek Kay, proved unsuccessful.

13 A full list of interviewees is included in Appendix B.

14 We acknowledge the importance of amateur music-making and that a clear divide between amateurs and professionals is not always possible, but follow the MU in concentrating on those musicians seeking paid employment.

Here it is possible to demarcate musicians through consideration of their employment patterns. In particular one key determinant is whether a musician has permanent, full-time, salaried employment or not. Following the merger that formed the MU in 1921,[15] the Union has had a membership within which a small minority have such positions, now largely focused in the UK's major orchestras. It was in the predominantly State-subsidised orchestras where the Union came closest to achieving a 'closed shop'[16] before the 1990 Employment Act effectively outlawed such arrangements. However, the total number of MU members employed in orchestras in 2013 UK was around 1,400, with another 1,550 working freelance (Kerr 2014). This was around 10 per cent of the MU's total membership of 30,718.[17] Self-employed and freelance workers form the vast majority of the Union's membership, with a 2012 report for the Union noting that 'only 10% of musicians are full-time, salaried employees. Half of musicians have no regular employment whatsoever. The vast majority of musicians (94%) work freelance for all or part of their income' (DHA Communications 2012: 14).[18]

Outside the orchestras some musicians may have permanent (if not always full-time) employment in places such as theatres, ballet and opera companies, and as music teachers of various sorts. Even musicians with recording contracts are *not* employees as such; rather they are contracted by record companies to provide services and products (such as recordings) in return for payment based on a percentage of sales once the company's investment (which may include advances to the artists) have been recouped.

There are numerous other types of employment involving freelance musicians, such as recording sessions, television and radio appearances, videos, one-off gigs, and concert tours. Here, the Union has negotiated on behalf of freelancers working in various contexts. As we show in Chapter 9, it continues to do so and has had a series of sector-wide collective agreements with major employers of such musicians. However, such agreements affect the daily workings of only a minority of its members.

Meanwhile musicians not permanently employed can be sub-divided into those whose musical jobs are negotiated on a *seasonal* or *time-limited* basis with employers such as orchestras, theatres, record companies, or broadcasters, and those who are *casually* employed on an ad hoc basis, generally as

15 In 1921 the AMU and the National Orchestral Union of Professional Musicians (NOUPM) merged to form the MU. See Chapter 3.

16 McCarthy describes a closed shop as 'a situation in which employees come to realise that a particular job is only to be obtained and retained of they become and remain members of one of a specified number of trade unions' (McCarthy 1964: 3).

17 www.certoffice.org/CertificationOfficer/media/DocumentLibrary/PDF/154T_2013.pdf.

18 For more see Taylor (2006, 2008).

non-affiliated musicians whose work consists of an accumulation of one-off, short-term engagements with a number of different employers.

Overall our approach is to treat musicians not simply as workers, but as *particular sorts* of workers seeking employment opportunities in industries wherein freelance working – often on very short contracts – is the norm and a wide range of working practices and contractual arrangements exist. What matters here is not so much whether our demarcations are water-tight, but the implications of musicians' varied working practices for the Union. These will become apparent as the book progresses and form a recurring theme,[19] often serving to undermine notions of a singular music profession.

Our emphasis, then, is not on musicians' talents, charisma, or personalities, but on their working practices. For the Union this often focused on their role as performers, as it was perennially concerned with maximising opportunities for performance, exercising as much control as possible over the conditions under which it occurred and seeking suitable amounts of remuneration for performers. An examination of the issues such workers confront reveals a number of overlapping issues that will now be considered.

Themes

A number of recurring factors can be seen as affecting musicians' working conditions, including technology, the contemporary state of the music profession and its related industries, changing musical tastes, competition, and gender. Such factors offer both generalities – the development of technology affects all music-making – and specificities – its impact may be mediated by legal and governmental contexts. While recurring throughout this book, they merit some introduction here.

Perhaps the most important theme to emerge during our research was that of technology. In interview, when asked what *the* major issue has been in the Union's history, current GS John Smith replied 'the *continual* battle with technology' (*2014*, emphasis Smith).[20] Numerous aspects of this could be examined, but our focus here will be on the effect on musicians as workers. There are at least three important aspects to this. The first is the most positive – technology is liberating. This can be seen in various areas. For example, consider the transformation of popular music that followed the invention of the

19 We share Batstone's view that three things contribute to workers' power – their ability to disrupt production, the scarcity (or otherwise) of labour, and their political influence (Batstone 1988: 223).

20 Citations to interviews are given in italics to distinguish them from references to publications. The list of interviews can be found in the Appendix.

electric guitar – perhaps *the* emblematic popular-music instrument (Waksman 2001). Then consider what effects pedals can add to the sheer range of musical possibilities the guitar has. Numerous other examples could be given: the point here is that technology enables these workers to perform all sorts of roles that were previously impossible.

However, there are also down sides to technology, of which two appear to be the most salient – de-skilling and replacement. The issue of de-skilling raises questions about the very status of being a musician. If one definition of musician involves possessing a particular skill set – that of being able to play a musical instrument to a certain standard and under certain conditions (primarily in public with others) – then as technology simplifies the music-making process, so the very status of musician becomes compromised. Once again history provides numerous examples – drum machines, synthesisers, samplers, and a range of modern computer-based technologies. Perhaps the paradigmatic case here is the role of DJs – which has moved from being about playing records, to being producers of music in their own right – something considerably aided by changes in technology. Thus when the Union began to admit them as members in the 1990s (Lee 1997) this was recognition that technology had changed their role and made musicians of those whose trade might previously have been seen as parasitic *upon*, or displacing, musicians.[21]

More problematic for the Union than de-skilling is the total replacement of musicians with technology. Over eighty years after the arrival of 'talkies' (films containing sound) in the cinemas in the late 1920s remains the emblematic example of this. It must be remembered here that 'silent' cinema was anything but silent and that the major films of the time were frequently accompanied by large orchestras. From the release of *The Jazz Singer* in 1927 the impact of the 'talkies' was dramatic and, as we show in Chapter 3, musical employment fell dramatically in ways that haunt the Union to this day.[22] The lesson learned was that simply being oppositional was unlikely to yield results. Tactics thus generally shifted towards attempts to control, combined with trying to maximise employment opportunities for musicians. Thus, while technological developments such as records, radio, television, and internet technology were rarely embraced, the real battle was to protect musical employment – either via the technology itself or via claims to the profits it generated.

21 Perhaps the most notorious case here concerns former Radio Luxembourg DJ Tony Prince. See www.dmcworld.tv/historyofdj/ for details.

22 In interviews both the current General Secretary (*Smith 2014*) and its orchestral organiser (*Kerr 2014*) spontaneously referred to the Union's response to the 'talkies' as something that should not be repeated.

The MU's actions in opposing technological innovation have been the subject of criticism. Street has said of the MU's approach to technological innovations that 'while inspired to protect members, the MU's policy appears as merely reactionary' (1986: 147). As will be shown, this entailed a range of tactics. However, it is important to establish that historically the MU has been at least as opportunist as it has been oppositional. While advancing technology remained a constant threat to musical employment,[23] it could be used as well as opposed. Thus, the Union's role became that of ensuring that it was either contained or monetised to the benefit of its members. Seeing all this through the prism of musicians as workers allows for a nuanced view of the MU's actions to emerge. Workers who are being threatened with replacement by new technology do not expect their union to stand idly by and this option was never open to the MU. It therefore strove both to mitigate the impact of new technology and to use it to preserve and create as many opportunities as possible for the employment of live musicians.

It is also necessary to acknowledge that technological innovations do not happen in isolation: they exist in societies with particular sets of social and economic arrangements. In short, for the MU, technological innovations occurred within capitalist economies characterised by varying degrees of competition and State intervention. They also occurred within a particular set of arrangements generally referred to as the 'music industry', another key theme. The book here inevitably bears our intellectual stamp and builds on our previous work and interests in the political economy of music. Of particular importance here is our conception of 'the music industries' (Williamson and Cloonan 2007, 2013).

In referring to 'the music industries' in a plural rather than singular form we made a somewhat polemical attempt to shift academic consensus away from a concentration on the recording sector as *being* 'the music industry' towards a more pluralistic approach. We adopt this approach here and suggest that a consideration of all the places in which musicians work soon shows how problematic a notion of a singular music industry is. The MU has to deal with myriad employment situations and workplaces every day and the complexity of its world is better reflected via such an approach. This has important implications for our emphasis. This is an account of the MU as a music industries' organisation. It is *a* history of the MU – not *the* history.

[23] For example in 2014 the Union was involved in a dispute over a production of *War Horse* at the National Theatre that terminated the contract of five musicians and replaced them with recorded music. See www.musiciansunion.org.uk/news/2014/04/25/save-the-war-horse-band-keep-music-live-in-theatres/.

We also distinguish between 'the music profession' as described by Ehrlich (1985) and our definition of the 'music industries'. Here we consider the former to comprise those who play music for a living, making them a part of the music industries, which also include those involved in the organisation and exploitation of their work. While accepting that such boundaries are porous, we trust they have some explanatory power. We are interested in musicians as workers, in different workplaces, with differing terms and conditions in constant evolution as musical trends come and go and supply and demand fluctuates – and in the politics that result from all this. This necessitates examining the state of the UK's music industries at any given point. One noticeable aspect of this is that recorded music has only ever provided significant income for a minority of the Union's membership. For the majority of its members 'work' consists primarily of live performance and, as noted above, the Union has long seen the provision of the opportunities for the employment of live musicians as its main aim. For the MU the longstanding motto of 'Keep Music Live' is no mere slogan, it is an underlying philosophy.

The changing complexion of the music industries has complicated matters here as it has shaped the increasingly diverse range of work that musicians undertake. In 1893 the AMU could work locally. It knew which venues employed musicians and would try both to recruit such people and to encourage major employers – such as music halls and theatres – to employ only its members. In essence 'the music industry' was then largely a local, live industry. However, the growth of recording and broadcasting, as well as new outlets for live work such as cruise ships and holiday camps, meant that the very notion of what constituted 'the music industry' changed and became more complex. Organisations such as the BBC and cinema chains emerged and employed significant numbers of musicians without necessarily being seen as part of 'the music industry'. While such philosophical questions were not the Union's concern, it had to deal with the implications for musicians *as workers*.

The Union's general response was to try to get agreements with major employers and, whenever possible, to ensure that such agreements covered both permanent employees and freelance musicians. Here an examination of the organisations with which the MU has collective agreements at any point in time provides a great deal of insight in to the state of the contemporary music industries. We illustrate how the Union has had to develop a range of relationships with major employers, and to adapt as the music industries have evolved through various entrepreneurial models, changing technology, and fluctuating public and private investment. In particular, as the recording sector rose and was underpinned by the exploitation of copyright, so the Union sought to ensure that performers enjoyed the fruits of such exploitation.

All this meant dealing with the realities of the music industries. Much could be said here, but one area that has been a constant issue for the MU is the question of over-supply of labour – that is, of competition for employment. While there are musicians whose talents seem to be unique, much musical work can also be viewed as routine, if by no means immune to individual input. Here the popular-music market is particularly competitive with the live sector including phenomena such as 'pay to play' gigs and a recording sector characterised by few contracts and a 'success' rate that rarely appears to have been over 10 per cent (Osborne 2014).

In short, the music industries are highly competitive. They also contain workplaces that are almost impossible to monitor systematically and where musical workers rarely enjoy the one real sanction usually available to workers – collective withdrawal of labour. There has never been an all-out strike of musicians in Britain, and where strikes have taken place they have been confined to particular workplaces over issues specific to that group of workers. The AMU's early days witnessed strikes in individual theatres, but the increasingly disparate nature of the music industries and the sorts of employment on offer within them meant that such actions became exceptional. When strikes occurred, they tended to be in places where workers were in full-time, permanent contracts – notably at the BBC. The most recent example of this was the 1980 BBC strike, which is dealt with in Chapter 7. Meanwhile freelance workers are inevitably less likely and able to withdraw their labour than those in large, organised workplaces. Lacking industrial muscle within the music industries the MU has often tried to convince employers and potential allies of the morality of its case. When unable to enforce, it has tried to persuade.

In addition, the MU has tried from its inception to limit competition. Initially this concentrated on trying to enforce local closed shops. As the music industries developed, it was also able to enforce de facto closed shops at various points in areas such as broadcasting, theatres, and orchestras, and reached agreements with employers enforcing them.[24] Prior to its illegality, the closed shop allowed for both protection of existing workers and some control over entry into the profession. However, it was only ever one tactic. Another was to try and curtail the activities of those deemed to be in direct competition with its members. Two main groups have been evident here. The first of these is military[25] and police bands. The MU Archive is full of evidence of attempts by the Union to convince the military and police authorities that

[24] For example, a 1983 agreement between the Theatrical Managers' Association (TMA) and the MU states that 'a manager shall not engage a musician under this agreement who is not a member of the Musicians' Union' (TMA files).

[25] See Countryman (1948) for similar concerns in the USA.

it should not allow public concerts by such bands as these were events that could equally be undertaken by its members.

Another form of competition was also a recurring issue – the importation of foreign musicians. This issue also arose early on with the AMU's first GS, Joe Williams, seeking 'to reduce competition, particularly from European musicians who had almost unrestricted access to work in Britain' (Jempson 1993: 8). During the First World War various local branches passed motions calling for the expulsion of members from enemy countries (and beyond),[26] and the following years saw calls for musicians from former enemy countries to be denied work permits. During the 1920s the growing popularity of American dance bands caused concern that they were performing roles that British musicians could equally do at a time when the American Federation of Musicians (AFM) routinely vetoed attempts by the UK to tour there.

In 1935 the MU's stance got official sanction when the Ministry of Labour agreed to stop issuing further work permits without the Union's approval, which was generally not forthcoming. The system was relaxed in 1956 when a series of reciprocal exchanges began. Based on 'man hours', the system allowed for musicians to be traded across the Atlantic (and elsewhere) and was in force until the late 1980s when the Government stopped routinely consulting the Union on permits. This story has been authoritatively told elsewhere (Cloonan and Brennan 2013) and we return to it below, providing evidence to show that this was merely one example of a number of protectionist measures that the Union was able to implement until well into the 1980s.

A final group of competitors were amateurs, some of whom had the potential to undercut the rates demanded by professional musicians. Examples of disputes around this appear to be comparatively rare and the opposition mainly rhetorical. However, overall it can be seen that the MU has adopted a dual approach of trying to limit competition as far as possible as well as trying to provide as many opportunities as possible for the employment of live musicians.

The final major theme that we examine in Chapter 9 is equalities, and we focus on gender and race relations. The absence of prominent women in the Union's history is a glaring one. While Joe Williams' mother, Kate, has been described as the 'Mother of the Union'[27] it appears that it bore comparatively few activist daughters. The EC and Biennial Conferences were an all-male preserve until after the Second World War, and in the Union's first hundred years

[26] On 11 June 1916 the Glasgow Branch passed a motion 'that no foreigners be admitted to membership of the Union' (MU, 4/2). The context for this was an influx of Belgian refugees to the city and fears that they might take work from local musicians.

[27] In an anonymous obituary in the MU *Monthly Report*, July 1931: 3.

only two women served on the EC. The first, Kay Holmes, served between 1948 and 1951, while the second, Barbara White, was not elected until 1990. Early correspondence in the MU Archive sees fellow members addressed as 'Dear Sir and Bro', and the lack of women within the Union can partly be seen as a reflection of the fact that for many years the music profession and its related industries were male dominated. This is certainly the case with instrumentalists, and while a number of woman singers enjoyed successful careers, most were members of another union, the Variety Artistes' Federation (VAF) which was incorporated into the actors' union Equity in 1967.

Over the years the situation would gradually improve, and by 2013 the Union's membership was 28.6 per cent female (MU 2013a: 6). This was aided in part by broader social changes following the sexual revolution of the 1960s and the impact of the feminist movement. However, overall, this will be a largely male-dominated history. Men have dominated the music industries and the musicians' representative organisation. However, any history is inevitably a process of inclusion and exclusion, and the exclusion of women from most of the Union's activities for much of its history is certainly a significant one.

Matters of race and racial discrimination have featured from the Union's early days, and we consider the accusations of racism levelled against the Union when it fought to protect its members from competition from foreign workers. Its later support for the anti-apartheid movement and opposition to colour bars in British venues provide a counterpoint to such claims and were among the first signs of the Union becoming a more diverse and tolerant organisation after the Second World War.

It should also be noted that the history that follows is often a London-centric one.[28] This is for two main, and overlapping, reasons. The first is that prior to the advent of processes of political devolution that began with the election of the Labour administration in 1997, the modern UK has had a highly centralised State. Laws affecting the lives of musicians emanated from Westminster, which was thus the focus of political lobbying. Relatedly, the music profession has long been centred in and around London, and so many of the major events – such as negotiations with the BBC and the Ministry of Labour – have taken place there. Since 1921 between a third and a half of MU members have been located in London. In addition, while we have generally sought to provide a UK-wide account of the MU, it is important to note that London is a significant city for the international music industries. The Union's membership has been skewed towards the city, and its Central London Branch was for

[28] For one account of the MU at local level see Thomson (1989).

many years the most important (*Morton 2014*; *Trubridge 2014*). Naturally our history extends to the provinces and we do not doubt that there are many important local histories still to be told. The MU Archive contains one way into this and we fervently hope that future researchers will delve more here. We are conscious that a history such as this inevitably has to play off breadth against depth. So we consider this history a start.

The themes of technology, the state of the music industries, competition, and equalities are, of course, hardly discrete. They overlap and interact, and can be seen as ever-presents that affect musicians as workers and that their representative organisation has tried to mediate for over 120 years. Its longevity, and central role in the history of the UK's music industries, makes the MU unique. However, as the next chapter shows, its precursor – the AMU – was not the first body to take up the mantle of organising and representing musicians.

1

Musicians' organisations before 1893

We begin by contextualising the work and organisation of musicians in Britain prior to the formation of the AMU in 1893.[1] To do so, we consider the challenges facing those working as musicians. These have long centred on the low pay and social status conferred upon professional musicians. Indeed, the very notion of music as work has often proved problematic, and work as a full-time (and adequately paid) musician has generally been attainable for only a small, elite group of musicians. The others have formed an often itinerant, insecure, and flexible labour force within which the supply of qualified players has frequently outstripped the demand for their skills.

Embedded within this predicament are the reasons for musicians organising in the first instance. Initially, musicians' organisations sought to offer forms of benevolence – making up for a lack of other provision elsewhere for times of hardship, illness, and old age – and to provide some form of entry to the profession via accreditation. However, as time progressed organisations were formed that also addressed the terms and conditions under which musicians were employed.

To begin, these were secondary to the main purposes of early musicians' organisations – to confer professional status on musicians and control entry to the profession. We examine these chronologically, starting with the first documented musicians' organisations in the fourteenth century and explaining the profession's journey towards trade unionism in three parts. First, we examine the historical precedents for organising musicians in Britain. Second, we pay particular attention to the wider socio-political changes in Britain in the nineteenth century concerning trade unions, employment, and working conditions. Finally, we discuss the formation of the AMU in 1893, emphasising not only the differences between it and previous musicians' organisations,

[1] The AMU was the predecessor organisation of the MU.

but also the lingering splits and differing attitudes towards trade unionism within the profession, as illustrated by the formation – also in 1893 – of the (London) Orchestral Association (LOA).[2]

Origins

The organisation of musicians in Britain can be seen as a progression from very loose, localised groups of court musicians to organised trade unions, growing in power and militancy between the fourteenth and nineteenth centuries, with the formation of the AMU being the culmination of this journey. Indeed, the changing names of such organisations illustrates their evolving nature: fraternities and brotherhoods in the fourteenth and fifteenth centuries, fellowships in the sixteenth and seventeenth centuries, benevolent societies[3] and protection associations in the late eighteenth and nineteenth centuries. While space prevents a detailed discussion of the history of the music profession in the UK, or of all the individual organisations representing musicians, it is fruitful to examine the changes in the nature of the profession, the bargaining power of musicians, and the various organisations that emerged.

To get a sense of the historic organisation of musicians in Britain it is important to consider the nature and geographic spread of musical work from the Middle Ages. Most professional musical activity was in London and centred around the royal court, with musicians surviving on royal patronage. There were also a small number of independent musicians (or minstrels) who were not directly dependent on court favours. Thus, while the main focus of the music profession was in London, Loft mentions early minstrel activity in the provinces in places such as Chester and Staffordshire (1950: 222). However, as late as the eighteenth century there were few opportunities for professional musicians in the provinces. According to Ehrlich these amounted to 'perhaps a few hundred rather tenuous jobs' (1985: 19).

As the music profession grew through the Middle Ages, town waits became the most significant group of musicians outside the court. Although they were primarily musicians, the exact nature of their role has been problematised by Rastall (2009), and Woodfill notes that they appear to have had several roles beyond music (1953: 33, 45–6). Their importance here is that they formed a

[2] This organisation was initially called the Orchestral Association (OA) but for most of its existence was the London Orchestral Association. However latterly it also went under the moniker of National Orchestral Association (NOA) and National Orchestral Union of Professional Musicians (NOUPM). After the merger with the AMU in 1921 it reverted to being the LOA and ran a members' club in London. Where possible we have referred to it as it was constituted at the time of reference.

[3] This tradition continues. See www.helpmusicians.org.uk.

significant group of employed musicians who were outside the court but were also tied to the State, albeit on a local level.

Accounts of musicians' organisations in this period are inevitably incomplete, speculative, and often contradictory (Wilson 2001). Here we focus on those aspects of their work that were of subsequent importance. Three things are of note. First, there was never one organisation that represented all musicians. Second, such organisations served primarily to offer benevolence to members in need. Third, they took on increasingly protectionist functions, wherein they sought to exclude non-members and 'foreigners'[4] from undertaking work that might impact on those already working in the profession. The significance of all this lies in the reoccurrence of such themes throughout the story of the MU some 500 years later.

These are also evident in the first of the musicians' organisations specifically named by Loft: the Fraternity of Minstrels in London, which he dates to 1350. It was established 'among ordinary, non-court players' in the City of London and had a limited purview, making 'no attempt to establish or enforce specific conditions of work in the craft'. Indeed, its most significant feature was the retention of 'a common treasury for the purposes of mutual aid', which looked after members in need – something characteristic of most subsequent organisations (Loft 1950: 216).

By the fifteenth century, splits in the profession and the increasing emphasis on protecting its workers were evident. A separate organisation representing the King's Minstrels (The Brotherhood of the King's Minstrels) had achieved guild status by 1449.[5] Loft characterises the decree as offering the King's Minstrels the power to 'protect the monopoly' of 'not only the court-players but also the general body of minstrels in England as a whole' (1950: 224). A subsequent charter granted to the Brotherhood in 1469 returned to the issue of competition from 'rude countryfolk and workers at various crafts in our kingdom of England (who) have pretended to be minstrels' (225), and sought to ensure that only trained, licensed musicians performed as minstrels throughout the kingdom. A further condition was that 'every professional musician is required to belong to the guild' (228).

While acknowledging the difficulties involved in tracing the lineage of the various musicians' organisations in the fourteenth and fifteenth centuries, Loft also notes the existence of an organisation called the Fellowship of Minstrels and Freemen in London in 1500, speculating that it was 'a continuation or

4 Referring not just to those musicians working in London from outside the city but also to those from outside the profession.

5 Loft merely notes that the guild already existed when King Henry VI issued a decree in that year (1950: 223).

at least an outgrowth of the 1469 group' (1950: 230), perhaps involving 'the civic musicians or 'waits' of London' (231). However, Wilson (2001) suggests otherwise, describing this as a separate grouping who 'occupied themselves with disputes with foreigners' but generally 'avoided disputes with the King's Minstrels'.

What is of importance, however, is that by the sixteenth century different groups of musicians had begun to organise in separate bodies, depending on the nature of their work. All these organisations seemingly shared an interest in controlling the supply of labour in the profession, albeit with generally limited success. In the first instance, they focused on the number of apprentices each member of the Fellowship could employ[6] and the control of 'foreign' musicians. According to Loft, these attempts at control failed miserably, and by 1574, the Fellowship had effectively disintegrated.[7] Thus, even where they existed, musicians' organisations were limited in scope, wealth, and power.

During the seventeenth century the end of the Tudor dynasty was the catalyst for the first substantive change in musicians' organisations in the wider context of what Loft describes as a 'period of extensive incorporation of the many crafts and trades' (1950: 236). In 1604, James I granted a charter to the (former) Fellowship of Minstrels under the title of the 'The Master, Wardens and Commonality of the Art or Science of the Musicians of London'.[8] This granting of a Royal Charter to what was previously the Fellowship of Minstrels and was now the Commonality of the Art or Science of the Musicians of London incorporated the new organisation as a guild with extended powers, described by Loft as a 'monopolistic authority over the craft' (238), albeit with the exception of the King's musicians, whose own brotherhood received a new Royal Charter in 1635. Three other things of later importance emerged as a result of the new Charter and its attempts to control membership of the profession. The first was the introduction of the right to examine both existing and potential new members for 'sufficiency and skill in the said art or science', the second was the creation of a minimum size of ensemble, and the third a rule preventing members from having any dealings with 'foreigners' (Worshipful Company of Musicians 1915: 33).

These can be viewed as protective measures designed to maximise the amount of work available to a relatively small number of musicians. By insisting that a minimum of four players be engaged for 'weddings, feasts,

6 A change to the Fellowship statutes in 1518 meant most musicians were forbidden to have more than one apprentice at a time (Loft 1950: 233).

7 Though it continued in name, meetings appeared to stop and its rules were routinely disobeyed by 'intruding' musicians (Loft 1950: 234).

8 Believed to be a successor of the Fellowship of Minstrels.

banquets, revels or other assemblies or meetings within the city of London' (Loft 1950: 39), Loft claims that the Commonality acted as a 'guard against underselling in the music trade' (248). Thus, as early as the seventeenth century, many musicians were employers of other musicians (their apprentices) whose interests were seen as being best served by the exclusion of 'foreign' musicians. However, the guild was still insufficiently strong to be able to police such regulations, and the dilution of the profession by non-members – with the consequent undercutting of rates – became another perennial characteristic of the music profession.

The eighteenth century heralded a number of changes in both the nature of musical work and the organisation of musical workers. At its commencement there was still a relatively small number of professional musicians and much of the demand remained in London.[9] However, the importance of the town waits decreased as the century progressed and there was a shift of emphasis from a patronage system to one that was increasingly reliant on the market – beginning what Ehrlich calls 'the gradual commercialisation of music' (1985: 3). Evidence of this came in the form of the growing number of music teachers, the launch of a number of subscription concerts, and the employment of musicians by larger theatres and opera companies. However, the profession remained relatively small in number, fragmented, vulnerable, and lacking 'sufficient coherence to form protective associations' (Ehrlich, 1985: 25). Such as it did, it was organised around a reconstituted version of one of the old organisations (the London Commonality) and an important new society (the Fund for the Support of Decayed Musicians).

Although the London Commonality had gone into decline in the late seventeenth century and apparently did not hold a meeting after 1679,[10] it re-emerged in 1700, when a new Act widened its scope to include 'dancing masters' as well as musicians (Loft 1950: 260). This reinforced the previous monopolies by insisting that only freemen of the City of London could be musicians or 'dancing masters' in the city, and furthermore it prevented its members from joining any other workers' association. The Commonality was reconstituted as the Worshipful Company of Musicians in 1750, though this too lost control of the profession because of a lack of resources to enforce both its rules and the desired monopoly. By the end of the century it 'was in a curious condition' (Loft 1950: 265) as a result of its membership policies. Desperately trying to boost its finances, it opened membership to non-musicians who wanted the associated right to work in the City of London.

9 Ehrlich estimates 'no more than 2,000' musicians in Britain in the late eighteenth century (1985: 24).

10 The last recorded meeting of the Brotherhood of King's Minstrels took place in 1677.

According to Ehrlich, of the 700 new members admitted between 1743 and 1769 only nineteen were musicians. While it survived – and remains as one of the traditional livery companies of the City of London[11] – its functions are largely ceremonial, and by the end of the century it had 'lost completely its old function as an arbiter in the music industry' (Ehrlich 1985: 268).

The other eighteenth-century musicians' organisation that has survived was formed in 1738 as the 'Fund for the Support of Decayed Musicians or their families'. A mutual aid society, it was established after three London musicians saw two destitute boys whom they recognised as the orphaned sons of a formerly successful colleague (Ehrlich 1985: 28). Initially, benefits from the fund were available only to full-time professional musicians, thus effectively excluding the majority of provincial musicians. Renamed the Society of Musicians, it received its Royal Charter in 1790[12] and remains an active charity involved in supporting musicians in need. However, like the Worshipful Company, it had no involvement in protecting musicians from the new type of employers that were emerging as the century drew to a close.

There is little evidence of musicians acting collectively to improve their working conditions during the eighteenth century other than on a small, localised scale. An example of this was a 'strike' by the four musicians at the Canongate Playhouse in Edinburgh in 1758. Having been asked, and having refused, to play at short notice on one of their nights off, the musicians met with the theatre owner to discuss their wages arrears, at which point they were dismissed for impertinence. In launching a campaign for the payment of the arrears they gathered public sympathy for their grievance and caused the theatre to be without music.[13]

While this was an isolated dispute, it did show that public support in combination with organisation and a limited supply of labour could be used to pressurise the growing cadre of theatre employers who were becoming increasingly important across the profession. However, the small numbers of musicians involved and their lack of organisation meant that striking was rarely a viable option in the eighteenth century.

The nineteenth century

The changing nature of musicians' organisations – from guilds and benevolent societies to protection associations and trade unions – during this following

11 The company received a new Royal Charter in 1950. See www.wcom.org.uk.

12 The Royal Society of Musicians of Great Britain was incorporated by Royal Charter in 1790 (and again in 1987) and remains active. See www.royalsocietyofmusicians.co.uk.

13 The full story of the strike can be found in the *Musicians' Journal*, January 1933, 8.

century was also a product of wider societal, professional, and legislative developments. The latter changes relate to trade unions and are dealt with in the next part of the chapter. However, they can only be viewed in the light of major changes in British society and, concomitantly, the music profession. The most important of these were the rapid growth of the population and of cities, which, along with rapid industrialisation, had a major effect on the music profession.[14] Such changes created an unprecedented demand for musical entertainment and tuition that saw the music profession grow at a rate that 'far outstripped the rapid growth of the country's population' (Ehrlich 1985: 51). Ehrlich estimates that between 1870 and 1930, while the UK's population doubled, the number of musicians increased sevenfold to around 50,000.

In the early 1800s even in some of the larger towns musical provision was still in the hands of a small number of waits, but these de facto monopolies were ended by the Municipal Corporations Act of 1835. This created a range of opportunities for independent musicians with an increasingly large number of places, events, and ways in which musical employment could be found. These opportunities arose largely from the growing demand for mass, commercial entertainment, which – combined with higher wages, lower prices, and greater ease of travel – made life as an itinerant musician more viable. Ehrlich also points to the huge increase in the number of orchestral concerts and the growth of opportunities to teach music: mostly privately, but latterly also in schools and colleges (1985: 70).

The parts of Ehrlich's account of most relevance to the subsequent organisation of musicians concern the nature of the work being undertaken and the raft of problems facing the profession. It was these conditions that gave rise to the need for trade union organisation among musicians. For such workers the most significant feature was the freelance nature of almost all the available employment. The growth of the profession had not yet provided permanent employment in fixed places of work, and this was to have a considerable impact on musicians' organisation. Ehrlich describes the emergence of a cadre of professional, specialist instrumentalists, almost exclusively based in London (1985: 46). Playing in scratch orchestras, as accompanists for star singers, in various musical societies and at any event that could afford their fees (48), they established 'patterns of life and work which were to survive almost intact to the present day' (46).

With only a few musicians able to make a living from playing in such ensembles, teaching became increasingly important for others as either

14 The population of Great Britain in the 1801 census was 10.5 million; by 1901 it was 37 million (www.ons.gov.uk).

their sole source of income or, more probably, a supplementary one. Ehrlich notes that by 1900, except in London, 'the overwhelming majority of the "profession" were now teachers in a new and a limited sense' with 'little or no experience of public performance' (1985: 52). Thus, by the time the AMU formed in 1893, the profession was increasingly fragmented with not only different types of work performed by musicians of varying capabilities, but also a diversifying range of workplaces and conditions.

Ehrlich's description of the most pressing issues for nineteenth-century musicians will be strangely familiar to contemporary musicians, and they have been the focus of musicians' organisations ever since. Specifically, these were the discrepancies between the top earners and the majority of musicians, the low socio-economic status of the profession and the poor terms and conditions under which musicians were being made to work. Despite the growth of the profession, music was 'still, as it was a century before, a possible career to contemplate; but if a mastery of notes might prove remunerative, a mastery of letters was socially indispensable' (Ehrlich 1985: 44). In short, an abundance of musicians and some unscrupulous employers meant that pursuing a career as a musician was still likely to bring neither great financial reward nor enhanced social status.

However, that the changing nature of *some* of the work brought about the conditions that allowed musicians to organise for their own betterment can be seen in the organisations they formed in the latter part of the century. The key factor here was the growth in size of the workplaces. Large theatres and music halls emerged in the second half of the century, often employing orchestras. Importantly, the presentation of entertainment generally – and music specifically – was no longer connected to patronage, but was now part of an emerging sector that was unquestionably a 'profit-seeking venture' (Ehrlich 1985: 60).

Unsurprisingly, this rapid industrialisation of the profession had a detrimental effect on musicians' pay and conditions. Ehrlich estimates that by the mid-1860s there were over 30 large halls in London and between 200 and 300 smaller ones, with an additional 300 in the provinces. He describes 'broadly similar, miserable working conditions', with hall owners regarding the engagement of musicians as a necessary evil (1985: 58). David-Guillou outlines the 'ruthless management' within the theatres and music halls, where directors' 'entrepreneurial thirst was rarely tainted by human feelings'(2009: 293). The work was generally hard and conditions poor. Competition for work was fierce; the work itself was short-term and often terminated on a manager's whim or as a result of poor ticket sales.

Musicians' societies

The initial outcome of the growth of the music profession was a divide between the two groups of musicians previously portrayed – the highly trained, mainly London-based specialists who worked in conservatories or universities and could command high fees for private performances, and the new breed of musician, often based in the provinces, working in halls and theatres, poorly paid and enduring hazardous conditions. The emergence of groups of what Ehrlich distinguishes as 'gentlemen' and 'players' (1985: 121, 142) – and the antagonism between them – was reflected in the types of organisations that musicians subsequently formed towards the end of the century.

Rather than combining for the benefit of the profession as a whole, organisations were formed largely to protect the interests of particular sections. This betrayed different conceptions of the status of musicians and, relatedly, how they should be organised. The 'gentlemen' organised in musicians' societies to preserve a notion of the profession based around musical technique and exclusivity, while the 'players' organised in protective associations and, eventually, a trade union, opening up the profession to all of those working in music, regardless of status, pay, or even ability. For the first time, the question of what it was to be a musician was being seriously considered, and the differing interpretations were evident in the new musicians' societies and organisations.

These included the Society of Musicians and the Musical Graduates' Union.[15] For the most part these organisations were a modernised version of earlier ones, with a focus on conferring professional status and attempts to elevate their members' status to those of professions, such as law and medicine. Yet these organisations, along with the longstanding Royal Society of Musicians (RSM)[16] and the Worshipful Company of Musicians, offered little to the new cadre of musicians in theatres and music halls, almost all of whom were ineligible to join because of their lack either of qualifications or of musical ability. The organisations did all they could 'to distinguish themselves from mainstream workers' (David-Guillou 2009: 290).

This type of thinking was enshrined in their outlook. The Society began in Manchester in 1882, and although initially dismissed in some quarters as 'a group of nondescript provincial music teachers' (Ehrlich 1985: 127), it did harbour greater ambitions. Its leader, James Dawber, wrote to the *Musical Times* to declare that it would only be open to '*bona fide* professional

15 The latter was mooted in a circular in the *Musical Times* in 1892 and formed as the Union of Graduates in Music (UGM) in 1893.

16 The Society of Female Musicians, which was formed in 1840, merged with the RSM in 1866.

musicians', and added that 'although it aims at the advancement of the art, perhaps its chief objective may be better described as the guarding of the interests of the artists' (1882: 455). Initially it did this by establishing an examination system to regulate entry. Viewing musicians as skilled artists rather than as workers, within ten years the Society had grown to over 500 members. In 1892 it became the Incorporated Society of Musicians (ISM), claiming to be 'the only registered body of composing, teaching and performing musicians in this country' (cited in Ehrlich 1985: 128). However, Jempson correctly notes that, in reality, it was an elitist organisation, closed to 'the vast majority of musicians' (1993: 4).

The Union of Graduates in Music (UGM) was similar in outlook. Initially proposed in correspondence in the *Musical Times* in 1892,[17] it was constituted the following year. It was similarly restrictive in outlook, only allowing entry to those 'upon whom Degrees in Music have been conferred by one of the universities of the United Kingdom of GB and Ireland'. Using the completion of a music degree as a criterion for membership enabled it to exclude those guilty of what it called 'that glaring incompetence which at the present day is so often suffered to compete on equal terms with solid merit'. As well as this exclusivity, the UGM also appealed to a *moral* authority, stating that 'it will not be an aggressive institution: the moral influence of such a body of men will, it is thought, be quite sufficient to give weight to any resolutions it may pass' (Anon. 1892: 638).

The true nature of these new organisations was perhaps best captured in their willingness simultaneously to be dismissive of the bulk of their profession while attempting to advance the social status of their section of it. The Duke of Edinburgh was appointed President of the ISM in 1893, around the same time that it moved its headquarters to London. Overall, prior to the formation of the AMU, there were no organisations that would allow the overwhelming majority of 'players' in the pit orchestras to join, and certainly none that sought to improve working conditions across the entire music profession. However, the 'players'' conditions of engagement meant that there were plenty of reasons for them to organise, and the 1870s and 1880s produced the first signs of this. Some short-lived organisations from the 1870s and a one-off strike in 1886 provide evidence that, despite the prevailing economic climate being against them, certain musicians were considering taking radical measures to improve their lot.

The formation of these little-documented organisations in the mid-1870s was significant. Ehrlich mentions the founding of protective associations in

[17] It was formed in 1893, remained in operation until 1972, and was liquidated in 1975.

London and Manchester and the Birmingham Orchestral Association, speculating that their short-lived nature was due to 'unions in many trades suffering reverses during the mid-1870s' (1985: 145), but offers little further detail. Remaining minutes from the Manchester Musical Artistes' Protection Association (MMAPA)[18] are also somewhat lacking in detail. However, they refer to both the other organisations in passing and are of some help in understanding the MMAPA's aims and modus operandi.

Although a London association was already in operation, the emergence of such an organisation in Manchester in 1874 was significant. The MMAPA's first general meeting on 9 June proposed that 'we form a branch in Manchester in conjunction with the London Musical Artistes' Protection Association but that the Manchester branch keep its own funds' (MU, 2/1/1). While this plan was not agreeable to the London musicians, who sought a third of the Manchester subscription fees, it was clear that the two organisations were in contact and at least open to the possibility of creating a nationwide association.

The minutes also give useful insight into the type of musicians involved. The MMAPA's committee comprised representatives of eleven orchestras in the city covering the various theatres, music halls, and public spaces where they were employed.[19] Each committee member collected subscriptions from members in their own orchestra, while the organisation's secretary collected payments from those employed elsewhere. Significantly, the association was open to all musicians – including amateurs – who were to be 'admitted and accepted as members of the association' (minutes, 16 June 1874 (MU, 2/1/1)). Subsequent meetings of the association showed no evidence of any applicant being refused membership. However, despite meeting regularly over the next two years, a meeting on 22 June 1876 dissolved the Association.

The minutes provide examples of the issues affecting the theatre musicians. These centred on payment for extra performances and rehearsals and the growing problem of over-supply of musicians. The MMAPA argued for 'all extra performances in theatres to be paid in full in the same proportion as the regular performances' and wrote to the London Branch warning its members against taking engagements at the Manchester Theatre Royal, where 'the present members (of the orchestra) are threatened with unjust dismissal through the wish to improve the conditions' (MU, 2/1/1).

18 Recorded in the same minute book as the AMU's first EC meetings (MU, 2/1/1).

19 An additional, unattached member of the twelve-man committee represented 'miscellaneous' musicians. Among the orchestras represented were those from the Theatre Royal and the Alexander Music Hall, Mr C. Hallé's Orchestra, Mr De Jong's Orchestra, and the Casino Orchestra.

It is here that the MMAPA's importance becomes apparent. Not only was it open to all musicians, it is also the first documented musicians' association explicitly to stand up for workers' rights when faced with attacks from employers. It also betrayed its role as a protectionist organisation when warning the London musicians against taking work at the Royal, as 'there are already more musicians in Manchester than we have employment for' (MU, 2/1/1). In this respect the MMAPA was more important in the history of the trade unionism in the music profession than Ehrlich allows for. It was actually an important precursor of the AMU, with Williams acknowledging a debt to previous organisations in Manchester almost twenty years after the MMAPA's demise (see below, 44).[20] Meanwhile, Manchester and other cities in the north of England had the highest concentrations of theatre musicians outside London and, therefore, the greatest scope for organisation. The MMAPA had also sought to work with other musicians around the country and its experience suggested that Birmingham might prove to be a fertile location for the unionisation of musicians.[21]

London was less so, but even in the capital there was growing evidence of unrest among the non-elite musical workers. In 1886 the first significant strike by musicians in Britain took place at Her Majesty's Theatre. The musicians, who had not been paid, refused to continue after two acts of a performance of Gounod's *Faust*, inviting the audience to assist in their predicament by throwing money on stage. However, there is no evidence that the strike had a wider impact, beyond garnering some local public sympathy and perhaps inflicting some damage to the theatre owner's reputation. These were to be important tools in subsequent disputes, as was the fact that the musicians were supported, in this instance, by other theatre workers (the stage hands). But while the power of organised musical labour was becoming increasingly apparent both in the UK and further afield,[22] it would be another seven years before a musicians' union was formed in Britain. Explaining why requires examination of the position of trade unions in the UK around this time.

Moves towards unionism

Musicians became increasingly organised as the UK's population and its number of musicians grew exponentially during the nineteenth century. However,

[20] While not specifically naming them, he almost certainly was referring to the MMAPA as 'brave pioneers' (AMU minutes, 9 December 1894 (MU, 2/1/1)). There must have been some connection between the two for the minute book to be shared, though it is not clear what this was.

[21] One of Williams' first moves on forming the AMU in 1893 was to ally with similarly disgruntled musicians in Birmingham.

[22] The National League of Musicians was formed in the USA, also in 1886.

for most of this period forming a trade union for musicians was either illegal or unlikely. To understand fully why the AMU formed in 1893, it is necessary to look at broader patterns of trade union activity in the UK and then specifically at a combination of legislative, economic, and industrial conditions during the 1890s. Of particular importance were the rise of 'new unionism', the growth of other craft unions, and the emergence of the first white-collar unions. Within the music profession, the problem of locating its workers within the wider workforce and the diverse means of entry resulted in a fragmented response to the question of organisation.

Webb and Webb's description of the functions of the early-eighteenth-century trade societies and clubs among professions such as 'curriers, hatters, woolstaplers, shipwrights, brush-makers, basket makers and calico-printers' seems to present a pattern familiar to the music profession. They describe the typical 'trade club' of town artisans as being 'an isolated ring of highly-skilled journeymen', which resulted in a 'long maintained ... virtual monopoly of the better paid handicrafts in an almost hereditary caste of "tradesmen" in whose ranks the employers themselves had for the most part served their apprenticeship'. Besides protecting the craft from outsiders, the groups' activities included some 'haggling' with employers for better pay and 'the provision of friendly benefits' (Webb and Webb 1920: 45).

They locate the 'pioneers of the Trade Union movement' as being the 'extensive combinations of the West of England woolen-workers and the Midland framework knitters' (45) and proceed to detail the attempts of various combinations of workers to lobby Parliament for better pay and conditions throughout the late eighteenth century. However, the prevailing mood of the legislature was one that outlawed various combinations of workers, a process that culminated in the wide-ranging Combination Acts of 1799 and 1800. Prior to their repeal in 1824 and 1825, trade unions were effectively illegal in Great Britain.[23] In addition, until the Conspiracy and Protection of Property Act in 1875, 'the legality of many of their activities was at least doubtful and precarious' (Clegg *et al.* 1964: 43). The repeal of the Combination Acts removed the threat of prosecution for criminal conspiracy, but limited trade unions to negotiating hours and pay, and expressly forbade 'violence, threats, intimidation, molestation and instruction' (44).

While there also remained a variety of legislation that could be used against organised labour, during the middle part of the century trade unions nevertheless embedded themselves within a range of industries. Attempts dating

[23] Although this did not entirely prevent workers from organising, as Clegg *et al.* explained that 'it was left for employers to instigate proceedings and they were often unwilling to do so' (1964: 47).

back to 1818–19 to form a general union continued throughout the century and culminated in the formation of the TUC in 1868 (see Webb and Webb 1920: 115). The Trade Union Act of 1871 removed unions from possible prosecution for restraint of trade, while the Conspiracy and Protection of Property Act (1875) ruled that acts carried out by 'two or more persons in contemplation or furtherance of a trade dispute' were no longer viewed as criminal conspiracies in law (Webb and Webb 1920: 45). For Clegg *et al.* the legislation of the 1870s left unions with 'a satisfactory legal status, by obtaining protection where they most needed it' (1965: 46).[24]

The strengthened legal position of trade unions did not, however, result in a steady growth in union membership. Instead membership fluctuated, something Clegg *et al.* attribute to 'the trade cycle, since unions tend to flourish in prosperity and wither in depression' (1964: 4). Economic recession in the early 1880s resulted in a situation whereby 'British trade unionism had lain fallow for over a decade' (89). Indeed, it was the simultaneous emergence of new forms of trade unionism later in the decade that was to provide the opening for Williams to organise a musicians' union in 1893.

New unionism

The growth of trade unions and, in particular, general workers' unions (Hobsbawm 1949) following the upturn in trade in 1887 came to be known as 'new unionism', something described by Clegg *et al.* as 'one of the most colourful and baffling phenomena in British trade union history' (1964: 55). The mixture of improved economic conditions and the organisation of workers previously excluded from the traditional craft unions resulted in a raft of industrial action, with a record number of days lost to strikes in 1889.[25] With the number of trade unionists growing,[26] unions were increasingly embedded in large workplaces, co-operating with each other and creating closed shops in these workplaces to consolidate their power.

According to Clegg *et al.*, the consequences of this were 'a readiness to employ coercion against non-unionists and blacklegs [strike-breakers]' and 'a tendency to look to parliamentary and municipal action to solve labour's problems' (1964: 92). The most significant aspect of the phenomenon for musicians was that it substantially broadened the type and number of workers who felt comfortable belonging to a trade union. Unions were no longer

24 There were some further changes to the 1871 Act in the Trade Union Act Amendment Act (1876).

25 Largely down to the Great Dock Strike of that year.

26 The Board of Trade estimated the number of trade unionists in 1888 had reached 750,000, or around 5 per cent of the 'occupied population' (Clegg *et al.* 1964: 2).

the sole preserve of skilled, highly qualified workers. This served not only to create unions for previously non-unionised 'general' workers, but also to change the nature of organisation among workers who were formerly either organised by craft or reluctant to organise. This had specific implications for musicians.

At the crux of this was where to locate music as a profession. We have already seen that this was a source of conflict and it was later to cause problems in relations with other groups of workers.[27] Prior to 1893, all musicians' organisations had been built around the idea of musicians being skilled craftsmen qualified to enter the profession by either the granting of degrees or the serving of apprenticeships. The majority of the previously discussed organisations could be seen to fit Clegg *et al.*'s description of craft societies as ones 'built on custom to delimit a preserve of craftsman's work' (1964: 25), which were also 'defended against the unqualified, against changes in the techniques or organisation of the product, and against encroachments by other crafts' (5).

It was against this backdrop that musicians began to organise during the 1890s. As the profession had grown, the importance of the qualifications and training required to work as a musician had diminished. In effect, what had once been a closely gated profession now offered opportunities to individuals from a much wider range of abilities and backgrounds and in a much greater variety of locations. Also of importance here was the extremely porous nature of the profession. Many musicians also worked in other (non-musical) jobs or flitted in and out of work, meaning that subsequent organisations had to reflect this and so incorporated characteristics of both craft unions and the type of general union that had emerged during the 1880s. Ehrlich places musicians in the mid-nineteenth century as being 'ranked socially with artisans, not bourgeoisie' (1985: 50), and while the existing musicians' societies still sought to advance the social status of elite musicians, this was hardly a consideration for the growing number of professional and semi-professional musicians. Rather than elevating the status of the profession as a whole, their interest was in improving working conditions and pay.

In this respect it is perhaps more helpful to view musicians as white-collar workers, a group that had also begun to organise into trade unions in the late 1880s. Lockwood describes these groups of workers as being traditionally closer to the 'master class, with whom they worked in a close and personal relationship', and 'socially isolated from one another and dependent on the

27 At the 1929 TUC Congress, the MU's motions were shouted down and their members accused of being 'double jobbers' (Dambman 1929).

goodwill of particular employers' (1958: 57). As noted above, Britain's music profession began in this way, and although it changed irreversibly in the nineteenth century, social isolation and reliance on (frequently non-forthcoming) goodwill from employers remained a feature in 1893. As a result of this the contemporary profession was split between those who still did not wish to be 'tainted by association with manual workers' (Jempson 1993: 4) and a growing number who saw the formation of a trade union as the only viable way to advance their cause.

The OA and the AMU

One such musician was Joseph Bevir (Joe) Williams, a clarinet player in the orchestra at the Comedy Theatre in Manchester. From a family of theatre musicians,[28] Williams responded to an incident at the Gaiety Theatre in Manchester by producing an anonymous circular and distributing it amongst Manchester musicians. It asked them to attend a meeting on 7 May 1893 to 'discuss forming a Union for orchestral players' (cited in Teale 1929a: 8). Having decided to embark on the task of organising the union, Williams set out its purpose as being to establish:

> a protecting Union, one that will protect us from Amateurs, protect us from unscrupulous employers and protect us from ourselves. A Union that will guarantee our receiving a fair wage for engagements. A Society that will keep the amateur in his right place and prevent his going under price. A Union that will see you are paid for extra rehearsals and in time raise salaries to what they ought to be (8).

He set out four rules: that the Society be called the Manchester Musicians' Union, that entrance fees would be 3s and subscriptions 5s per year, that each member had to be proposed by two existing members, and that amateurs could join on 'payment of the entrance fee and half the annual subscription' (Teale 1929a: 8). Williams asked those interested to sign the letter and return it to 'Anonymous', 32 Clifford Street, Old Trafford. Around twenty musicians turned up to the meeting. Williams' vision had already extended beyond his home city as he had made contact with like-minded musicians in Birmingham. The AMU was then constituted and grew rapidly across the north of England. the Midlands, and Scotland over the next few years. The rest of this book tells the story of its subsequent journey.

[28] His father and three brothers all played in theatre orchestras; his mother was from a theatre family.

Prior to that it is worth considering the importance of Williams' initial vision of the Union and why it continued to alienate some within the profession. The two things of prime significance about the AMU's formation are its inclusiveness and geography. Unlike all the previous musicians' organisations, it was open to *all* musicians with no potential members turned away on the grounds of either ability or income. Even amateurs, one of the groups the Union was formed to protect against, were allowed to join on the grounds that they would be easier to control inside the organisation than out. While this inclusiveness was to provide the Union with the size of membership and finance that were subsequently to make it the largest representative body of British musicians, at first its growth was restricted by geography and the different concerns, working conditions, and aspirations of London musicians.

The AMU initially made few inroads into London, where the largest number of musicians (and all of the most successful ones) resided. This was primarily a result of the near-simultaneous formation, by Fred Orcherton, of the OA. Prompted by concerns about the influx of foreign musicians into the capital, it was formed after a mass meeting of orchestral musicians at the Royal Academy of Music on 25 May. Significantly, the Association chose its name after deciding that 'the word Union was not advisable' (LOA 1962: 5). Its approach to employers was more conciliatory than that of the AMU. Thus, while the Association offered help 'in any disputes occurring between members and their employers', it was strongly resistant to the methods used by trade unions, seeing these as incompatible with another stated aim: 'to enlighten public opinion upon matters orchestral with a view to raising the social status of the *orchestral* musician' (5, emphasis ours).

Compared to the AMU, the Association's initial aims were modest and its membership limited by geography and, to a lesser extent, professional status. It was, however, still a protection association, and moved a substantial number of London musicians a major step away from the professional societies of the past and towards trade unionism. Although the nature of the profession in London prevented its musicians from unionising as quickly as elsewhere, 1893 marked a huge shift in the way that musicians thought of themselves. Over 500 years after they started organising in Britain, the changes in the profession during the late nineteenth century meant that musicians had formed organisations that reflected a change of worldview. By finally thinking of themselves alongside other workers, musicians were at last on a path that would result in their being able to improve the terms and conditions under which they worked.

However, this long-coming change of perspective did not immediately result in a unified or more militant profession. Indeed, the aforementioned fractured history and its enshrined attitudes remained an impediment to full organisation of the musical workforce. This was evidenced by the ensuing conflicts between its two new representative bodies – the AMU and the OA.

2

Early days: the Amalgamated Musicians' Union, 1893–1918

Joe Williams (see Figure 1) was just twenty-one when he decided to try and form the union that he was to dominate for the next thirty-one years. His youth and lack of status in the music profession, coupled with a longstanding resistance to trade unionism among professional musicians, meant that the success of his venture seemed unlikely. But an examination of the working conditions of his contemporaries was to prove his hunch that 'on all sides it is admitted that one [a union] is necessary' (cited in Ehrlich 1985: 146). This, along with Williams' tactical astuteness, was to establish the AMU over the next three decades, despite considerable obstacles.

This chapter explains how this was achieved by detailing what happened in the period immediately after the Union's formation. It begins by describing the musicians' working conditions in the 1890s before outlining the formation itself. To do the former, it will draw on first-hand accounts of employment in the theatres and music halls found in the early publications of both the AMU and the rival OA. The second part focuses on the AMU's foundation and its rivals and opponents within the profession. It also reflects on the purpose and internal configurations (and disputes) of the formative Union. The chapter then considers the key issues for the Union during its early years and the tactics it employed to achieve its desired outcomes. In short, it outlines what the Union actually did – nationally and locally – in the late nineteenth and early twentieth centuries, considering both the headline-grabbing and mundane aspects of its activities.

The chapter concludes by considering the disruption caused to the music profession by the outbreak of the First World War in 1914. After the steady growth of the Union during its first twenty years, the war was the first of a series of major disruptions to musical employment that – along with the Union's responses to them – constitute the backbone of this history. While many musicians served in the war and 201 AMU members perished, it was

Figure 1 Joseph Bevir Williams, founder of the AMU (MU, 5/2).

also a period that confirmed the Union's importance and embedded it at the centre of the UK's musical life. By 1918, the AMU had moved from being one of many organisations representing musicians to the dominant one, with 15,000 members and a reputation among employers as a fierce negotiator. Here we show how Williams steered the Union from its modest Manchester origins to being a powerful, national organisation whose policies and style of leadership 'ultimately dominated industrial relations in music throughout the country' (Ehrlich 1985: 146).

Musical work in the 1890s

Fully understanding the conditions that facilitated the formation of the AMU in 1893 necessitates some consideration of where its potential members worked, who employed them, and the conditions under which they were engaged. One useful source for establishing this is the price lists created by individual AMU branches during its first two years of operation. For example, a price list drawn up by the Newcastle Branch suggested that the bulk of work was in (variety) theatres, though the rates members would expect to be paid per week were determined by the stature of the theatre and whether the engagement was seasonal or occasional. In addition, a small number of members performed on stage as part of opera performances,[1] but most employment came via one-off engagements or short seasons in myriad venues or contexts that had an occasional need for musical accompaniment. These included assemblies and dances, balls, church services, bazaars, garden parties, wedding receptions, and performances in public parks and halls. While most musicians tended to work in and around their place of residence, there was also seasonal migration with musicians moving to seaside resorts to play during periods when theatres traditionally closed over the summer.[2]

The nature of the work meant that the majority of musicians were competing for short- or medium-term employment in local labour markets where supply (including that from amateurs and semi-professionals) outstripped the number of jobs available. Those unable to find work in a theatre orchestra had to make do with sporadic work in different places of entertainment, or by occasionally deputising for orchestra members. The deputy system was itself a product of job insecurity. With musicians taking on more work than they could actually perform, it became common practice for those faced with a double booking to organise for a deputy to fulfil the less well remunerated one. Ehrlich (1985: 31) dates this system to the 1760s, and while it often did little for the quality of the orchestras, managers accepted it as a means of maintaining cordial industrial relations.

These were, however, fraught at the time of the AMU's formation and had been for many years. Among the common complaints detailed about orchestral conditions of the time were low pay, cramped conditions, long hours, unpaid rehearsals, and heavy-handed management. Ehrlich's account notes that, until this point, orchestral players had 'generally been anonymous creatures' (1985: 143) who had received little scrutiny from outside the profession, operating as a necessary but largely hidden backing for singers and variety stars.[3] He also notes that the over-supply of labour was to present

1 Shorter-term engagements were usually paid at a higher weekly rate than longer-term ones. Appearing on stage usually resulted in a higher fee than performing in the orchestra pit, while theatre orchestras generally paid more than music halls (AMU, *Musicians' Monthly Report and Journal* [*MMRJ*], May 1895: 84).

2 Similar employment patterns existed amongst contemporaneous American musicians (Preston 1992).

3 Neither of these groups was considered eligible for membership of the AMU, either joining their own professional organisations/unions or remaining non-unionised.

the biggest obstacle facing those trying to organise the music profession, and effectively suppressed any 'demands for higher wages and better working conditions' (143).

The negative attitudes towards and surrounding theatre orchestras were made apparent by formation of workers' organisations. An early edition of the *Orchestral Association Gazette* gives a snapshot of such attitudes from both the public and managers. According to the (anonymous) author, while musicians traditionally performed during plays or at their intervals, 'it is too often the case that the band is regarded as a necessary evil, and that a good reason for dispensing with it altogether would be welcomed by most managers' (MU, 1/8/2). Unsurprisingly, dissatisfaction with management within theatres and music halls was widespread, as managers often delegated all responsibility for musicians to conductors or bandleaders. The same article claimed that the typical manager had 'not a note of music in his head yet he dictates what is and what is not good in music', while conductors were portrayed as having 'not a rudimentary acquaintance of how to handle an orchestra' (MU, 1/8/2).

Working conditions naturally varied among venues and in different parts of the country, as did the level of attention paid to the individual bands. It was clear that, while the public wanted and expected high-quality musical performances as part of theatre productions, the theatre managers' focus was more on suppressing costs. Ehrlich describes the theatre in the 1860s as 'a sweated industry' (1985: 144) and there was little evidence that this changed substantially in the years running up to 1893. Despite unsocial and variable hours (rehearsals were often arranged at the last minute), cramped and dirty working conditions, and low pay, the insecurity of their positions ensure that, with a few exceptions,[4] musicians remained supine.

There is one further point to note about the nature of employers in the theatre in 1893 – they were mainly small-scale, local entrepreneurs and it was with these that the Union initially came into contact. However, the growth of large theatre chains was imminent. Sir Edward Moss opened the Empire Palace Theatre in Edinburgh in 1892 and, in collaboration with Sir Oswald Stoll, incorporated Moss Empires Ltd in 1899. Within four years they controlled seventeen theatres across the UK, presenting a much more formidable obstacle for the Union when it came to bargaining over wages.

While the working conditions cried out for a response from musicians, in 1893 they were divided as to how to advance the profession. Such splits were a result of a mixture of self-interest, geography, and deep-seated ideological differences as to how to advance the lot of orchestral musicians.

[4] Such as the 1886 strike at Her Majesty's Theatre, London, covered in the previous chapter.

Union or association?

Subsequent to the founding of the AMU, events were fundamentally to alter the music profession in the UK. By attempting to organise in an effort to improve pay and conditions, musical workers in the UK were, for the first time since the failed attempts of the protection associations in Manchester and Birmingham in the 1870s, forming groups that focused on working conditions and not on the type of professional validation and control of entry into the profession offered by the ISM and UGM. Inevitably, such attempts resulted in schisms across the profession, as individual musicians and their representative organisations fought for power and influence. Though the AMU was ultimately to become the dominant musicians' organisation, it only reached this position after considerable opposition.

It is also unsurprising that the attempts to organise in 1893 came in the same cities as in the 1870s, with Birmingham and Manchester at the forefront of moves towards unionisation. While the accepted narrative is that Williams formed the AMU when he produced the anonymous circular described earlier, there is some evidence that by this point Birmingham musicians were already organised. Two years later a member at an AMU Conference of Delegates held in Leeds disputed Manchester's claim to be the parent branch of the AMU, claiming that 'I was one of the active workers and the Union was in existence before you heard of it. Birmingham is the leader of this movement. We got one started on March 17 and yours was sometime later than that' (MU, 1/1).

While the Birmingham meeting, which was chaired by Sam Tute (later an AMU EC member), certainly preceded Williams' meeting, it remains unclear how the two groups got together and at what point the name the Amalgamated Musicians' Union was first used. Initially both Tute's and Williams' ambitions were largely parochial, based on organising musicians in the theatres and music halls of their home cities. More details of Williams' ambitions remain, especially in the circular that he produced and distributed amongst the orchestra pits of Manchester's theatres. Williams' aims for the Union were largely protective, but a key aspect of his plan was that the Union would be open to *all* musicians willing to pay an entrance fee and subscription.

Tellingly, his first demands focused on both pay and conditions of work. They were those of pursuing 'a fair wage for engagements … a society that will keep the Amateur in his right place, and prevent his going under prices (and ensuring that) … you are paid for extra rehearsals' (cited in Teale 1929a: 8). Raising salaries more generally was seen as a longer-term ambition. The circular also made the case for organised labour in the music profession, provided a list of proposed rules for the new Union and suggested a date for a first meeting.

Williams' proposed rules set out his vision of the Union and further highlighted the issues facing working musicians.[5] A key proposal was that, unlike that of other musicians' organisations, membership would also be open to amateurs, who would pay half the rate of full members. While this was seemingly at odds with the Union's declared aim of protecting its members from such musicians, it was a tactic designed to control their activities. Indeed, it is uncertain how amateurs would have benefited from membership, as other rules seemed loaded against them. For example, members were prevented from sending non-members to deputise for them and from sending amateurs 'if a professional is disengaged'. Amateurs were also not allowed to take up regular engagements. The remaining rules focused on payment for rehearsals, calls for morning performances, and the setting of rates for 'Balls and Assemblies' (Teale 1929a: 8).

While only twenty or so musicians from the city's various orchestras turned up to the meeting on 7 May, this was sufficient for Williams to move ahead with his plan. Having lifted his veil of anonymity, he became the AMU's leader, appointing the London-based Yorkshire violinist J. T. Carrodus as its President[6] and Dr William Spark[7] as its patron. While these appointments were largely designed to bestow credibility on the Union, Williams' mother, Kate Leigh, took on a much more practical role, acting as an assistant to her son prior to the appointment of E. S. Teale to the position of Assistant Secretary in 1896. Kate's involvement at the Union's General Office continued long beyond Teale's appointment, making her the only prominent woman in the Union's early history.

The Union quickly changed its name from the Manchester Musicians' Union to the Amalgamated Musicians' Union as it connected with other musicians around the country. The first branch was formed in Dundee on 8 June 1893, and by the end of its first year the Union had 1,093 members with branches in Glasgow, Liverpool, and Newcastle-on-Tyne. Membership continued to grow, reaching 2,421 by the end of 1894, with a further seventeen branches forming, mainly in cities in Scotland, the North of England, and the Midlands.[8] The Union held its first General Meeting in Manchester on 29 October 1893 and its first Delegate Conference took place in Liverpool on 11 November 1894. The latter gathering was attended by nineteen branches and Williams reported that 'the progress of the Union during the past year has been in the

5 Williams' mother, Kate, seemingly assisted in the preparation of the circular (Teale 1929a: 8).

6 Confusingly, Carrodus was also to be appointed to the same position in the OA (*Musical News*, 4 November 1893: 396).

7 Spark was organist at Leeds Town Hall for over forty years as well as being a conductor and composer.

8 The furthest south of the initial branches were in Bristol and Cardiff.

highest degree satisfactory' (AMU *Monthly Report*, January 1895: 1). An EC was appointed and met for the first time on 9 December 1894.

Teale later described the AMU's early years as being about 'getting together the framework of the administrative side of the organisation, forming Branches, getting an EC together, appointing Trustees, and deciding on Rules' (1929a: 9). But this was far from a trouble-free enterprise for Williams and a pivotal moment came in 1895 when members of the Manchester Branch challenged his authority. The dispute began over the Union's *Monthly Report*, which was to be distributed by branches and which members were compelled to purchase. Disapproving of these instructions, the branch initially complained that it did not believe that members should be forced to buy the report. This soon escalated into complaints about Williams' stewardship of the Union. Given the trivial and imprecise nature of the complaints (there were also suggestions that Williams was profiteering from AMU work given to printing companies), there is much to suggest that Teale was correct in his assessment that the issue was rather based on the resentment of some malcontents in orchestras who saw the leadership of the Union as 'an EC composed mostly of music hall and theatre musicians, plus what was considered to be a boy GS in an inferior orchestral position' (1929a: 9).

Williams responded forcefully to something he saw as being both an attack on his character and 'against the spirit, and injurious to the wellbeing of the Union' (MU, 2/1/1). The Manchester officials were suspended and a Conference of Delegates was organised for 19 May 1895 to resolve the matter. With the exception of the three Manchester delegates, the Conference backed Williams' handling of the matter, with the Newcastle Branch typical of the strength of feeling of the Conference in their exhortation to Williams that 'you cannot deal too strongly with the Manchester people. They have come here to waste time and bring forward irrelevant questions' (MU, 1/1).

An offer by Williams to resign was rejected by delegates and he was subsequently able to consolidate his power within the Union. Thereafter, any dissent was intermittent and unco-ordinated, usually focused on individual branches resenting the Union's centralised power structure. From 1894 onwards, the major threats to Williams' power were from litigious employers and those musicians remaining outside the Union. The latter grouping seem to comprised those guilty of musical snobbery and/or holding the belief that trade unionism was incompatible with working as a musician, something that was embedded in the OA's ethos. Following the General Meeting in October 1893 Williams reached out to the Association, seeking affiliation with them. This was not immediately forthcoming – the OA preferring a less formal working agreement – thus highlighting the differences between the two organisations.

The Association enjoyed the status conferred by the fact that its founder, Fred Orcherton, was a member of the Queen's Hall Orchestra (and a member of Queen Victoria's private orchestra) and that some of its members were well known in established orchestral circles. Its respectability was further evident in the location for its initial meeting, which was held at the RSM, after Orcherton had, like Williams, issued a circular. In this instance around sixty musicians attended. However, a subsequent meeting, held at the Royal Academy of Music in June 1893, attracted some 500 musicians.

Ehrlich describes the Association as being 'like the AMU, but with far more decorum' (1985: 153), and evidence of this is provided by its aims and objectives. While it shared the AMU's protectionist aims, and saw itself as being 'for the protection of the best interests of orchestral musicians' (MU, 1/8/1), it adopted restrictive entry criteria, specifying that membership was open to 'all *professional* orchestral players, resident in the UK and of good character' (MU, 1/8/1, emphasis ours). If the OA was less accommodating of amateurs than the AMU, it still relied on musicians *declaring* themselves to be professional. Many of its aims overlapped with the AMU's, including the organisation of funds for sickness and funeral benefits, provision of legal assistance in disputes, and working as an unofficial agent providing orchestras for events and institutions. The key differences between the two organisations lay in their attitude to amateurs and their general approach to employers. The OA refused to strike and adopted a more conciliatory tone, 'keeping industrial disputes at a distance, and allowing time to calm tempers and induce compromise' (MU, 1/8/1).

Many orchestral musicians greeted the Association enthusiastically. A report on their first Annual General Meeting in August 1894 noted that membership had risen to 1,100 (MU, 1/8/3), including some members outside London in the Hallé, Scottish, and Carl Rosa Orchestras. In its early years, the Association produced a directory and provided legal help for some members, while being careful to maintain its distance from trade unionism. By registering as a company – and not a union – the Executive stated that its aim was to 'bring to bear upon all connected with our branch of the profession a wholesome influence rather than a wholesale coercion' while stressing that they viewed 'the professional status and interests of orchestral musicians as matters which should and may be conserved in a higher plane than Trade Unionism' (MU, 1/8/3).

This loftier approach did not prevent it from being viewed – like the AMU – as a threat to the profession by the established organisations that represented London's musical elites, with the UGM and ISM both using musical journals of the time to dissuade musicians from involvement with either. The most redoubtable attacks on the AMU came from Ebenezer Prout in the *Monthly Musical Record*.[9] He responded to Williams' request to be a patron of the AMU by attacking both its particular aims and those of the wider trade union movement. Prout's main objections were based around the Union's threat of force and its desire to interfere in labour markets, which he believed should be regulated only by supply and demand. He described trade unions as a 'system of organised tyranny' (1893: 146). Furthermore, he claimed that any musicians' union was doomed to failure, that Williams was 'utterly mistaken in his ideas', and that the existence of a union would 'aggravate rather than alleviate' the problems facing orchestral musicians (147).

Five months later Thomas Southgate, the Secretary of the UGM, extended the attack to include the OA in the *Musical News*, in an article entitled 'Questionable orchestral associations'.[10] Transparently self-interested, this highlighted the perceived threat to the musical establishment caused by the AMU and OA. Southgate saw the OA as 'a more harmless affair' than the AMU, but regarded both as being superfluous in the context of the ISM and UGM exerting 'a very considerable influence on the welfare of those professing music, and indirectly on the art itself' (Southgate 1893).

Southgate was particularly riled by the AMU's acceptance of amateurs, suggesting that this would result in the Union's membership being 'a strange collection of skilled and unskilled entities, and the most objectionable features of the Trades' Unions will be adopted, viz. all are reduced to one level'. Likewise, he took aim at the OA for admitting 'anybody who chooses to call himself a professional musician and has 8s in his pocket', before launching a patronising claim that 'a union of orchestral players properly thought out and with the right sort of people at the head of it would be most valuable and useful', and recommending that his readers avoid both organisations (Southgate 1893).

These high-profile attacks on organised labour were quickly rebutted as the OA's *Gazette* summarised Southgate's article as 'keep the band down' (December 1893: 24). However, his intervention highlighted the impact that the new organisations had made in a very short period of time. Crucially, the AMU and OA had radically challenged pre-existing notions of what it was to be a professional musician. By treating musicians as workers, and seeking an improvement in their conditions, the two organisations were diametrically opposed in outlook to those, like Prout and Southgate, who were beneficiaries of limited entry to the profession.

9 Prout was a well-known composer and a professor of music at the Guildhall School of Music, having previously held a similar position at the Royal Academy of Music.

10 Southgate was also the editor of *Musical News*.

Despite the opposition they faced from elements within the profession, both the AMU and OA survived their early years and retained a solid base of members. The AMU's membership grew rapidly and exceeded 3,000 in 1895. This level was more or less unchanged until 1907, and established the AMU as the more powerful of the two organisations.[11] It was from this base that Williams was able to define the main issues facing the Union and the tactics that it was to employ in order to deal with them.

Defining the issues

When the AMU's executive met for the first time at the end of 1894, the Union had already begun to identify the most pressing concerns for its members, with a number of themes emerging that were to remain prominent throughout its history. Williams' initial aims of protecting members' employment prospects from the interventions of amateurs, unscrupulous employers, and fellow musicians were soon extending to combating competition from military and police bands and foreign musicians. Although amateurs were (along with all other non-unionised labour) part of an over-supply in the job market that kept rates of pay low and conditions poor, the Union's initial concerns about military and police bands were largely aesthetic and based on combating the widespread perception that they could play to a higher standard than many theatre musicians. This was largely a provincial problem, but when the Union established a London Branch in 1896 it became increasingly aware of the displacement of members by foreign musicians.[12] Regardless of the types of non-unionised workers involved, such issues persisted, becoming most prominent during periods of high unemployment and echoing age-old concerns over regulating entry to the profession.

Problems around competition were first noticeable in the early years of the twentieth century when the AMU's *Musicians' Monthly Report and Journal* (*MMRJ*) blamed amateurs for a lack of job opportunities in London. It claimed that 'hundreds of pounds' worth of business is being carried out by amateurs', who were described as 'blacklegs of the worst description, as they are employed in government offices by day, and in receipt of good salaries. In the meantime, disengaged lists are being sent round London theatres every week with some hundred odd names of professional men upon them' (*MMRJ*, March 1903: 3).

11 This was partly due to geography. Although the AMU had made some inroads by setting up branches in London, prior to 1909 the OA largely limited its recruitment to the London area.

12 The majority of foreign musicians in the UK moved to London because of the perceived job opportunities, though many left disappointed (David-Guillou 2009: 294).

The reference to these musicians working at other jobs was part of a broader concern that musicians were 'double-jobbers'. This became a perennial problem for the AMU, internally with its unemployed members and externally with some other trade unionists, who perceived musical work as being a largely part-time occupation. When Williams addressed the Manchester and Salford Trades Council in November 1894, seeking their support in his campaign against the deployment of military musicians in civilian contexts, he was immediately quizzed by members of the Typographical Association as to 'what proportion of the members of the Musicians' Union earn their livelihood from music only?' (*Manchester Courier*, 16 November 1894: 3). Whilst in this instance the AMU was supported by other unions, there remained a widespread suspicion that it was preaching one thing while its members practised another.

Despite amateurs' impact on the availability of work causing ongoing concern, the Union spent less time on dealing with this than it did with other threats to employment. Amateurs' seemingly limited ability meant that the vast majority were unlikely to be a serious option for most employers. The well-trained musicians in the army and police bands were seen as far more likely to displace Union labour and thus became a far greater source of irritation. Williams quickly identified this as an issue, writing in 1894 to the Commanding Officer of Salford barracks and lobbying the local trades' council about four cornet players from the barracks taking part in shows by the Carl Rosa Opera Company at Manchester's Prince's Theatre for rates that were 'less than a fourth' of what professional musicians would have been paid for the job (*MMRJ*, February 1895: 25). Similar protestations were made in Glasgow, when the Union wrote to Colonel Oxley of the Gordon Highlanders in Maryhill and to Campbell Bannerman, the Secretary of State for War, complaining about the use of military musicians in theatre orchestras. The Union's concern was not simply the undercutting of expected pay levels, but the fact that this competition was being subsidised by the State. Williams argued that military bands 'secure their engagements not because they play better, but by means of their uniforms, which are I believe, the property of the State', and compared their lot with those of civilian musicians (25).

Williams observed that Union members had to pay for both instruments and tuition, contrasting this with military musicians who 'are taught free, have their instruments paid for, and, being soldiers, are provided for' (*MMRJ*, February 1895: 25). Charles Jesson, an early AMU activist, noted that military musicians were also perceived as being 'more skilful than civilian bands' (*MMRJ*, 5 May 1895: 83), this resulting from them having time to practise with the same musicians and not – like their civilian counterparts – being called upon to sight-read in hastily put-together 'scratch' bands. Military bands were to remain an issue for the Union, partly because of the public appetite for them and partly because of the military hierarchy's reluctance to place too many restrictions on their charges' extracurricular activities. Although they frequently made reassuring noises to the Union, there was little evidence of any fundamental change in policy at either the War Office or local level, and military musicians continued to permeate theatre orchestras.

In their attempts to raise awareness of the issue, the AMU printed 500 circulars for the TUC in Edinburgh in 1896, where Williams attempted to convince delegates of the 'unjust competition' from military and police bandsmen. Meanwhile individual branches of the Union began to form their own professional military bands.[13] In 1909, the Union organised a protest at the House of Commons, where they launched a barge on the Thames festooned by banners highlighting the issue. However, the response was one that suggested a limited degree of public and political sympathy for the Union's stance.

A second threat to jobs came from the growing number of European musicians who were working in London. The appearance of a Blue Hungarian Band as part of Queen Victoria's Golden Jubilee in 1897 produced the first occasion on which the Union wrote to the Government over the issue. In 1901 a petition was raised to King Edward VII urging action to prevent what the Union described as the 'wholesale importation of foreign bands'. In an attempt to limit the number of foreign musicians working in orchestras, it imposed a by-law that allowed membership to foreigners only if they had been resident for two years or were 'already a member of the MU in their own country' (*MMRJ*, May 1901: 3). This issue was also to recur throughout the Union's history, notably during the First World War and its aftermath.

If competition in the labour market from various types of non-Unionists occupied much of the AMU's time in its early days, it is important to emphasise that this was only part of a range of issues surrounding pay and conditions. Elsewhere the Union's initial focus was on trying at least to ensure that existing pay and conditions did not deteriorate when threatened by individual theatre managers. Its ability to achieve this over a number of years was the result of its own decisions and tactics combined with a number of external interventions and events from which it was to benefit.

The AMU's initial strategies were generally similar to those employed by its contemporaries, concentrating on maximising the number of members both in individual workplaces and across the profession in order to create advantageous conditions for collective bargaining over pay and conditions. This could

[13] The first of these were reported in the *MMRJ*, formed in Liverpool in 1896.

only be achieved via a high density of Union membership and by threatening of industrial action where disputes arose. Simultaneously, unions worked to strengthen their support by local, national, and international engagement with the wider labour movement and by communicating the benefits of membership to both existing and potential members. The AMU adapted its tactics to the nature of the music profession, and its initial approach can be characterised as a combination of recruitment and industrial action, litigation, communication, and political lobbying.

Recruitment and industrial action

The fragmented nature of the musical workforce presented the AMU with a number of specific problems. Whereas in other industries it was possible to achieve a high density of membership because of the relatively small number of employers and high numbers of workers in some individual workplaces, this was difficult to achieve across a profession characterised by both a large number of employers and differing attitudes to trade unionism.

From the start of the Union, many musicians worked in a number of different jobs, for a number of employers, and frequently on a short- or medium-term basis. This made trying to establish a closed shop – a tactic deployed by larger, more industrial unions – virtually impossible for the early AMU. It was to remain an insurmountable challenge for the Union, but it is worth noting that orchestras, as the largest groups of musicians, were always a prime recruiting ground for the AMU. Most of the Union's initial members were in theatre or music hall orchestras and these remained the most unionised parts of the music profession, while remaining a small percentage of all potential members.

The nature of musical employment has also dictated the type of industrial action across the profession. Any strikes in which the Union has been involved have tended to be relatively small-scale and localised. The first AMU-organised strikes covered a range of issues in a number of cities and were of varying durations and outcomes. While detailing all of them here is impossible, we will provide an overview of some of the various disputes and their effectiveness.

The first recorded strike was at the Liverpool Court Theatre in the summer of 1894, when the theatre owner offered musicians in the orchestra a pay cut of 5/- in return for keeping the theatre open for four of the eight weeks during which it was normally closed during the summer. With Williams (who was working there at the time) as the main instigator, the dispute was resolved when the management restored full wages for all the musicians except four horn players, whose wages were topped up by contributions from the other members of the orchestra (Teale 1929b: 27).

A more typical and important dispute came the following year at the Leeds Grand Theatre, which was described retrospectively by a delegate at the Union's May 1895 Conference as 'our pioneer struggle' (MU, 1/1). Significantly, the successful tactics employed by the Union were to create a template of sorts for future actions. The dispute was triggered by the takeover of the theatre by John Hart, who had already established himself as a fierce anti-Unionist when, as manager of the Bradford Theatre Royal, he had threatened to sack any musician joining the Union. At Leeds one of his first moves was to reduce the level of pay to the same level as he paid in Bradford. When the Leeds musicians walked out he immediately sacked them, and replaced them with non-Union members and three of the original band who went back to work.

The strike began at Easter and lasted fifteen weeks before, faced with declining audiences,[14] Hart was forced to reach into a compromise. For the strike's duration the Union had provided support for striking members, partly funded by a levy of 1/- per month imposed by the EC. The striking musicians were paid £1 per week for the first month of the strike, 15s for the second and 10s for the third, making it easier for the Union to retain the support of members. Those striking picketed the theatre, using handbills and sandwich boards to convey their message and appealing to fellow trade unionists not to patronise the theatre. Support from other unions and the local trades' councils were an essential part of the striking strategy, as was the Union's provision for its members.

Further disputes in Leeds (1895, 1897) and Oldham (1897) occupied the Union briefly, but a report on a strike at the Opera House in Northampton (1908–09) suggests that the nature of industrial action was largely unchanged. In this case, a new owner (Milton Bode) sacked a number of Union members and imposed stricter working conditions, resulting in a strike that mobilised local trade unionists in a boycott of the Opera House. Faced with declining audiences, the Union members were reinstated after twenty-three weeks of strike action, during which the non-Union musicians who replaced them were also targeted.

Although localised disputes were to remain a feature of the Union's activities, the changing nature of musical employment meant that it soon became engaged in less parochial disputes. Initially, this was because of the growing popularity

14 The *MMRJ* reported that 'even Sarah Bernhardt could not fill the pit and gallery' (August 1895: 151).

of the music halls and variety theatres. Russell describes the growth of the halls, noting how, in the early twentieth century, they managed to 'penetrate even those smaller towns previously regarded as uneconomic', citing 1910–14 as 'the zenith' of their popularity (1997: 294). This, along with the increased willingness of the Government to become involved in the resolution of industrial disputes, enabled the AMU to gain some considerable advantages in the wake of the 1907 Music Hall strike.

This was instigated by the VAF,[15] which launched a charter for improved wages and conditions that put it in dispute with the hall managers. The strike involved over 2,000 VAF members and was supported by those AMU members working in the music halls. Lasting two weeks, it affected twenty-two theatres and importantly saw major stars of the day, including Marie Lloyd and Arthur Roberts, on picket lines. Lloyd's involvement was to be pivotal when the strike was referred to the Board of Trade under the Trades Disputes Act (1896). Her evidence at the conciliation hearings conducted by George Askwith[16] was seen as pivotal in producing an outcome that greatly improved the pay and working conditions of artistes, stage employees, and musicians working in the halls. For Jempson, this represented a 'major victory for all those who worked in London theatre' (1993: 11).

Here the AMU was a beneficiary of the VAF's power and the esteem and popularity of stars like Lloyd. Askwith's pay award imposed a minimum wage of 30s per week for all musicians in London's music halls with additional payments for matinees and special rehearsals.[17] While this represented a huge advance for *some* musicians, Askwith's remit was limited and he made 'no order with regard to deputies or any other claims on behalf of musicians'. Additionally the award did not apply to musicians in provincial halls as it was claimed 'no dispute exists at the present time' (*The Era*, 15 June 1907: 1). However, Askwith was to remain an arbitrator in music hall disputes, and through this was further to advance the pay and conditions of musicians. In 1911, an amendment to his original award granted a pay rise of 1/- per week to London musicians and achieved wage parity for drummers. A further award for provincial musicians in 1912 did not set minimum rates, but placed a number of obligations on the employers, including a maximum working week of twenty-six-and-a-half hours as well as payment for matinees and additional rehearsals.

15 Formed in 1906, by the time of the strike the VAF had approximately 4,000 members.

16 Askwith's findings were published in June 1907, following twenty-three formal sittings and evidence from over 100 witnesses.

17 Drummers were only awarded a minimum of 28/- per week, while theatres that opened during the period of the agreement had to pay a minimum of 32/- (30/- for drummers).

Ehrlich claims that Askwith's interventions in the music halls acted as 'an effective recruiting sergeant' for the AMU (1985: 182). Despite competition from both the OA and the newly formed National Federation of Professional Musicians (NFPM),[18] AMU membership increased from 3,839 in 1907 to 8,757 in 1913, adding to the Union's financial reserves and industrial muscle. Both were integral to the Union's longest-running battle in the pre-war era, with Sir Oswald Stoll, who unsurprisingly saw the Union's influence in his expanding variety theatre empire as a malign one and whose powerful position highlighted the challenges faced by the AMU.

The Stoll dispute began at the end of 1912, when the Union decided to seek a minimum wage of £2 2/- a week, only to be undermined by the engagement of many non-members across Stoll's Moss Empires venues on considerably less. Beyond being a dispute about wages, it developed into one that focused instead on the Union's desire to create a closed shop among musicians working for Stoll. Having dragged on with little sign of movement on either side, this came to a head at the start of 1914. A localised strike at the Middlesex Music Hall, caused by a member of the AMU promising to support strike action and then defecting to the OA, was escalated when musicians at the Chiswick, Hackney, Shepherd's Bush, and Wood Green Empires walked out and raised the prospect of what the *Daily Herald* described as 'a general strike involving thousands of men in London and the provinces' (6 January 1914: 8). While this did not fully materialise there was further support from musicians at the Hippodrome and Ardwick Empire in Manchester, who stressed that they had 'no grievance as regarded wages and conditions' but 'felt bound to support their fellow members in London' (*Manchester Courier and Lancashire General Advertiser*, 8 January 1914: 7). Union anger at military musicians was increased by reports of their 'blacklegging' at some of Stoll's halls during the disputes, and Williams called on fellow trade unionists to boycott Stoll's halls (MRC, MSS 292/20/2/50–9 and 112–20).

Despite sympathy actions by fellow musicians and the growth in size of the Union, the strike served to highlight the enduring problems of non-membership and splits in the profession. During the Stoll dispute, amateurs, military bandsmen, and members of the OA all filled the positions of the AMU members, allowing Stoll to continue operations and creating division within the music profession. If this was a tactic utilised by many employers, it was one that would only work where there was either an over-supply of labour or a

[18] Founded in 1907, the NFPM registered as a trade union and sought to include only 'competent musicians of good moral character' (Ehrlich 1985: 181), excluding amateurs and 'double-jobbers'. Williams accused them of being 'an association of seceders and excluded members' (MRC, MSS 292/20/2/50–9).

relatively low density of Union membership. In 1914, for all its advances, the AMU was still struggling on both fronts, and the dispute was resolved after the intervention of Ramsay MacDonald.[19] Stoll waived the damages awarded to him against the musicians and offered the prospect of re-employment if vacancies arose (MU, 1/8/48). This allowed both sides to claim victory. For Williams 'the biggest fight the AMU has ever entered into' had resulted in 'its reputation [being] enhanced' (*MMRJ*, August 1914: 1) although its finances were severely depleted in supporting the strike.

The AMU in the courts

The cost of strikes was not the only item of expenditure to which the Union's income was being allocated. From the beginning, litigation costs were a major drain on its financial resources.[20] The Union was particularly enthusiastic in its use of the law to establish itself and spent many thousands on legal fees, resulting in criticism from both members and other organisations.[21] Nevertheless, Teale's history of the AMU boasts that Williams 'received so many writs he could paper his house with them' and that 'we could furnish a decent-sized library with bound volumes in our various legal cases' (1929b: 27). Ehrlich also notes that Williams claimed that by the end of the lengthy Williams–Dallimore case in 1914 he had already appeared before six judges (1985: 183).

The cases in which the Union became involved all centred around either trade disputes or reputational damage inflicted by slander or libel. While the former yielded some positive outcomes, the readiness of Union leaders and officials to make derisory public comments about their opponents often led to damages being awarded against them. Early examples offer a flavour of what was to follow. In 1895 a slander case was brought against the Glasgow Branch Secretary, Henry Vollmer. The plaintiff was Edward De Banzie, the musical director of the Royal and Royalty Theatres in Glasgow, who raised the action after the suicide of the one of the musicians working for him, Gottfried Hepner. Vollmer had been quoted in a letter as claiming that 'De Banzie's tyrannical way is the cause of the death of Hepner' (*Edinburgh Evening News*, 24 October 1894: 2) and De Banzie sought damages. During the court case the characters of the disputants were examined in great detail

19 A friend of Stoll, MacDonald was leader of the Labour Party and in 1924 became its first Prime Minister.

20 In 1914 Williams petitioned the TUC's Parliamentary Committee for financial support for the AMU's legal cases (MRC, MSS 292/20/2/50–9).

21 The NFPM pointedly claimed that its membership fees would 'not line lawyers' gowns' (Ehrlich 1985: 183).

and the judge eventually ruled in favour of De Banzie, awarding him £5 damages (and expenses) and noting that 'the defender [Vollmer] wrote a letter that was slanderous and defamatory' (*MMRJ*, March 1895: 55). Although this was a reverse for the Union, the final award was a fraction of the £500 damages claimed by De Banzie. The Union's willingness to provide legal support for its members and officials – even in contentious circumstances – was also established.

By way of contrast judges ruled in favour of AMU members in disputes in Hull (1895) and Leeds (1896) when theatre managements had sought injunctions preventing them from, respectively, distributing handbills and urging a boycott of the venue (MU, 1/1). These set important precedents for the Union, and neither occasional reverses nor substantial legal bills dampened its enthusiasm for a legal fight.

Despite the costs incurred, Teale's account argues that such expenses 'were not by any means lost. They have helped to establish the status of the musicians and of the AMU, and taught those concerned that the organisation was one to be reckoned with' (1929b: 28). Williams personally also suffered and benefited from his engagement with the courts. In 1906 he was bankrupted after being unable to pay damages awarded against him when, in his role as a Manchester City Councillor, he made slanderous comments about police administration in the city. A later unspecified case allowed him to 'recover a goodly sum in damages' (Teale 1929b: 28), which allowed him, in 1921, to buy a house in Veyrières in France, to which he later retired.

Getting the message across

Much of the remainder of the Union's work during its first twenty-five years focused on communicating with and assisting members. As with other trade unions, considerable resources were spent on print material to relay information and ensure that the benefits of membership were sufficiently apparent to both existing and potential members. Early records suggest that this was a struggle, with branch meetings frequently dominated by the expulsion (and sometimes readmission) of members who had gone into arrears. The nature of musical employment made for a high turnover of members, with individuals joining and leaving regularly, depending on their employment status and whether they needed to be a member of the Union at any given point.

The first edition of the AMU's *Monthly Report* was published in January 1895, with its declared aim being to allow the Union to 'be better able to effectively unite our members' (*MMRJ*, January 1895: 1). It contained a report on the Congress of Delegates, along with articles written by Williams and individual Branch Secretaries. Members were obliged to buy a copy from their branch at a cost of 1d and the initial print run extended to 3,000 copies. Sales of the report and a directory of members, which Williams had compiled in 1894, were the initial source of funds for the Union's Benevolent Fund. These were supplemented by the proceeds from concerts organised by individual branches and, on occasion, levies applied for short periods to all members to support those who were unemployed or on strike.

Thus, from the outset, the Union attempted to provide for members with a range of benefits. From 1895 funeral benefits were paid to families of members who had died. A short-lived unemployment benefit was introduced the following year, as was an instrument insurance scheme. Prior to 1906, these schemes tended to be organised on a local level, but the EC was also able to make discretionary payments from central funds in unique circumstances, such as when it authorised the payment of £5 to the Glasgow Branch in 1895 to help members who had been put out of work as a result of a fire at the Theatre Royal.

A more ambitious project sought to build a convalescent home for musicians, but this was never completed and the monies raised for it were diverted towards the families of the eight musicians who had perished when the RMS *Titanic* sank on 15 April 1912. In addition, the AMU produced a print of the *Titanic* musicians that sold over 80,000 copies and members took part in a memorial concert for the musicians at the Royal Albert Hall.

Political lobbying and campaigning

It was apparent from an early stage that Williams in particular was aware of – and wanted to engage with – not only other musicians' organisations but also the wider labour movement with a view to increasing the AMU's influence on both local and national government policy.

Evidence of this can be seen in his repeated overtures to the OA with a view to a merger from the inception of both organisations. Approaches by Williams to merge, affiliate, or amalgamate in 1894, 1904, and 1909 were rebuffed, as the OA retained its ideological opposition to the methods of trade unionism, even if some of its members recognised the value of a united profession. A Joint Committee made up of members of the Executives of the two bodies was finally set up in 1915 with a view towards affiliation, although a combination of the war and continued differences ensured that the journey towards merger was a slow one.

The AMU affiliated to the TUC in 1896 and Williams was happy to form an alliance with both the VAF and the stagehands' union (the National Association of Theatrical Employees) during the 1907 music hall strike. At a local level, the support of trades' councils was vital in disseminating musicians' grievances to both other trade unionists and the wider public, and Williams spent much of the first few years of the Union travelling the country speaking to trades' councils. While his message was often greeted with some suspicion, there is little doubt that the support of other trade unionists was vital to the success of AMU industrial action.

Beyond the trade union movement, some AMU officials became politically active. Williams, J. S. Ratcliffe, and Charles Jesson were elected to Manchester, Glasgow, and London County councils respectively, with Jesson going on to be MP for Walthamstow West between 1918 and 1922, representing the National Democratic and Labour Party (NDLP).[22] During the war, Williams campaigned for the formation of a separate Trade Union Party to stand in parliamentary elections. However, this idea gathered little support from other unions, and the AMU supported Jesson and the NDLP in the 1918 election.

Williams was also quick to recognise the value of international co-operation with other musical workers' unions. He made contact with the American musicians' union in 1895[23] and embarked on his first visit to the Congress of French Musicians in 1903.[24] At the 1904 Congress, an international alliance of instrumental musicians' unions, the International Confederation of Musicians (ICM) was formed, and Williams gave a speech arguing that 'musicians cannot and must not think about borders. The interests of each musician, whatever his nationality, must be the common interest of every musician' (cited in David-Guillou 2009: 301). This perhaps idealistic view was still to be tested by both the growing number of migrant musicians and the First World War. While there was evidence of substantial numbers of European musicians arriving in London in the 1890s,[25] this became a bigger issue when, in 1904, a dispute in New York saw employers threatening 'to employ European musicians if American musicians did not accept the conditions they were offered' (David-Guillou 2009: 302). An open letter from the AFM was published in the journals of both the French and British unions and the dispute was ultimately resolved in favour of the American musicians. However, tensions among international musicians' unions caused by migrant labour would later reappear in more dramatic forms.

22 A short-lived, pro-war party, it enjoyed some success at the 1918 General Election. However, by the end of the parliamentary term, all nine of its elected representatives had joined the National Liberal Party.

23 This predated the formation of the AFM in 1896. At the time, it was known as the National League of Musicians.

24 The Fédération des Artistes Musiciens de France, formed in 1902.

25 See David-Guillou (2009) for a detailed account of the formation of, and early relationships among, British, French, and American musicians' unions.

Meanwhile Williams continued to represent the AMU at the conferences of both the French Fédération and the ICM, and made a number of trips to the USA to foster relationships with the American union, whose growth and militancy were watched with some admiration by their European counterparts. Williams had been seeking a working agreement with the AFM since its formation, and visited their Congress in Atlanta in 1911.

War

The developing international relations were one of many aspects of the Union's activities that were severely disrupted by the outbreak of war in 1914. The changing conditions of employment during the war were the first major disruption to the AMU's routine operations, and were to prove the value of Williams' leadership when faced with conflicting attitudes within the Union towards the war itself and the Union's responses to the problems it created for working musicians. Understanding the war's impact on the AMU requires wider contextualisation of how it affected trade unions generally. Despite the prevailing sense that trade unions were 'done' by the State at the end of the War (Webb and Webb 1920: 643), the outcome for the music profession was less disastrous. Indeed, Ehrlich argued that the war's impact on the British music profession, 'though immediate and spectacular', was 'neither profound nor long lasting' (1985: 186). Remarkably, the Union's membership increased from 8,608 in 1914 to 14,649 in 1918.

Yet at the start of the war trade union leaders found themselves in an unenviable position and were understandably fearful of the likely outcomes. Many had taken part in anti-war rallies, but were faced with pressure from both the Government and some of their members to respond to their patriotic duty and support the war effort. Indeed, the TUC rapidly agreed to drop industrial disputes and be largely supportive of the war in return for guarantees of work in many industries (primarily those directly supporting the war effort) and promises that outstanding issues would be resolved on its conclusion. As well as those who stayed at home and produced supplies for the war, many trade unionists joined the forces and fought for their country. Webb and Webb argued that compromises by Union leaders meant that, for the first time, trade unions had become 'part of the social machinery of the state' (1920: 635).

The outbreak of war saw Williams act decisively. Afraid of widespread job losses, he rapidly called off disputes and reached agreements with major employers to reduce pay in the hope of sufficiently improving their economic position and thus keeping their halls open.[26] This hasty and autocratic decision was undertaken without consulting the EC and did not play well with some Union members, who soon realised that the actual impact of the war on the music profession was much less than Williams (and others) had imagined. But Williams defended his action on the basis that if he had waited for due process many musicians would have been laid off immediately by employers worried about the economic consequences of war.

Williams was also quick to deal with some of the recurring issues surrounding competition, especially from military and foreign musicians, which were exaggerated by the unique conditions of the time. As thousands of AMU members joined the forces, its officials were horrified to find that many army bandsmen were still at home, officially to help with the recruiting process, but according to the Union working 'in places of amusement, whilst civilians are walking about unemployed'. Despite representations to the War Office, the Army Council told the Union that it 'saw no reason to interfere in the matter', an illustration of the limited nature of the Union's power (*MMRJ*, October 1914: 1).

While the problem of foreign labour was not exaggerated by the war, it was one in which Williams' intervention was important. Here, his attempts to dampen what Ehrlich describes as the 'antipathy to foreigners' (1985: 189) and 'displays of xenophobia' (187) evident among musicians did have some impact. The war caused many foreign musicians working in London, especially those from the Central Powers, to return to their home countries. However it was also responsible for an influx of refugees from Belgium and France, including some musicians. Although there is no data on the number of musicians involved, concerns about their impact on the profession were voiced at branch meetings across the country and especially in Glasgow, where a number of Belgians had been relocated (MU, 4/2). This was to result in the Glasgow Branch making representations to Glasgow Corporation's Belgian Refugees Committee in June 1916 on the issue and subsequently tabling a motion to the Union's Executive that all foreign musicians should be prevented from being members (MU, 4/2).[27]

Williams, however, pursued a much more nuanced line and remained true to his previously stated internationalist views, supporting the French and Belgian musicians' right to work in the UK, albeit with some caveats. As well as describing them as 'comrades in arms', he reminded members of the horrors

[26] He agreed 'a maximum reduction of 20% with a minimum basic salary of 30s a week' (*MMRJ*, October 1914: 2).

[27] For more see Farmer, Box 67.

of the war in their countries and even offered to help form an orchestra of Belgian and French musicians to tour the country to raise funds. Williams also promised their Unions that the AMU would help them so long as it was 'without injuring our own members' interests' (*MMRJ*, October 1914: 2). Perhaps inevitably, this also found little favour with some AMU members, and the Manchester Branch soon passed a resolution condemning Williams' conciliatory tone (*MMRJ*, November 1914: 1).

The unprecedented turnover of working musicians during the war was expected to have negative consequences for the profession, but the decreased supply of musicians (as foreign musicians returned home and British ones enlisted) was offset by an increased demand for entertainment (Ehrlich 1985: 186). This allowed amateur, foreign, and female musicians to get a foothold in the profession that had previously been denied them, provoking some anger and a number of condemnatory articles in the *MMRJ*. However, the growth of the profession both during and immediately after the war meant that this was less of an issue for the Union than it might otherwise have been.

The expansion of both the Union and the profession during the war had another significant result – a narrowing of the differences between the Union and the OA. As noted above, a Joint Committee was formed in 1915 with a Working Agreement signed the same year (Farmer, 67/24). This was intended to result in affiliation, but new disputes between the two parties erupted and further delayed the process. However, the relative strength of the AMU and the awareness that employers – especially Stoll – were playing the organisations off against each other meant that, by the end of the war, some sort of conciliation was inevitable.

Conclusion

The AMU's first twenty-five years were marked by periods of growth, consolidation, and then further expansion. But perhaps Williams' greatest achievement was to break down the hostility to the very notion of musicians as workers and trade unionists. In this regard, the nature of the majority of musicians who joined – usually in peripheral, poorly paid positions – was integral to the Union's appeal. The initial resistance from the musical elites to the idea of a musicians' trade union became increasingly marginal as both the Union and profession grew in size. Put simply, the type of musician who was opposed to the very idea of trade unionism went from being in the majority in 1893 to a small minority by 1918.

The Union's success in embedding itself within the British music profession was a result of Williams' vision and leadership and a number of triumphs, some of which had been at the Union's behest, others a result of strategic alliances with other unions and/or the prevailing political climate. Williams dominated the Union during its early years and throughout this period was able to win both internal and external battles using a mixture of reason, threats, and force of personality. Meanwhile the greater density of Union membership across the profession steadily increased the AMU's bargaining power, especially following the 1907 music hall strike.

The benefits of both an alliance with other unions (where the musicians benefited from the presence of the stars of the VAF in the dispute) and the stronger legal position of trade unions[28] marked something of a watershed for the Union, and the attendant pay increases and the Union's growing influence in London were responsible for a substantial rise in membership even during the uncertainty of the war.

In many ways this period represented one of stability for the Union both internally and externally. It maintained a core of personnel who had enough respect to be able to quell any internal disputes. Meanwhile the music profession expanded via the increased popularity of music halls and, by the end of the period, cinema orchestras. Generally, pay and conditions had improved considerably, but for much of the period the Union's negotiating power was constrained by an over-supply of labour and its inability to form a closed shop across the profession.[29] These challenges – embodied by the omnipresent threat to employment from amateurs, service bands, and foreigners – would not disappear. However, the period also saw the first stirrings of far greater challenges and opportunities facing both the profession and the AMU. These could be largely characterised as a result of overlapping developments in musical tastes and technology. The growth of dance music and the formation of new orchestras[30] were to combine with developments in broadcasting and recording to ensure the next part of the Union's story was considerably less stable or predictable.

[28] Union power was still partially dependent on the Government policy and various legal rulings. By the time of the music hall strike, both the Conciliation Act (1896) and the Trade Disputes Act (1906) had greatly strengthened the unions' hands. The latter judgement in the case of the *Taff Vale Railway Company* v *Amalgamated Society of Railway Servants* (1901) decreed unions could be liable for losses incurred by employers during strikes.

[29] One example of this came in the Union's Musical Directors Section, which stipulated that its members must employ only AMU members (Farmer, 67/10).

[30] The London Symphony Orchestra, formed in 1904, was the first self-governing orchestra.

3

Boom and bust: 1919–1933

The decade following the war witnessed a period of unprecedented demand for musicians in the UK, with cinemas, dance halls, restaurants, cafes, and broadcasters providing work for players of all abilities. The results of changing musical tastes and technological advances in recording and broadcasting ensured that the music profession opened up in previously unimaginable ways, leading to the first 'talk of a shortage' of musicians (Ehrlich 1985: 186).

Unsurprisingly, this was to have huge consequences for the AMU, which found itself having to adjust quickly to a number of internal changes while simultaneously attempting to cope with dramatic social and technological developments. After a decade of plenty for musicians, the situation it faced in 1929 could hardly have been more different. A global recession and the displacement of thousands of musicians' jobs in the cinemas on the advent of the talkies found the Union struggling for both strategies and survival.

This chapter deals with this complex and fraught period in the Union's history by first considering the developments in the Union itself, notably the merger with what was by then called the National Orchestral Union of Professional Musicians (NOUPM)[1] to form the Musicians' Union in 1921, its fluctuating membership,[2] and the changes in leadership following Williams' resignation in 1924. It then discusses the external factors that were to affect the music profession, especially the inter-connected issues of changing musical tastes, new technology, and the perennial problem of competition in the labour market.

[1] The NOA joined with the NFPM in 1918 to constitute itself as a trade union.
[2] This peaked at 22,685 in 1921 after the merger and dropped to 7,989 in 1933.

From the AMU to the MU

By the end of the war, there were already sufficient changes in both the music profession and in audiences' tastes for leaders of musicians' organisations to recognise the need to adapt. The NOA and AMU had moved closer towards merger, but were still embroiled in disputes over work at individual venues. When the 1915 Working Agreement between the two organisations expired in 1917, Williams proposed a new agreement, but this was rejected by the NOA, partly because its leaders viewed the AMU's attempts to establish closed shops with big employers as attempts to oust its members.[3] However, the war had engendered closer contact. For example, in 1917, a mass meeting of members of both took place at Essex Hall so that Williams could report on his attendance at the Joint Committee of Representatives of the Entertainment Industry, which had been set up by the Director General of National Service to advise him on the 'matters affecting employees in theatres, music halls and cinemas' (OA, *Monthly Report*, April 1917: 4).

While Williams was always keen to seek alliances, much of the impetus for merger came from the NOA. In 1918 it changed its name and officially became a trade union (the NOUPM) making merger between the two easier legally. In addition, a change of leadership meant that the NOUPM under Fort Greenwood was more alert to the need for unity across the profession, especially when his members frequently found themselves being used in attempts to drive down the fees demanded by AMU members. Aware of the potential financial advantages to his members of a Union representing the entire profession, he continued dialogue with Williams until an agreement was reached in 1921.

After years of dithering, the merger was finalised with remarkable haste. Williams had argued for such action on the basis that employers – especially the Cinema Exhibitors' Association (CEA) – were trying to play the organisations off against each other in order to 'smash trade unionism'. After the executives of both unions had 'by a unanimous and enthusiastic vote, agreed that the two Unions should be amalgamated into one society, to be called the Musicians' Union', their members voted overwhelmingly in favour. Of the NOUPM's 2,695 members, 1,361 voted for merger and 20 against. The AMU reported that it had 'obtained even larger majorities in favour' (*Musicians' Journal*, August 1921: 1).[4] Little attention was paid by the press to what was a momentous event in the history of the UK's music profession. Ehrlich

[3] This centred on the dispute with Sir Oswald Stoll/Moss Empires at the Hippodrome in London, discussed in chapter 2.

[4] The *Musicians' Journal* was the new Union's publication for members, replacing the AMU's *MMRJ*. The first edition was published in August 1921.

Figure 2 The AMU EC just prior to merger in 1921. Williams (seated, centre) is immediately surrounded by two important figures in the early years of the AMU and MU. Charles Jesson is seated to his left and William (Bill) Batten is behind him on his right (MU, 5/2).

attributes this to fatigue with the story of a merger that had seemed inevitable for some time (1985: 193). Only the first edition of the *Musicians' Journal* gave the merger due prominence.

The outcomes of the merger for the MU's two predecessors were contrasting. The AMU closed with a farewell dinner, hosted by Williams and his wife on 1 July 1921, at which he was presented with 'a beautiful silver fruit dish suitably inscribed' (*Musicians' Journal*, August 1921: 1). Williams then formally became the first GS of the MU,[5] with a provisional EC made up of members of the two existing executives, but dominated by former AMU members (see Figure 2). Henceforth, apart from odd bouts of nostalgia in MU publications, the AMU's achievements and tribulations were largely confined to history.

By contrast, the OA lived on, both in name and in bricks and mortar. Despite its smaller membership, the NOUPM ended with a healthier balance sheet as a result of owning a property at 13–14 Archer Street in London,

[5] The branches nominated eight members as potential candidates for the post of GS, but none of them asked the candidates' permission. Two were deemed ineligible to stand, and the others declined, leaving Williams unopposed (*Musicians' Monthly Report*, September 1921: 1).

which it ran as a members' club. Because of its proximity to the many theatres in the West End of London, both the club and Archer Street (see Figure 3) more generally had become a hub for musicians, and the club continued to operate under the auspices of the OA until the late 1960s. Of those members of the last NOUPM Executive, only Greenwood and James Whitaker were to play a lasting part in the MU.

Figure 3 Musicians gather in Archer Street, whose hostelries acted as a meeting point and unofficial labour exchange from the 1920s to the 1960s (MU, 5/1/2).

Williams resigns

If the formation of the MU was ultimately rapid, the other major organisational change of the period was more protracted and damaging. Williams' decision, less than two years after the triumph of merger, to announce first his partial withdrawal from Union activity and subsequently his resignation was both drawn out and never fully explained. The saga began in 1923, reaching a conclusion, of sorts, some four years later. The surprising aspect was not that Williams wanted a break following an extended period of dedicating himself to the Union,[6] but that it came at the peak of his career. The merger witnessed the music profession accepting his vision of trade unionism and he became leader of a union that was more powerful than any previous musicians' organisation. Williams had won the respect not only of fellow trade unionists, but also of some major employers.[7]

In early 1923 Williams announced that he was planning to go into semi-retirement from the start of the following year. Although Ehrlich suggests that ill health was behind his decision (1985: 194), it was initially attributed to 'family reasons' (MU, 2/1/5) and appears to have been driven as much by Williams' desire to devote time to both his sick wife and his house in France. The ineffectual response to his bombshell announcement illustrated the extent to which the Union would become rudderless without him. The EC sent a memo to Branch Secretaries, seeking their approval of a scheme whereby Williams would be employed for half the year, conducting negotiations during the winter months and attending all full EC meetings, while acting as 'consultative adviser' (MU, 2/1/5) during the remainder of the year on half salary.

The branches responded by voting 62 in favour and 8 against, with 17 offering alternative suggestions. Despite this strong endorsement, the EC decided that 'more satisfaction would be given and the position more stabilised if the members individually expressed their opinion by a ballot vote' (*Monthly Report*, November 1923: 4). This duly took place and, almost a year after Williams announced his intention and nine months after it was first discussed at the EC, a majority of members (3,655 to 1,238) approved the plan to retain him as GS for six months of the year. But this did not close the matter, and the Union's *Monthly Report* told members:

6 Williams had also faced a number of personal problems during the period, including his bankruptcy and his son Joe's death shortly after his eighteenth birthday.

7 Williams had been voted Chair of the TUC's General Council in 1922 and was also a member of its Parliamentary Committee. A general meeting of the Society of West End Theatre Managers (SWETM) on 18 December 1924 unanimously agreed to send a letter expressing regret at his retirement.

> We regret to announce that the General Secretary has found it necessary to intimate to the EC that owing to the state of his health he finds it imperative to give notice that he cannot continue as GS after the March quarter, 1925. We feel sure that all our members will join us in expressing deep regret that such a cause should make it imperative for the GS to sever his lifelong connection with the musicians' organisation. (March 1924: 1)

By the end of the year, Williams had penned his farewell to the Union, his tenure as GS ending in January 1925. His leaving article gives no explanation for his decision, instead reflecting somewhat blandly on the Union's achievements, wishing its members well and claiming that 'I left no enemies' (*Monthly Report*, January 1925: 1).

This seems to tell only part of the story, as EC minutes from 1923 and 1924 suggest that Williams had indeed been ill at various points, spending time in France and failing to attend meetings. This caused some disquiet, and there is also evidence of policy disagreements between Williams and the EC in 1924 when he formally submitted his resignation letter. The Executive regretted 'having to take note of the GS disagreement with EC policy', but argued that this should 'not be an occasion for resignation, but rather of closer co-operation between the GS and the EC' (MU, 2/1/5). Although the minutes do not make the bone of contention explicit,[8] the most likely explanation is a disagreement over salaries, as much of the EC's time in the preceding months had been spent dealing with issues surrounding officials' pay and expenses. The Union's leadership was further interrupted during this period by the absence of many of its key officials. Both Williams and Teale were absent for large parts of 1923 and 1924, while other significant figures in the Union, Bill Batten[9] and Bertram Newton Brooke,[10] were also in dispute with the Executive and absent from their duties at various points.

Faced with Williams' imminent departure, the Executive put in place arrangements for the election of a successor. The Union's first ever leadership election attracted seven candidates, with Teale duly becoming the MU's first elected GS, gathering 3,228 votes – almost ten times the amount of the runner-up, Glasgow Branch Secretary Walter Murdock. Having comprehensively defeated not just Murdock but also Greenwood, Batten, and Newton

8 Williams' letter of resignation is reported but not archived.

9 Bill Batten served continuously as Secretary of the Union's Central London Branch between 1914 and 1940, and was heavily involved in negotiations with both the BBC and the Ministry of Labour in the 1920s and 1930s. After the Second World War he served on (and briefly chaired) the EC and remained interested in Union affairs, attending a Biennial Conference in 1967 at the age of ninety-four.

10 Bertram Newton Brooke was a Union official from the 1920s to the 1950s.

Brooke, Teale had the mandate – if not the capacity – to resolve the Union's leadership problems. Older than Williams,[11] he also had serious health problems and his twenty-nine years as Assistant General Secretary (AGS) were later characterised by Henry Farmer[12] as being ones in which 'he had little opportunity of exercising his own will or individuality' (1931: 3). Teale's six years as leader were scarcely more distinguished. He was ill for most of his tenure and for the latter part of his tenure the AGS, Fred Dambman, appeared to do much of the GS's work (Farmer 1931: 3).

The start of Teale's reign was overshadowed by Williams' lingering presence. Despite their differences, the EC, perhaps mindful of Teale's condition, sought to retain Williams' experience and expertise in some capacity. He was offered the position of Chair of the EC, given a retainer of £5 per week to be available on a consultative basis, and appointed Chair of a Consultative Conference the Union had planned for 1926.[13]

In reality, Williams' involvement was limited by his own health problems and his relocation to France. He attended infrequently, and the EC's frustration was evident in a resolution at their meeting of 11–12 February 1927 that 'it is not in the best interests of the Union that its Chairman should reside in a foreign country, and that it is incumbent upon them to have a Chairman more accessible to urgent calls' (MU, 2/1/5). Williams was duly informed that he was to be removed from his Chairmanship, though his retainer initially continued. He was also offered a position as Honorary Vice President of the Union, his last documented interaction with the Union he had founded.

The subsequent deaths of the Union's first two leaders within two years ended the direct link between the Union and its Manchester origins, allowing the candidates in the 1931 GS election to offer a realistic prospect of change unencumbered by the presence of dominant figures in the background. However, the outcome was to privilege continuity and stability, with the AGS (Fred Dambman) again being elected to the top position. Having joined the Union in 1902 and been Manchester Branch Secretary prior to his appointment as AGS, Dambman was elected with over 65 per cent of the votes cast in an election that pitted him against Batten, John Briggs (a London Branch member), and Whitaker, who had chaired the EC after Williams. The result highlighted the schism between London and the rest of the country. Batten based his campaign on the premise that 'the policy that has succeeded for London can succeed for the whole country' (Farmer, 67/9–28) and accumulated the vast majority of his 1,481 votes from within the capital. Dambman

11 He was sixty-three when he became leader. Williams resigned at the age of fifty-eight.

12 See the Appendix for details of Farmer and the archive of his work.

13 This took place in Birmingham in January 1926 (MU, 1/7/1926).

instead pitched his campaign to provincial members and secured his majority by highlighting the differences between the working lives of musicians in London and elsewhere.

His election also prompted the Executive to implement a series of reforms to the Union's structure, further cutting costs in the wake of declining membership. These included cutting permanent officials' salaries[14] and reducing the number of both permanent officials and districts.[15] This placed greater responsibilities on the Secretary-Organisers who were to be based in Glasgow, Leeds, Manchester, Liverpool, Birmingham, Bristol, and London.[16] Plans were also made to move the General Office from Manchester to London. Later in the year, Walter Murdock was appointed AGS, the Midlands and South West Districts were merged, and the General Office took direct control of the North-East District. The immediate outcomes of these personnel and structural changes were both a streamlining of Union activity and a period of relative internal stability that was to last until after the Second World War.

The profession

The essentially reactive nature of musicians' organisations is nowhere more evident than in the way that both the AMU and MU responded to many of the major social and technological changes that reached their zenith post-1918. Ehrlich correctly argues that many of the advances in musicians' pay and conditions prior to the war 'owed little to the protective efforts of unions and professional organisations' (1985: 186), and even the *Musicians' Journal* accepted that 'many musicians fail to realise to what extent their protection is governed by circumstances entirely extraneous to themselves, and entirely outside the controlling power of their organisation' (July 1925: 5). Despite this, the ways in which the MU reacted to the social and technological changes during this period were to have long-lasting effects on both the music profession and the emergent music industries.

Although the likelihood of being able to get gainful employment as a musician had increased substantially by the 1920s, the expansion of the musical labour market was not without problems. In much the same way as the profession had divided in the 1890s along the lines of what music musicians

14 Dambman's salary of £8 per week was less than that of his predecessor (*Musicians' Monthly Report*, April 1931: 1).

15 The Union had organised in some areas by districts as well as branches since the early part of the twentieth century. The earliest district minutes of the AMU belong to the Scottish District in 1904. On the formation of the MU in 1921, new districts were formed and these were frequently reorganised until their dissolution in 2005.

16 The London Branch's size led to its having two Secretary-Organisers, Batten and Greenwood.

played and where, the demand for dance music was one that caused concern amongst the ranks of established Union members.

Before the war the majority of musicians were employed in orchestras, performing in theatres, concert halls, music halls, and cinemas. They were generally not the main entertainment and their audiences largely remained seated. Each of these types of work had its particular instrumental requirements, meaning that the prospect of musical work was often down to instrumental specialism. For example, brass players were in particular demand at ice rinks, while cinemas created 'a demand for an abnormal number of special instruments, pianists, violinists and cellists' (*Musicians' Journal*, July 1925: 5). Thus, in order to remain employed musicians often had to adapt or learn new instruments.

Though cinemas remained the largest employers in the 1920s[17] – bolstered by their ever-increasing size and concomitantly scaled-up orchestras – the real boost to musical employment came from what Ehrlich calls the sudden 'craze for "American" music which was sweeping the country at every social level' (1985: 201). This saw the engagement of bands for dancing (in cafés, hotels, restaurants, and nightclubs) augmented by the opening, across the country, of large new dance halls in the style of the Hammersmith Palais de Danse (which opened in 1919). Their popularity meant that they inevitably became 'a focus of big business interest' (Nott 2002: 148), with dancing their core activity and musicians significant beneficiaries.

With demand for such music fuelled by the advent of radio broadcasting, dance music rapidly became not only hugely popular but also big business – often at the expense of other forms of musical entertainment. Ehrlich cites the financial troubles of the Bournemouth Symphony Orchestra in 1924 as an example. Attendances at their concerts had dropped to 100 people while 4,000 were 'at dances on the same night' (1985: 201).

The emergence of a new cadre of musicians engaged in dance halls created a number of problems for the Union, relating to friction within the profession, money, and organisation. The disdain with which dance musicians were treated by some longstanding members was evident in a *Musicians' Journal* article in 1925 that described them as 'an entirely new breed, their demeanour crass, their training inadequate or non-existent' (July 1925: 5). From this starting point, it was hardly surprising that the better rates of pay for what were perceived as inferior musicians also caused resentment. However, that this was an inevitable consequence of simple market forces is shown by

[17] Ehrlich estimates that 50 per cent of Union members were working in cinemas in 1924 (1985: 199).

the importance of such musicians to the dancing industry coupled with the large amounts of money it was generating. The same article lamented the fact that 'baton musical directors in some forms of entertainment find themselves assessed at a portion of the value of jazz drummers or solo saxophonists', but nonetheless retained a degree of pragmatism, recognising that for musicians 'the only remedy is adaptability or extermination', and that the Union would 'have a poor chance of success against the public demand' (*Musicians' Journal*, July 1925: 5).

The final aspect of disgruntlement with the new breed of musicians was the difficulty in organising them, as many were seemingly satisfied with their conditions and saw little need to join a Union whose members appeared hostile towards them. *Melody Maker* highlighted the differing attitudes towards trade unions among what it delineated as 'straight' musicians and those playing 'what they are so fond of calling "jazz"'. It described how 'straight' musicians working in theatres 'are all members of the Union, otherwise they would find it very difficult to earn their living', contrasting this with the dance musicians 'who have not thought it worthwhile to join' (October 1929: 991).

The other substantive changes in the music profession during the 1920s were technologically rather than stylistically driven. At their heart were developments in broadcasting, recording, and cinema technologies, all of which were to have different outcomes for both the profession and the Union.

The arrival of broadcasting

Nowhere was this impact more positive than with the advent of the British Broadcasting Company in 1922, as it required large numbers of musicians to fill musical slots on its schedules.[18] Although it presented an immediate work opportunity for musicians, there were a number of reservations across the profession about the potential impact of radio, especially the effect it might have on audiences for public performances. In this instance, the MU's stance was more progressive than both some of its international allies and some theatre owners and concert promoters. For example, the *Musicians' Journal* reported that the French union 'forbid their members to play at any theatre, variety hall, cinema or other place of entertainment where it is intended to broadcast the whole or any part of the performance' (October 1923: 1). Meanwhile William Boosey,[19] acting in his capacity as managing director of

[18] The British Broadcasting Company began broadcasting in 1922, received a Royal Charter in 1926, and became the British Broadcasting Corporation from 1 January 1927.

[19] Boosey was a music publisher and entrepreneur who later appears in this story as Chair of the Performing Right Society (PRS).

the Queen's Hall, was initially resolute in his opposition to the BBC's activities. According to Briggs, he 'maintained that broadcasting would ruin the concert world and that people would never pay for concerts when they could sit comfortably at home' (1995: 253). He also refused to allow the BBC to use the Queen's Hall and prevented musicians working for him from accepting work from the Company.

By way of contrast, the Union's EC discussed the possibilities and threats from broadcasting and produced a much more nuanced response that, remarkably, promoted the approach to broadcasting that it has employed ever since. A *Musicians' Journal* editorial raised many arguments for its proposition that 'the broadcasting industry must not be opposed, but controlled' and that the Union's job was to 'control the salaries and everything else will adjust itself'. In coming to this conclusion, the article reflected on the futility of opposition to technological developments in other industries and argued that audiences wanted the experience of both seeing and hearing live performances, meaning that broadcasting 'will never displace living musicians to such an extent as to cause grave injury to our profession' (October 1923: 1). Contrary to Boosey, the Union suggested that far from reducing attendances at orchestral concerts, the exposure granted by radio would generate interest amongst people who had not previously attended them.

Though the Union later partially backtracked on this optimistic view, its lack of opposition was a contributory factor in the rapid expansion of musical employment at the BBC. It was also to its advantage that many venue owners, concert promoters, and musical organisations shared its view that the BBC should be seen for its immediate opportunities, rather than its potentially harmful longer-term effects. Both the British National Opera Company (BNOC) and the Proms[20] were initial beneficiaries of BBC patronage and the publicity that came with subsequent broadcasts.

The BBC's employment of musicians was initially somewhat ad hoc. However, on receiving its Royal Charter in 1926, the Corporation was able not only to employ hundreds of musicians, but to do so on a basis that transformed working conditions within the profession. The first BBC orchestral broadcasts involved relatively small numbers of musicians,[21] but grew quickly. Briggs describes how 'all the main stations had their own orchestras, consisting of about eighteen players' (1995: 253), with these based in London

[20] The 'Proms' are the annual Promenade Concerts, which were founded by Sir Henry Wood and Robert Newman in 1895. These had been held at the Queen's Hall and were in danger of closing before the BBC's involvement was agreed in 1927.

[21] The first, on 23 December 1922, consisted of eight musicians, though this increased to eighteen when the Company moved to larger premises in 1923. An orchestra of forty performed for broadcast in November 1923 (Briggs 1995: 252).

(2LO Wireless Orchestra) and in major cities including Glasgow, Manchester (2ZY), and Belfast. Other forms of music were also reflected in the BBC output, including light music ensembles, choirs, and dance bands broadcasting on a regular and semi-regular basis.[22] The 2LO became the most significant in terms of employment. Members were offered full-time contracts from 1924, ensuring both security of employment and an end to the deputy system. Subsequently, part-time BBC musicians were also contracted (with fewer guaranteed performances) and this model was followed when the BBC vastly increased its musical output after 1927.

The ten years following the award of the Royal Charter saw the launch of a dizzying array of BBC orchestras, both nationally and regionally.[23] They were organised by location (e.g. Welsh Orchestra, Northern Wireless Orchestra, Scottish Studio Orchestra, Midland Orchestra) or by style (Symphony Orchestra (BBCSO), Dance Orchestra, Theatre Orchestra, Military Band), but each provided secure and comparatively well-paid employment for musicians, becoming much-coveted positions. The largest was the BBCSO, which was founded in 1930 and was to provide employment for 114 musicians. It had been planned for a number of years, initially under the guidance of Sir Thomas Beecham, to whom had been delegated both recruiting the musicians and negotiating with the Union. His withdrawal from the process saw Adrian Boult take over as the BBC's Director of Music and permanent conductor of the orchestra, the formation of which he duly accelerated.[24] Recruitment of the best players was easy because of the terms on offer. These had been designed by Julian Herbage and Edward Clark prior to Boult's arrival[25] and saw the BBC become the first employer to offer year-round contracts with a fixed number of hours,[26] holiday provision, and a salary of £11 a week for rank-and-file members.

The BBCSO enjoyed instant success. Its first performance at the Queen's Hall in October 1930 attracted glowing reviews (Kenyon 1981: 56) and Briggs argues that Boult 'built up the BBCSO to be one of the great orchestras of the world' (1995: 159). The MU was a key beneficiary of these developments and soon saw the merits of public sector broadcasting. At the start of what was to be an exceptionally difficult time for the Union and the music

22 For more detailed accounts see Briggs (1995), Doctor (1999), and Nott (2002).

23 A list of BBC orchestras is given by Witts (2012).

24 Beecham (with Malcolm Sargent) later formed the London Philharmonic Orchestra (LPO) in 1932 as a rival to the BBCSO, and became an outspoken critic of the BBC.

25 Herbage and Clark both worked in the BBC's Music Department and had devised a policy scheme called Comprehensive Orchestral Organisation, which set out the terms and conditions of employment.

26 144 hours every 4 weeks.

profession, it was appreciative of the BBC's employment of 197 musicians at an annual cost of £112,840 (Kenyon 1981: 44). The BBC's terms also represented a considerable improvement on anything offered by employers in the past. *Melody Maker* proclaimed that 'BBC musicians had struck oil ... with high pay, unprecedentedly generous holidays and interesting work' (July 1931: 611).

This reorganisation of the orchestral world meant that 'within a decade of its formation, the BBC had not only become the most significant music disseminator in Britain, but also the foremost employer of British musicians' (Doctor 1999: 16). According to MacDonald, by the mid-1930s 'it was the world's biggest employer of musicians – possibly the biggest in history' (2010: 4). Its terms and conditions were generally superior to those offered elsewhere, and even if some bands were able to pay more, the prestige of playing for the BBC provided sufficient stimulus for musicians to join.[27] Henceforth the MU's fate was to be intertwined with that of the Corporation.

Recordings

The second great technological issue facing the music profession was the development of the recording industry and the possible threat it posed to the employment of live musicians. In this instance, it is telling that, at least initially, the record companies and venue operators appeared to be more alert than the Union to the potential disruption recordings might cause. Applying the same logic that it had to broadcasting in the early 1920s, the Union's stance was summed up in the *Musicians' Journal* when it answered the rhetorical question 'Why has the gramophone not injured the musical profession?' with the bold claim that 'man is a sociable being and wishes not only to hear but also to see the artistes' (October 1923: 1). Its stance was that, far from harming musicians, gramophone recordings were attracting new audiences to live performances. This position was undoubtedly influenced by the fact that a very small number of MU members were involved in recording sessions.[28] This was to change as the BBC sought the right to record its orchestras and record companies sought to take advantage of the increased demand for records for use in dancing.

[27] In interview, former MU EC member Nick Tschaikov (*2014*) recalled his father, Anissim, working for the BBCSO in the 1930s for the prestige, despite having a better-paying offer from Geraldo's band. Tschaikov joined the MU in 1942 and his father was a member of the BBCSO from 1930 to 1947.

[28] Many of the available gramophone recordings of the time were either made by singers (who were not in the MU) or non-British musicians. It is likely that the majority of those making records saw payment for this as additional to their core income from playing live.

Pivotal to the Union's lack of awareness of the potential threat posed by the recording industry was its somewhat one-dimensional view of the recordings themselves. It shared the widespread view that records were designed for home entertainment,[29] and that so long as they were confined to personal use by those affluent enough to buy both playing equipment and the records, their impact on the employment of live musicians was, indeed, limited. However, when combined with the other technological developments in broadcasting and in the quality of both the hardware and software used, recordings soon presented a very real threat to live performance. By the end of the decade, their use by broadcasters and in public places became a genuine problem for the Union, and at the centre of all subsequent negotiations between it and the recording industry.[30]

These did not begin in earnest until the formation of PPL by the record companies in 1934. The events leading up to this highlight the differing worldviews of the record companies, who saw the public use of records as a threat to their profits, and the Union, which initially did not see any threat to musicians' livelihoods. Two issues were at stake here: whether the public use of recordings should be paid for and, if so, how the monies this generated should be distributed.

These debates can be traced back to the Copyright Act of 1911, which introduced copyright on sound recordings. While there is no evidence in the Union's archives of its being an interested party in the discussions preceding this, the major record companies gave evidence to the 1909 Copyright Committee. The Gramophone Company[31] told the tribunal that 'public performances [of records] are a great advertisement to the music, and the author would be very sorry for us to discontinue them'. When asked by Lord Gorrell whether 'the purchaser of a disc should not merely acquire the right to use it in his own private surroundings like the singing of a song but to use it in public', the Company responded 'yes' (Copyright Committee 1952: 50).

This was a response to the position the Company found itself in when a recession had resulted in a serious downturn in sales from 1907. Martland notes that by the following year, its 'usually handsome profits were reduced to almost nothing' (1997: 102), thus forcing the recording industry to seek all available means of boosting its turnover. The increased public performance of its output was one way, at least indirectly, of achieving this.

29 For example, in 1948 an inquiry into BBC–MU relations held that 'Gramophone records are primarily recorded for private use' (Forster 1948: 84).

30 The Union also reached numerous agreements with the BBC on recording of its musicians. For early examples see WAC, R8/123/1–9.

31 The Gramophone Company was founded in 1897 and at this point was the UK's largest record company.

Around the same time, the music publishers had moved to make a more direct connection between public performance and income, setting up the Performing Right Society (PRS) in 1914 to collect payments for the public use of songs.[32] This meant that publishers and composers were remunerated when their works were used in public, but record companies and performers were not. Inevitably, this was to prove an attractive model for the record companies and we consider the importance of this in the subsequent chapters – from the formation of PPL in 1934.

Nevertheless, the initial interactions between the Union and the developing music industries during this period set important precedents. Although the Union had a number of run-ins with the PRS and its Chairman, William Boosey, in its early days,[33] its relationship with the music publishing industry was to be of less importance than that which it subsequently formed with the recording industry. The explanation for this lies in the 1920s. Here it is worth considering that, at the time, a very small number of MU members were also composers,[34] meaning that PRS income was of little concern for the players who dominated the Union's membership. In addition, until this point, Union members had not viewed the use of recordings as a threat to the live performances that were their primary source of income.

The post-war expansion of the recording industry and the advent of radio broadcasting changed this, and when the more widespread use of records began to have an adverse effect on live performances, it became obvious that the Union and the recording industry would have to reach some form of accommodation. Three specific things were influential in paving the way to such an understanding: the first deals between the record companies and the BBC; the Dramatic and Musical Performers' Protection Act (DMPPA) 1925; and the case that the Gramophone Company took against Steven Carwardine, a Bristol café owner who had been playing music on his premises.

The first use of gramophone records by the BBC was a clear test of whether record companies still maintained their 1909 view that the public use of their records promoted sales. Perhaps because of their declining sales – largely attributed to the growing popularity of radio – there was evidence that their stance had changed. Briggs notes that by the time the BBC launched a weekly programme of new records, *The Week's Concert of New Gramophone*

32 For more on the origins of PRS see Peacock and Weir (1975), McFarlane (1980), Ehrlich (1989).

33 This story is told in more detail by Davison (2012) and McFarlane (1980).

34 This grew in subsequent decades when jazz, folk, and rock musicians began increasingly to write their own material.

Records, in 1924,[35] 'one large gramophone company supplied its records to the BBC free of charge, but copyright fees were regularly paid by the BBC to the copyright owners' (Briggs 1995: 255). Informal agreements continued before a written agreement was made in 1933. Records were supplied for free, but the BBC was obliged to give full details – including the catalogue number – of the records played (WAC, R21/74/1). The announcing of catalogue numbers was soon abandoned (WAC, R21/74/3). The first agreement with PPL came in 1935 and allowed the BBC to use records for fourteen hours a week for a £20,000 annual fee over a three-year period (WAC, R21/74/3). This formalised a relationship between the record companies and the BBC that was subsequently to become of major importance to the Union.

The DMPPA was to prove similarly important, although again the Union was passive in its instigation and implementation. It forbade the recording of artists' performances without their permission. While the Gramophone Company was behind its route through Parliament (Evans 1966: 245), the Union was soon using the limited rights granted to performers by the Act in its battle against another technological threat – the talkies. By granting performers the right to take criminal proceedings against anyone manufacturing their work without their consent, the Act both recognised, and provided a basis for the future pursuit of, performers' rights in sound recordings. This advance was something of a mixed blessing for recording musicians as the contracts issued by the record companies assigned all the rights in the recordings (including those of the performers) to the labels.[36]

The outcome of the Carwardine case was to determine the future remuneration from public performances of gramophone records. This was a test case,[37] heard in December 1933,[38] which the record companies hoped would establish their right to receive payment when their records were used in public places. The judgment that Carwardine was not entitled to play recordings owned by the companies in his café without their consent provided the basis for the formation of PPL and the timely opening-up of a new stream of revenue for the record companies, which is explored further in Chapter 4.

35 The BBC began using gramophone records in 1922, but according to Briggs 'there was no reliance on gramophone record programmes which were such a useful, low-cost staple of local American broadcasting' (1995: 255).

36 Our evidence here is a blank Gramophone Company contract from this period contained in MU, 2/5.

37 *Gramophone Company Ltd* v *Stephen Carwardine* ([1934] Ch. 450 (Ch.D.)).

38 The ruling was published the following year – a full report can be found in *The Stage*, 21 December 1933: 7.

Crisis in the cinemas

The changes in the recording industry and the economic crisis that had prompted the record companies to go 'casting around anxiously for an additional form of income to bolster their sagging profits' (McFarlane 1980: 132) were to have long-term consequences for the Union. However, the arrival of the talkies was to have a far more immediate, and disastrous, effect.

By the time *The Jazz Singer* (the first 'talkie') was shown in the USA in 1927 (1928 in the UK) the film conglomerates had already been planning the weakening of the film industry's reliance on musicians. Mermey describes how, in the 1920s, music was the one thing the cinemas 'could not do without', and how 'the orchestra was virtually the most important part of the movie programme, the main attraction' (1929: 302). The film companies had an obvious interest in ending this situation. Their mechanism for doing so was the Vitaphone system, which, with its improved fidelity and amplification, allowed Warner Brothers to move towards replacing 'live music in the movie theatres with mechanical recordings' (Hubbard 1985: 430).

Despite the limited number of cinemas with the technical capacity to play them, the talkies' success soon 'seriously wounded the status of live music in movie theatres' (Hubbard 1985: 432). Ehrlich gives some sense of the scale of the cinema orchestral displacement in the UK between 1928 and 1932, citing figures for 9,500 unemployed musicians in the 1931 census. By 1932, 4,000 British cinemas were capable of playing talkies, and only 900 remained silent and in need of musicians (1985: 210). Fox stopped making silent movies in 1929 and other film companies soon followed.

Musicians' unions in both the UK and the USA had benefited hugely from the expansion of cinema. Their response to the talkies reflected a lack of experience in dealing with such a scenario, encompassing initial outright opposition, followed by a suspension of disbelief and, eventually, an outbreak of realism. They began by working to protect the profession from what was disparagingly referred to as either 'canned' or 'mechanical' music. In the USA, the AFM appealed to its members to 'help in any way you can to arouse public consciousness of the threatened rape of the musical art' (cited in Mermey 1929: 306). Estimating that 50,000 American musicians were put out of work by 1928, the AFM responded by establishing a fund to fight the talkies, and organising a number of strikes. At best, these delayed the inevitable, and Hubbard argues not only that *The Jazz Singer* 'seriously [wounded] the status of the live musicians in movie theatres' (1985: 432), but that the AFM 'suffered a considerable defeat' (438) in trying to reverse, or even stall, the advance of technology.

In the UK the response from the Union's leadership moved rapidly from denial to resigned acceptance, covering most points in between. As early as April 1929, Greenwood[39] was repeating a familiar mantra: that outright opposition to new technology had to be tempered and that 'a wiser course is to seek to control it and turn it to our advantage' (*Melody Maker*, May 1929: 518). In other recurring themes he also lamented the apathy of British musicians and pointed to copyright legislation as a possible means of obstructing the talkies' progress.

The following month, the London District Branch called a Special General Meeting at King George's Hall on Wednesday 15 May to discuss 'The Kinema Crisis'. This event sought to 'consider the position arising out of the introduction of mechanical music and the talkies' (MU, 3/2) and was most notable for the anti-American rhetoric that predominated. The agenda highlighted how 'mechanical music gains impetus from day to day and is already responsible for the dismissal of several West End Orchestras'. Blame for this was put firmly down to the 'dictation of the American capitalists trying to install their talkies on the threat of the supply of silent pictures being immediately cut off'. The Union's belief that British cinema owners would have either delayed or refused the talkies were it not for American pressure seems as naive and misguided as their proclamation that 'while unemployment is still extremely severe, there are signs that matters have reached their worst' (MU, 3/2).

As matters progressed the Union continued with an outpouring of propaganda that suggested 'The Kinema Crisis' was coming to an end and musicians would be re-employed in the cinemas. In 1930 the Union's publications[40] featured a series of cartoons (see Figures 4 and 5) attacking the talkies and their perceived crimes against both the English language and the music profession. A typical cartoon showed a cinema orchestra entering a cinema with the caption 'Picture of a cinema returning to sanity' (*MU Monthly Report*, March 1930: 1), while the rhetoric inside matched the optimism of *Melody Maker*. The magazine viewed the talkies as something of a fad, the success of which was 'due almost entirely to its novelty'. Moreover, it suggested that 'in the long run the sound film will not seriously harm the music profession' (1 November 1929: 413).

Two years later, and despite declining membership and finances, the *MU Monthly Report* was still pursuing the optimistic view that 'the human

39 Then Joint Secretary of the MU's London District Branch.

40 The *Musicians' Journal* was published between 1921 and 1930; the *Musicians' Union Report* began a new series in 1930 and ran until 1950. Although it was generally published monthly this varied depending on finances and external circumstances.

Figure 4 Cartoon from the *Musicians' Journal* (October 1929) highlighting the Union's belief that the public preferred films accompanied by orchestras to the talkies (MU, 1/3).

element [will] prevail in our profession in spite of everything' (July 1931: 1). Though history would show that both the profession and the Union would ultimately survive and thrive, this appeared completely at odds with both the unemployment levels in the profession and the scaling down of the MU's activities in 1931.

Competition

While the shifts in musical taste and technological disruptions were new and urgent problems, they merely added to the longstanding competition issues in the labour market where considerable energy was spent highlighting – and attempting to minimise – the presence of military musicians and foreigners in positions that would otherwise be taken by Union members.

Military bands were still clearly a source of irritation, but the growing number of foreign musicians working in the UK after the war soon became

THE TURN OF THE TIDE.

Figure 5 The imaginary orchestra depicted on the cover of the MU Monthly Report (March 1930) was one of the few to return to cinema work after the advent of the talkies (MU, 1/4).

more pressing. The focus here was largely on American musicians who were coming in to help meet the demand for dance music. The MU believed that any foreign musician entering the UK displaced a UK musician. It continually argued that, with a very few exceptions, anything a foreign musician could do, a British one – given time – could match. Thus importation was largely unnecessary. Its views were summarised by Teale in a letter to TUC General Secretary Walter Citrine in 1929:

> as citizens of Gt Britain we are entitled to the protection of our country against displacement by Alien work-people in our own land. We have no anti-foreign feeling in the matter based merely on insular or national prejudices; we welcome the best that art can send us from abroad, we recognise the benefit to ourselves and to our country of a judicious and well-regulated influx of world ideas, but with all such advantages we still decline to say that foreign citizens have the right of asylum irrespective of the harm their activities may do in exercising it. (MRC, MS 292b/103.21/1)

The Union focused its attention on the Ministry of Labour, which was responsible for implementing the Aliens Order (1920).[41] This laid down that any foreigner seeking to work in the United Kingdom must 'produce a permit in writing for this employment issued to the employer by the Ministry of Labour' (cited in Batten 1929). The Union's concern was that the Ministry was continually being too liberal in issuing permits to 'alien' musicians whose work could equally have been done by British ones. It thus continually lobbied to be consulted and to restrict entry.

In 1922 the Ministry assured the Union that it would be consulted on the issuing of permits (MRC, MS 292b/103.21/1). When, in 1924, the Union prevented the Viennese Opera Company from bringing its entire orchestra with it for performances at Covent Garden and ensured that British musicians were employed in some positions, it hailed this as 'a great victory for the Union' (London Branch Agenda, 22 February 1924). The same year a proposed tour by the American bandleader Paul Whiteman was only approved after the Prince of Wales had intervened (Parsonage 2005: 181),[42] and a series of conditions were attached to the granting of work permits. The most important were clauses insisting that 'where an American band was employed in a ballroom or nightclub, an English band had also to be employed', and 'where any American musicians were employed in an otherwise English band, there should be an equal number of British players' (Moore 2006).

Central to the Union's objections were that applications from major employers including Moss Empires, the Kit Kat Club, the Covent Garden Opera House and the Savoy Hotel were rarely, if ever, refused. By the end of the decade, Dambman was complaining about the 'maladministration of the Aliens' Order' and suggesting that 'a long indictment could be drawn up showing the partiality of the Ministry of Labour for foreign musicians' (1929: 14). Matters came to a head in 1929 when *Melody Maker* reacted to a proposed visit by Abe Lyman by arguing that his band was 'just about the type of band which can teach us nothing' and suggesting that UK bandleader Jack Hylton was his superior (March 1929).[43] Hylton then became the focus of attention when he was unable to play a series of lucrative shows in New York following suggestions that local musicians would strike if he did so (*Daily Mirror*, 26

[41] The Aliens Order was part of the major piece of immigration legislation, the Aliens Restriction Act (1914).

[42] When Whiteman played London's Tivoli Theatre in 1926, the Union successfully insisted that thirty-three members of the resident band be retained (MRC, MS 292b/103.21/1).

[43] Lyman was allowed entry on condition that the British band at the Kit Kat be retained and its numbers increased to match those of Lyman's band (*Daily News*, 26 April 1929).

April 1929).[44] It was also reported that because of such threats from the AFM 'no British stage band has visited America' (*Morning Post*, 26 April 1929),[45] a situation Hylton described as being 'unfair' at a time when, he said, there were 'something like 80 highly-paid American musicians working in London' (*Daily Sketch*, 26 April 1929).

The Union had hoped that the return of a Labour government[46] in 1929 would mean that its stance on 'aliens' would be received more sympathetically, and it enlisted the help of the TUC in lobbying the Ministry – Teale arguing that, as the matter could not be resolved by 'ordinary Trade Union activity', so 'we must appeal to those representing bodies of citizens to assist our cause' (MRC, MS 292b/103.21/1). However, a succession of meetings with the Minister, Margaret Bondfield, failed to resolve matters, with the Ministry generally arguing that the numbers involved were small, that the American musicians offered something their British counterparts could not, and that taking a harder line might damage the prospects of UK musicians working abroad (MRC, MS 292b/103.21/1).

While it appears that the Ministry acted even-handedly throughout, Batten argued that Bondfield had dashed 'the hopes of those in the Labour movement who thought things would improve under a Labour minister'. Such was the MU's frustration that in March 1930 it wrote to the TUC suggesting that further meetings with the Minister would be futile (Batten 1929). Instead the Union turned to international action, convincing Citrine to write to the American Federation of Labor (AFL) to clarify matters surrounding the entry of foreign musicians into the United States. This elicited a letter of 27 May from Joe Weber, the AFM's President, which offered little prospect of compromise. Weber pointed out that musicians were beyond the scope of existing US contract labour laws, meaning that the Federation, rather than the Government, was responsible for the refusal of entry to foreign musicians, and that it was merely seeking the same control as the British Union pursued. Weber ended his message with the assertion that 'musical employment in England should certainly be given to English musicians' (Batten 1929).

If such intransigence was a blow to MU members seeking to work in the USA, a further problem for the Union was that its argument that British musicians could do anything that a foreign musician could was increasingly undermined by exceptional musicians with particular racial origins. Jazz's

44 A fee of $5,500 a week was widely reported.

45 Arthur (2003) reports similar protectionist measures by the Australian Musicians' Union at this point.

46 Labour had briefly been in power in 1924, but both then and between 1929 and 1931 it ran a minority Government.

first stars were black Americans who possessed ability and originality that could not be replicated by their British peers. The Kit Kat Club successfully argued for uniqueness in 1925 when it applied for work permits for a number of American musicians, a move that the Union opposed. Though Batten wrote to the Ministry of Labour claiming that 'only a few very special American musicians are in any way superior to ours' (TNA, AR/278/41/1925), the Union found that the Ministry, British musicians, and audiences all disagreed (Parsonage 2005: 218).

By 1930 the Union's Dance Band Section (see below, pp. 85–6) was calling for 'tightening restrictions upon the entry of aliens and the ultimate exclusive employment of British musicians' (*Melody Maker*, September 1930: 739), but some of its leading members – including Hylton, Jack Payne, and Bert Ambrose – saw advantages in the creation of a reciprocal exchange that would allow their bands to visit America in exchange for UK visits by their US equivalents. While in the short term transatlantic union intransigence rendered this impossible, it was to remain an important aspiration.

It also appeared that British musicians might be closing the musical gap. A meeting among the MU, the Ministry of Labour, and various employers in November 1930 concluded that 'the improvement of British bands was such that whole American bands had less to offer in terms of entertainment or educative potential for British musicians', but that 'importing some American individuals and bands could still be justified' on the grounds of inspiring new ideas (Parsonage 2005: 220). According to Parsonage, the outcome was application of 'a flexible policy ... whereby American bands could perform in variety halls and in dance halls only when the resident British band was retained' (220). Thus displacement was a key criterion.

This fragile truce allowed Louis Armstrong to perform in 1932 and Duke Ellington in 1933.[47] However, the latter's shows inadvertently became a catalyst for the pursuit of tighter restrictions on the importation of American jazz musicians. Hylton had brokered the deal that brought Ellington and his band to the UK, reaching what *Melody Maker* described as 'a reciprocal agreement' with Ellington's agent, Irving Mills, in December 1932, where the two agreed to 'represent the other's activities in their respective countries' (April 1933: 327). Although Parsonage notes some 'undoubtedly philanthropic' motives behind Hylton's involvement in Ellington's 1933 shows, she also argues that it had the potential to assist in his campaign to play in the States (2005: 253).

[47] Both played residencies at the Palladium – a variety venue. While Ellington brought his own orchestra, Armstrong was eventually backed by 'a complete band of coloured musicians from Paris' (*Melody Maker*, August 1932: 10)

Meanwhile, it should be noted that this era witnessed the peak of xenophobic and anti-American sentiment in the Union. Despite protestations that 'British musicians have no feelings against foreign musicians as such' (*Musicians' Journal*, April 1925: 7), during the 1920s the *Journal* became full of inflammatory grandiloquence and unsubstantiated claims. The foreign, predominantly American, musicians were accused of 'underselling their services' (April 1925: 7), 'drawing huge salaries', and not paying tax, as well as flouting the conditions of their work permits (*Musicians' Journal*, January 1926: 6). The latter quotes come from an uncredited article entitled 'The growing menace of alien musicians', reprinted from the *Empire Record*. This invoked race and, despite lacking any evidence, reported that:

> a revolting phase of this alien competition is that in some cases – all too frequent – the British musician has to give way to a negro. It is understood that this has actually happened in orchestras engaged for private houses. Or again, he may have to submit to being trained by a black. Naturally he will not, and one more alien gets a job and one more Britisher is unemployed. (*Musicians' Journal*, January 1926: 6)

Although this does not appear to have been written by an MU member, its publication in the *Journal* is worthy of consideration. In addition an article by Batten in 1930 was headlined 'Alien menace', and racist sentiment has been suggested in Batten's other work (Batten 1930; Cloonan and Brennan 2013: 288).

It is now difficult to ascertain how widely such views were held, and the general antipathy towards foreign musicians has to be placed in a wider context. The loss of jobs caused by the talkies had decimated the Union and it was extremely wary of further displacement of its members. In this context the denial of the uniqueness of American players was something of a desperate last stand. Moreover, it was far from alone in its antipathy towards migrant workers, as its stance was replicated in the United States and Australia (Dreyfus 2009). More broadly Winder notes that the TUC 'passed several resolutions calling for strict legislation against the immigrants who were stealing their members jobs' going back to the turn of the century, and that 'forty-three trade unions supported some form of anti-alien legislation' (2004: 257). Such lobbying had influenced a number of pieces of protective legislation.[48] In such circumstances the identification of xenophobic views within the MU remains unfortunate, but perhaps not unexpected.

48 The Aliens Act (1906) and the Aliens Restriction Act (1914) were the most significant.

More challenges

The issue of foreign workers was closely connected to other challenges faced by the Union in the 1920s and 1930s, especially those posed by changing tastes and new technology. The MU's response was primarily organisational, with the formation of two important bodies and a reappraisal of its relationship with the wider trade union movement. Formed in 1930, the Union's Dance Band Section recognised the changing nature of musical employment in the palais and ballrooms, as well as concerns around foreign labour. The Musical Performers' Protection Association (MPPA) was formed in 1928 (see Figure 6 encouraging members to join) as a specific response to concerns around the 'mechanical reproduction' of members' work on records, and quickly turned its attention to the emergent problem in the cinemas.

Both these responses show that – in a reverse of Williams' earlier tactics – the MU was now turning inwards rather than outwards for solutions. As well as internal restructuring, including the move of the head office from Manchester to London in 1931, the Union distanced itself from former allies in the labour movement – as we now show.

Figure 6 An advert from the *Musicians' Journal* of April 1929 urging members to join the MPPA (MU, 1/3).

The Dance Band Section and MPPA

As the availability of work in cinemas declined, the MU's formation of a Dance Band Section was a somewhat belated attempt to bring such musicians into the fold. Previously, they were under-represented in a Union whose core membership remained that of orchestral musicians. However, as the 1920s progressed, many orchestral musicians had to adapt to playing music for dancing. Coupled with the decline in membership prompted by the cinema crisis, this accelerated the Union's efforts to organise among those playing dance music in cafés, restaurants, and ballrooms. A meeting was called at Victory House on 8 August 1930, for which the Union had enlisted a number of well-known bandleaders including Hylton, Payne, and Ambrose. The outcome was the formation of the Dance Band Section, which was rapidly constituted over the course of two further meetings in August and September.

An eighteen-strong committee was appointed that included some of the bandleaders, and rules and objectives were set out. The Section was 'an organisation within and subject to the rules of the Musicians' Union', open to any '*bona fide* dance players'. Its primary aim was 'to secure the complete unionisation of dance musicians for their mutual benefit and protection' (*Melody Maker*, November 1930: 925). The most important aspect of the Section's work was a refusal of the bandleaders involved to employ non-Union labour. This attempt to create a closed shop among dance bands was largely applicable to the most high-profile (and London-based) bands, but set a working template.[49] However, the Section soon collapsed and did not meet again after February 1931.

The MPPA was an attempt to alert members to the growing threat from technology and to rally them to take action. Organisationally, it was set up as a limited-liability company controlled by the Union, because laws governing the conduct of trade unions prevented it from 'undertaking the duties which the Association will perform' (*Melody Maker*, January 1929: 12). *Melody Maker* described the MPPA as 'a project likely to be one of the most far reaching and important ever conceived for the benefit of musicians' (January 1929: 12). It adopted a similar approach to that employed with the broadcasters, seeking to control the use of members' recordings via the authorisation of licences for use in return for payment.

Musicians were encouraged to sign up (for free) to the Association, and by June 1929 it had recruited 5,200 members, the vast majority in London.

[49] For example, various SWETM/TMA minutes reveal that in 1920 the Union was seeking to enforce a closed shop and in 1924 the Union attempted to enforce a rule in theatres that its members would not play with non-members. Both attempts were resisted. For the fallout from an attempt to enforce a closed shop in the late 1920s see Cloonan (2012).

However, a significant problem for the Union was that in the cinema crisis it had no UK employer with which it could negotiate. It had hoped that the MPPA could use the limited rights granted to performers via the DMPPA both to obstruct the advance of the talkies and to secure additional payments from the use of recordings in other public contexts. However, its legacy was much more pronounced in future negotiations with the British recording industry than in its attempts to stop the talkies.

The Association failed in its one attempt at the latter, when it took out a test case against British International Pictures (BIP) to establish whether the performing rights of those MPPA members who had performed on the soundtrack of the BIP film *Blackmail* were in fact invested in the Association, and whether members could perform on film soundtracks without its permission.[50] The judge in the case, Mr Justice McCardie, found 'no merit' in the MPPA's case and argued that a ruling in their favour would have given the organisation too much power to impose its own conditions (*Melody Maker*, July 1930: 644). After the failure of the case, and the gradual realisation that the talkies' popularity was irreversible, both the Association and the Union gradually applied their energies elsewhere.

Attention duly turned to the recording industry, where concern focused on the move of records away from being used purely domestically to their growing presence within public places and airways. Here the principles established by the MPPA formed the basis for the Union's approach to industrial relations in the recording industry for decades afterwards. Although the Association did not endure, its aim of collecting and distributing money for additional uses of recordings, and controlling such uses, soon became incorporated into the MU's ethos and negotiating position. Meanwhile, other external concerns loomed.

The trade union movement

Financial problems caused by declining membership and a problematic relationship with the TUC saw the Union becoming increasingly self-reliant and inward-looking. In 1929 the TUC's conference considered three MU motions – around unemployment, foreign musicians, and 'mechanical music'. The first resolution was passed, but Dambman reported that it was 'treated with scant attention' (1929: 14). The motion on foreign workers was better received, but referred to the General Council. The resolution on mechanical music was opposed, as other unions facing similar problems felt that 'the

[50] Alfred Hitchcock's *Blackmail* (1929) is generally considered to be the first all-British talkie.

introduction of mechanical music was progress, and that to oppose it was like turning the tide back' (Dambman 1929: 15).

Following the Belfast experience, it was perhaps unsurprising that the MU took a step back from the TUC. It stopped paying affiliation fees shortly after the conference[51] and officially resigned from the Congress in 1935, although this was attributed to the Union's financial position rather than to the apparent ideological differences (EC minutes, 25–28 April 1935). However, when this was combined with continuing discontent over Labour's failure to address the 'aliens' issue, it left the Union more estranged from the labour movement than at any previous stage in its history.[52]

Conclusion

This period saw the Union struggling to deal with both its first major internal changes and unprecedented technological change. In addition, the perennial issues surrounding competition from police, army, and foreign musicians remained high on the Union's agenda, particularly during periods of mass unemployment.

The protracted nature of Williams' departure did little for the Union's internal stability. While Teale's weak leadership was not responsible for the external issues that were to confront the Union during his short tenure as GS, it *was* a contributory factor when the Union's responses seemed either slow (the embrace of dance musicians) or reactionary (the initial response to the talkies). However, as the broadcasting and recording industries grew in importance and engendered new threats to the provision of live performances, the Union's reaction was comparatively enlightened. In both cases it sought to control employers' activities and to maximise payments to members, while recognising potential employment opportunities. In broadcasting this hunch was proven correct, as by the mid-1930s the BBC became the UK's largest employer of musicians.

The prospects of meaningful work for musicians in the recording industry perhaps seemed less encouraging, as by 1933 the Union and industry both appeared to be in irreversible decline. In fact, the basis of recovery in both was sown in the period. The Union (with the formation of the MPPA) and the record companies – globally with the formation of the International Federation of Phonographic Industries (IFPI),[53] and nationally with the

[51] It continued to pay fees to the Scottish Trades Union Congress (STUC).

[52] TUC officials were generally supportive of the Union and sought to retain it. See MRC, MS 292/91M/184.

[53] The IFPI was formed in Italy in 1933.

formation of PPL – both saw the importance of copyright as a means of potentially reviving their respective fortunes.

Finally, the problem of competition, especially from abroad, continued. Not only were 'star' American musicians in demand among British audiences, and less well-known American musicians working in British bands, but the Hylton case brought to the fore the issue of British musicians seeking to work in the USA. Ehrlich argues that 'the early 1930s were watershed years for professional musicians', relating this to 'technology, patronage and the collapse of domestic music making' (1985: 209). From our perspective of musical labour, it was the confluence of changing public tastes, technology, and immigration that made this era so important for the Union. Between 1919 and 1933, the professional, industrial, and employment landscape for musicians changed irrevocably, and planted the seeds of many of the organisations and agreements that were to be pivotal to industrial relations in the music profession for much of the remainder of the twentieth century.

4

The politics of dancing: 1934–1945

Following Ehrlich's assessment that the 1930s were a 'watershed moment' for the music profession, we argue that 1934 was a significant turning point for the MU. With the first signs of a reversal of the dire consequences of the talkies and recession for the profession, it was also the year in which the recording and broadcasting industries reorganised in ways that were to prove integral to the Union's immediate survival and long-term future. This chapter concentrates on the period of revival that made this possible. We argue that a politicisation of the profession, particularly among dance musicians, was largely responsible, and that, unlike many of the previous successes and failures of the Union, this reversal of fortunes was as much down to the mobilisation and radicalisation of its members as it was to the circumstances to which they were reacting.

We begin with a general overview of the profession at the start of the period before concentrating on the matters that were to preoccupy the Union and shape British musicians' working lives before and during the Second World War. We split these between the internal machinations and politics of the Union, and external factors such as the continuing problem of foreign musicians, building relationships with the broadcasters and record companies, and the war's impact.

Working life

The events of the late 1920s and early 1930s changed the British music profession in ways that were as dramatic as they were unforeseen. This was visible in both the mass unemployment of musicians and the changing nature of the work for those who remained employed. Among the more obvious outcomes of this was a growing inequality across the profession, which was to have a huge impact on both the Union's membership and its operation. If the years between 1928 and 1933 saw the talkies decimate both the profession and the Union, 1934 marked the start of resurgence brought about by a mixture of the changing outlets for music and organisation within some branches of the Union.

Although the extent of the unemployment among musicians was difficult to measure (Ehrlich 1985: 210), Union membership was one of the more reliable indicators, as those who became either unemployed or under-employed within cinemas ceased to pay subscriptions. The scale of displacement across the profession was therefore evident in the shrinking size of the Union, which decreased by two-thirds between 1926 and 1934, suffering eight years of consecutive decline. With only 6,772 members in 1934, and over half of these in London, this inevitably impacted on the Union's finances and organisation.

There are two important points to note here. The first, made by Ehrlich, focuses on the specifically *technological* nature of the unemployment. Unlike other industries, where unemployment was essentially cyclical and likely to be reversed, there was no guarantee that this would happen for musicians. Moreover, he notes that technology had broken 'the firm link which had always existed between a demand for music and the simultaneous employment of musicians'. This was a turning point for the profession and meant that 'those who found work in recording, broadcasting and film studios were singularly favoured' (1985: 211). For many Union members, this was to remain a source of resentment for decades to come.

The second point is that focusing on the musicians being made redundant in the cinemas risks neglecting the considerable growth in other parts of the profession, especially among broadcast orchestras and the higher echelons of the dance music business. The nature and complexity of this are covered in more detail later, but throughout the 1930s the BBC's orchestras grew in number and the Corporation increasingly engaged other musicians on a casual basis. Tschaikov highlights the BBC's importance, claiming that 'in its first fifteen years, the BBC's enlightened music policy profoundly affected musical life in Britain' (2009: 20), among not only musicians but also audiences who, through radio and television, were exposed to an increasing amount and range of music (Baade 2012).[1]

The most popular dance bandleaders – among them Hylton, Payne, Ambrose, and Billy Cotton – had, by the mid-1930s, sold several million records and been able to secure lucrative residencies and tours, the result of increased exposure through new technology.[2] Consequently, like the BBC

[1] The first BBC television broadcasts were in 1936.
[2] The best and most detailed account of this period is by Nott (2002).

musicians, those working in the leading dance bands enjoyed pay and conditions unimaginable even a decade before, while many of their former colleagues drifted from the profession or found themselves in less appealing places of employment (Tschaikov 2009: 10).

Over-supply of labour meant that theatre engagements were few and far between, and musicians were increasingly drawn to employment in cafés, restaurants, and – further afield – in holiday camps and on cruise ships. With each of these dominated by large employers like Lyons, Butlin's, and Cunard, there was also a huge supply of non-unionised workers willing to undercut Union rates. Unsurprisingly conditions in these new places of work were poor and the MU relatively powerless.

Nevertheless, by 1935 there was some evidence that the Union had moved beyond blaming the talkies for the depressed state of the profession, and even some talk – at least in London – of an upturn in the availability of work. The *Musicians' Union Report* recorded successful shows at the Drury Lane and Palace Theatres, with Newton Brooke writing that 'it means the panic of the talkies is finished. It means that musicians no longer regard the Union as "off the map". It means that confidence is coming back' (Newton Brooke 1935).

Whether such positivity would have resonated with many Union members – especially those working in the provinces – is questionable. Just one month earlier, *Melody Maker* had reported on the formation of the General Musicians' Association, which sought to address 'the grave state of unemployment in Lancashire's dance music circles'. This reported that around 370 of the estimated 2,000 dance musicians in Manchester had signed up, and that a Liverpool Branch was being formed to deal with the transformation of the city from 'the provincial Mecca of dance musicians' to one in which conditions were 'heart-breaking' (1 December 1935: 9). While the organisation was short-lived, its formation and initial success highlighted both the reality of conditions outside London and the apparent lack of response from the Union.

Reports from provincial branches in the *MU Report* offered little solace for the Union's leaders. The Leeds Branch said that 'the provinces are being starved in order to keep London and the General Office in existence' (April 1935: 1), a theme that was also being pursued with some vigour by the Glasgow and Edinburgh branches (January 1936: 1).[3] A letter from the Nottingham Branch painted an even starker warning of the Union's position

[3] The Scottish branches had long felt removed from the Union's leadership and had intermittently sought greater autonomy. For example, in 1915 Fred Young of the Glasgow Branch wrote proposing a 'Home Rule Bill' for Scotland within the AMU (*Musicians' Monthly Report*, February 1915: 3).

outside London, claiming that 'in many branches the MU is practically a dead letter in the lives of musicians' (October 1935: 5).

As well as being divided by geography, the Union was also split by music and politics. Here the formation of the Dance Band Section had done little to reduce the internal tensions between the 'straight' orchestral musicians and those playing jazz or dance music. Such attitudes were evident in a 1936 *MU Report* article by Charles Bohm, which blamed the new breed of musicians for some of the problems facing the profession and Union. His disparaging attitude towards some jazz – 'the noise of indiscriminate banging and harmonic clashes' – whose performers were 'mainly "stunt" merchants and their performance ... more of a novelty than an actual profession' (July 1936: 4), was accentuated by bitterness about the fees that some such musicians commanded. He reported that their terms 'were far in excess of the accepted Union standards' and that this attracted a huge influx of semi-professionals and amateurs into bands that were both largely devoid of MU organisation and willing to undercut its rates. He also reported that a lack of work elsewhere was driving many dance musicians to relocate to London, resulting in 'fierce competition for fewer engagements' within the capital (July 1936: 4).

Though Bohm's analysis drips with contempt, his primary target was non-Union musicians, rather than dance musicians specifically. In addition he recognised both the growing inequality across the profession and the need to do something about it – regardless of the type of musicians involved. This drew him and a sizeable number of London musicians towards the CPGB, with significant implications for the Union. Initially the CPGB influence was the catalyst for a revival in Union membership;[4] latterly it was to produce internal strife.

Politics and internal machinations

Disillusion with both working conditions and the Union leadership's ineffectual response had been brewing for a number of years. The lack of dance musicians in the Union was widely identified as a problem and, as Bohm noted, many of them saw the Union as an irrelevance. Evidence of this is found in an anonymous letter in the *MU Report* that argued that the relatively brief boom in cinema employment had merely been a disruption of the established order, wherein the Union had primarily served those musicians employed in 'theatres, music halls and concert halls'. With the coming of the talkies the Union had, it was argued, 'reverted to its original type', acting 'only on behalf of the former classes' (January 1934: 2).

[4] In 1936 this dropped to 6,741 – the lowest since 1912.

This was the thinking behind a call to action in July 1935, when the *MU Report* announced the formation of a Voluntary Organising Committee (VOC), allegedly the result of an Archer Street café conversation among a group of dance band musicians bemoaning conditions within the profession and the MU's apparently weak response to them. It was reported that two musicians had mooted the idea of a separate dance musicians' union and this became the catalyst for what the *Report* called an agreement among those present 'to put their backs into the work of campaigning for a 100 per cent Musicians' Union'.

The urgency being sensed, action was prompt and a meeting was held at Victory House on 29 April with support from 'members and non-members alike'. The meeting received the crucial endorsement of the Union's London District Committee (LDC) and the London Trades Council. Tellingly, the Union's paid officials and leadership were not involved in the organisation, which quickly cut a deal with the LDC to reduce the entrance fee from £1 1s to 10s on the grounds that 'a campaign for increased membership would only be effective if the entrance fee were within the means of those who had struck a bad patch' (July 1935: 1; see Figure 7). Besides increasing membership, the VOC published a monthly magazine, *Crescendo*,[5] and independently pursued better terms for musicians working for the Lyons chain, which had previously refused to negotiate with the Union.

The VOC had a sizeable impact on both the size of the Union and its longer-term political leanings. Over 500 new members signed up in London between April and July 1935, and VOCs were set up in Glasgow, Leeds, and Manchester, marking the start of the reversal of the Union's fortunes. More significantly, they changed the power dynamic within the Union, shifting the balance away from older members to younger ones, from 'straight' musicians to dance musicians, and from the provinces to London. In doing so they also moved the MU's politics to the left. Despite some resistance, the VOCs formed an uneasy alliance with the Union's leadership. Dambman's position was weakened – but not threatened – by the upsurge in activism. Given the Union's perilous finances, it could barely refuse the shot in the arm offered by the VOCs, even if they were almost certainly pulling the Union in a direction some officials opposed.

This zeal of the new activism is captured in Morgan's description of the change in the LDC, where 'out went the bald-headed old guys ... and in came a younger breed of dance-band leftists, gathering in the small hours in West End

[5] The first issue appeared in June 1935 and sold out all 1,000 copies. Some copies are available in MU, 4/3/5/3.

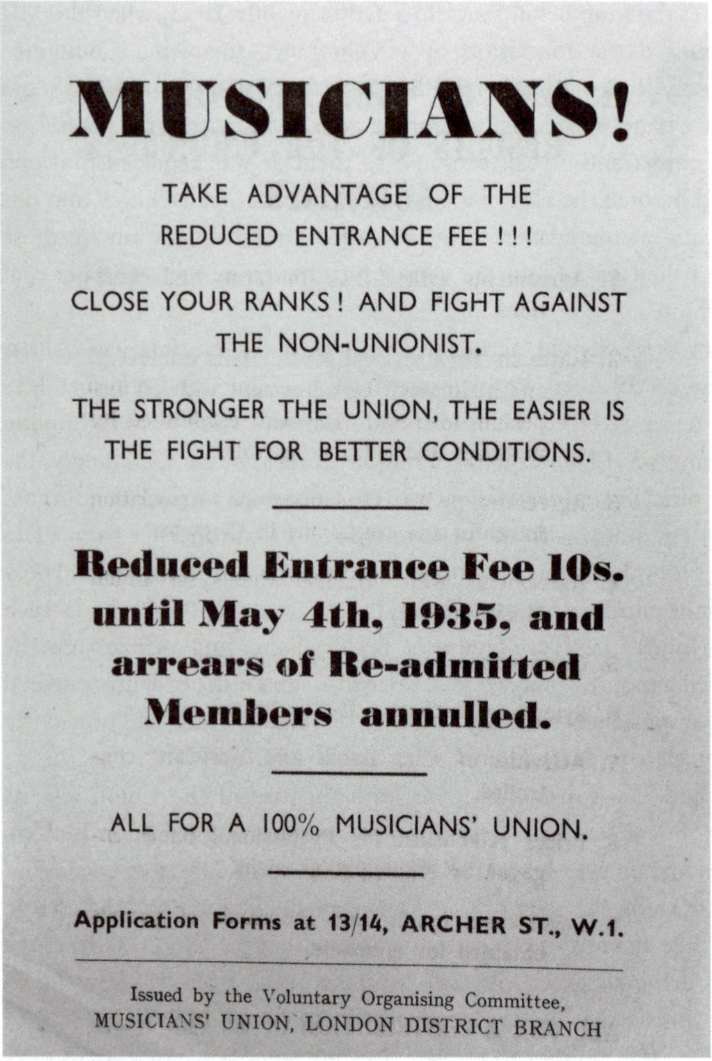

MUSICIANS!

TAKE ADVANTAGE OF THE
REDUCED ENTRANCE FEE !!!

CLOSE YOUR RANKS! AND FIGHT AGAINST
THE NON-UNIONIST.

THE STRONGER THE UNION, THE EASIER IS
THE FIGHT FOR BETTER CONDITIONS.

Reduced Entrance Fee 10s. until May 4th, 1935, and arrears of Re-admitted Members annulled.

ALL FOR A 100% MUSICIANS' UNION.

Application Forms at 13/14, ARCHER ST., W.1.

Issued by the Voluntary Organising Committee,
MUSICIANS' UNION, LONDON DISTRICT BRANCH

Figure 7 A flyer produced by the VOC of the MU in London, 1935 (MU, 1/9).

cafes and then setting their alarm clocks for the next morning's union business' (1998: 128). This period saw the emergence of some figures who were to play sizeable roles in the Union's subsequent history: Hardie Ratcliffe, Jack Dearlove, Alex Mitchell, Charles Bohm, Van Phillips, Harry Francis, and Ted Anstey.[6] Each came to hold positions of power and all were involved, to varying degrees, with both the VOCs and the CPGB. That musicians were involved with leftist politics

[6] Van Phillips' full name was Alexander Van Cleve Phillips, Francis' was Henry Francis Major, and Anstey's Edward Henry Thomas Anstiss.

at this stage was unsurprising, but the number of Communists within the MU was such that during the Second World War the Security Service (MI5) kept a close watch on their activities with the assistance of informants inside the Union and the Metropolitan Police's Special Branch.

The reasons for support of the CPGB at the time were manifold but converged around issues of inequality in British society and 'concern about Fascism and a commitment to progressive politics' (Hanlon and Waite 1998: 69).[7] The Party therefore became a natural home for musicians, not least because of its inclination to 'take its cultural work very seriously indeed' (Croft 1998: 3) through associations like the Left Book Club, Unity Theatre, and the Workers' Music Association (WMA). By the start of the war, Communist leanings were evident across the profession and Morgan notes that by the early 1940s there was 'hardly a name dance band without its communist faction' (1998: 125). Among the orchestras, Thomas Russell and a number of members of the London Philharmonic Orchestra (LPO) were also known to be active in the CPGB (*Tschaikov 2014*).

It hardly took the resources of MI5 to see evidence of CPGB influence within both the profession and the MU. In the latter, this was most prominent in the *Monthly Report*, much of which was being written by members of the VOCs. Articles appeared in quick succession on rearmament and the cost of living (Dearlove 1937), the Soviet Art Workers' Union (Bohm and Mitchell 1937), and the Spanish Civil War (Green 1937). These provoked other members to voice their disapproval, with one writing that Dearlove's article 'revealed a political tendentiousness that smacked too heavily of the left' (*Monthly Report*, April 1937: 4).

A Special Branch report from 1941 noted that 'Communist infiltration into the Musicians' Union started about six years ago and from time to time the extremist element has set up a series of committees and political groups with the object of gaining control of the Union' (TNA, KV3/375). Having established this, the security services kept personal files on a range of Union officials and activists they believed to be CPGB members or sympathisers, including Bohm, Mitchell, Francis, and Ratcliffe, who had been appointed AGS on the death of Walter Murdock in 1937.[8] However, it was Party members Jack Dearlove and Van Phillips who were to become the focus of most detailed scrutiny after they were respectively appointed London Organiser[9]

[7] There were a large number of Jewish musicians in London, many of whom were involved in the CPGB.

[8] Mitchell took over Ratcliffe's former job as General Organiser at the same time.

[9] This was a full-time post, which in 1941 was combined with the job of full-time London District Branch Secretary.

and elected to the EC in 1940. They were also to become divisive figures within the Union. We will consider Phillips' activities in more detail in Chapter 5, and for now concentrate on Dearlove and the Union's London District.

Dearlove's allegiance to the CPGB was immediately tested when, on his appointment, he was asked to assure the Union's Executive that he would not 'propagate his political opinions when carrying out union duties' (TNA, KV3/376). In doing so, he upset his colleagues in the Musicians' Group of the CPGB, who were to seek his removal firstly from the Party[10] and then from the Union because of 'his inconsistency and suspected treachery' (TNA, KV3/376). His particular crime in their eyes was writing to the TUC for advice on how to deal with the Band Stewards' Organisation, a CPGB group within the MU that had attempted to organise a 'slate' for elections to the London Branch Committee at the end of 1941 (MRC, MS 292/91M/184).

Both attempts to oust him failed, but six CPGB members involved in the plot against him were charged with conspiring to 'usurp and undermine the authority of the Union' (MRC, MS 292/770/4). Their £10 fines and six-month suspensions were later overturned at a specially convened meeting on 5 March 1944. Meanwhile the power balance within the LDC constantly shifted. The high watermark of the CPGB's influence came at the end of 1942, when nine of the fifteen-strong committee[11] were known Communists,[12] causing Special Branch to warn MI5 that the CPGB 'is very strongly represented' and that 'there is every likelihood of a considerable increase in communist activity within the Union' (TNA, KV3/376). It was, however, short-lived, and a year later their representation on the committee was reduced to three after concerted attempts by the 'old guard' within the Union to organise against them.

Tellingly, Bill Batten and Vic Sullivan finished first and second in the elections to the LDC for 1944, and the CPGB never reached the same level of influence within the London District again.[13] Both Batten and Sullivan were strongly anti-Communist, with the former having scores to settle following his ousting as Secretary of the London Branch in January 1940, and they successfully reversed a situation whereby the Communists had politicised the meetings to an extent that drove many members away.

There are three important things to draw from the period. The first is that the CPGB had relied on a very small number of members in London and the

10 However it seems that the TUC took no action as the MU was not then affiliated.

11 Elections were held at the end of each year with the period of office being the following calendar year.

12 Of the nine, seven were under surveillance and had a file held on them by Special Branch.

13 Sullivan was a member of Hylton's band and was seen as being on the right of the Union.

apathy of their opponents to create a powerbase within the Union.[14] A number of strong individuals who were CPGB members played a major part in the Union's revised fortunes, causing disproportionate alarm within the press and the security services. Significantly, during the same period, the Union reaffiliated with the TUC in 1942[15] and affiliated with the Labour Party in 1943, meaning that the MU was once again connected with the wider labour movement.

The second point is that Communist support and activity among Union members during the period was not atypical. CPGB membership in Britain peaked at 56,000 in 1942, having risen from 15,570 in 1938 (Beckett 1995: 98), partly a result of wartime support for the Soviet Union. In short, the Party had become 'popular and respectable' (Beckett 1995: 98). The unique aspect of the MU was its position of extreme industrial weakness in the mid-1930s, which the Communists were able to exploit to mutual benefit.

Lastly, the declining representation of the CPGB members on the Union's committees did not mean an end to either their ideological influence or their occasional ability to divide the Union in the future. We return to this in the next chapter, but it is worth noting that many of those involved in the VOCs – notably Ratcliffe, Francis, Anstey, and Mitchell – retained positions of power in the Union until the late 1960s and early 1970s. Ultimately, the CPGB faction may not have taken over the Union at a national level or been the catalyst for revolution that MI5 had feared, but they did highlight divisions within the MU and undoubtedly moved its politics to the left.

Introducing a 'ban'

Given the level of unemployment among musicians in the 1930s, it was hardly surprising that competition from foreign musicians still caused the Union considerable concern. When this was combined with a feeling that UK musicians were being denied the opportunity to perform in the USA, resentment grew. Matters began to unravel in 1934, when Duke Ellington tried to return to the UK and a number of attempts by Hylton and other British bandleaders to appear in the USA were vetoed by the AFM. For the first time there was interest among American promoters, agents, and broadcasters in British jazz musicians, with *Melody Maker* running a series of stories about proposed trips by Hylton, Ambrose, and Ray Noble, and speculating that the

[14] Membership of the CPGB Musicians' Group was only sixty in 1943, although it was thought that not all members were registered (TNA, KV 3/377).

[15] The MU was allowed to reaffiliate for £100, rather than the £491 it owed (MRC, MS 292/91M/184).

latter 'would set a precedent that might result in a veritable flood of British dance musicians into the USA' (8 September 1934: 1). However, such visits remained blocked by AFM strike threats.

Meanwhile a return visit to the UK for Ellington had been mooted in the spring (*Melody Maker*, 19 May 1934: 1) but was beset by problems. The paper's editorial urged Ellington not to return so soon after his previous triumph (19 May 1934: 1) and revealed Hylton was suing Ellington's agent, Mills, for breach of the contract they had signed at the end of 1932. Although Parsonage attributes Hylton's opposition to Ellington's return to 'the refusal of the American union to allow him to play in America' (2005: 253), the legal dispute was probably a further mediating factor.

Without the two most influential supporters of his 1933 visit on board, Ellington's return to the UK was already on shaky foundations when he set sail in July 1934 for a series of shows at the Plaza Cinema on Lower Regent Street,[16] with assorted provincial venues planned for September. However, the Ministry of Labour refused him a work permit. *Melody Maker* was precipitous in reporting that the decision 'undoubtedly foreshadows a new policy in the consideration of applications for such permits', predicting that, as a consequence, 'it is now very unlikely that the Ellington aggregation will ever be heard in England again' (11 August 1934: 1).

While the MU was continuing to exert pressure, the refusal of Ellington's work permit was ultimately a Ministry decision. This was influenced not only by Union pressure, but also by the high level of unemployment amongst musicians and the AFM's unwillingness to contemplate reciprocal exchanges. In the latter case, Joe Weber's brief visit to London in 1934 may have been influential. Described by *Melody Maker* as 'the Mussolini of American musicians' (4 August 1934: 1), Weber told the paper that, while he was willing to allow Jack Hylton to enter the USA and conduct an American band, he saw no prospect of a wider arrangement allowing British musicians to tour, stating 'there would be an outcry throughout the country [USA] were foreign musicians to be imported at such a crucial moment' (*Melody Maker*, 4 August 1934: 1).

The AFM's position, and confirmation from the US Labor Department that it would no longer even consider work permits for British bands (Moore 2006),[17] ensured not only that hopes of US tours by UK musicians were crushed, but that the UK Government finally acquiesced to the MU's pressure

16 Initial reports had suggested he would be returning to the Palladium.

17 Previously they had been considered but vetoed by the AFM (Cloonan and Brennan 2013: 285).

in the opposite direction. A further application for Ellington to visit in 1935 became the final straw, and a press communiqué issued on 29 March 1935 stated that the Minister of Labour, Oliver Stanley, 'does not feel able to grant permits freely to American bands to take engagements of the Variety Hall type', with the only prospect of reappraisal being when 'he can be assured that no less favourable treatment will be accorded to British Bands seeking engagements in the USA' (cited in Parsonage 2005: 255).

Hylton was consequently unable to fulfil his long-held ambition of touring in America, while Ellington was not to return to Britain until 1948, when he appeared 'not with his orchestra, but as a solo pianist' (*Melody Maker*, 19 June 1948: 1).[18] As we show below, it would be 1955 before the restrictions were eased. The limitations on the transatlantic movement of musicians have previously been portrayed by Godbolt (1984) as an MU ban on American jazz, and both Oliver (1990) and McKay (2005) have pointed out the racial overtones of some of the accompanying rhetoric to a set of restrictions that excluded predominantly black musicians from the UK emanating from an almost exclusively white trade union. It is important to note, however, that while racist sentiment was not absent, the MU opposed *all* visits by foreign musicians regardless of their racial origins.

The understandable focus on jazz and American musicians in previous accounts has deflected attention away from the complexity of the arrangements for foreign musicians, which varied among countries[19] and types of music[20] involved. Although the number of foreign musicians working in the UK was greatly reduced, there was never a blanket ban. Cloonan and Brennan (2013) have challenged both the notion of an outright 'ban' and the MU's ownership of it. Indeed, while its instigation came after years of MU agitation, both the AFM and Ministry of Labour played major roles in establishing and operating the restrictions. Furthermore, commencement of war prevented any great movement of musicians for performances, and the full implications of the 1935 restrictions did not play out until after 1945. In summary, the 1930s saw the Union make progress in persuading the Government to protect UK musicians from foreign competition, but 1935 restrictions did not close the matter and we return to it below.

18 The MU's main concern was with combos, and a number of foreign musicians were able to tour as singers or 'entertainers' whose act included music. See Cloonan and Brennan (2013) for examples of the restrictions being circumvented.

19 Reciprocal arrangements were in place with some European countries, and musicians from elsewhere in the British Empire were allowed to work freely in the UK.

20 In 1952 a Visiting Orchestras Consultative Association (VOCA) was set up to deal specifically with visiting orchestras. See Chapter 5.

Shaping the Corporation

Besides the attempts to restrict foreign musicians, the single biggest concern of the Union's leaders was the relationship with, and opportunities presented by, the BBC. With the launch of the BBC Midland Orchestra (1934) and the BBC Northern Irish and Scottish Orchestras (1935), the Corporation had ten permanent orchestras in addition to the BBC Military Band. In addition to these contracted staff musicians, others were employed on an irregular basis for recordings and broadcasts for radio and, from 1936 onwards, an increasing number of television broadcasts. As the BBC moved towards using more recordings (both of its own concerts and of commercially available records), it offered the MU an opportunity for some additional revenue generation (via PPL) that had to be balanced against its fears that the playing of records would result in the loss of employment for live musicians.

The position of both the Union and the BBC in the early days of their relationship set the tone for negotiations down the years. Outwardly, the MU was at its weakest when the BBC began offering permanent contracts to musicians on the formation of the Symphony Orchestra in 1930. However, in the BBC the Union found an employer that was fundamentally different from those it had previously dealt with. Rather than seeking simply to minimise costs in order to maximise profits, the BBC's public service ethos – embodied by its first Director General, John Reith – meant that it valued music and musicians for their own sake. This was apparent both in the favourable terms and conditions the BBC's musicians received and in responses to the Corporation's music programming and policies from both its funders in government and the public.[21] While some newspapers (see Briggs 1995: 387) and elements among the music profession (see Doctor 1999: 305) made their objections known, the first major review of the BBC – conducted by Lord Ullswater in 1935 and published in 1936 – not only recommended its charter renewal,[22] but also heaped praise on its musical activities (Briggs 1995: 164). The BBC saw its duty as broadcasting music of all types, partly with the aim of educating its audiences. It told Ullswater that it saw its music policy as 'determined by the conviction that listeners would come to appreciate that which at first might appear uninteresting or even alarming' (cited in Doctor 1999: 301). Ullswater duly backed both the philosophical and practical aspects of the BBC's music policy and Doctor argues that this 'quashed the music profession's objections to BBC practices and policies' (305).

21 The BBC was funded by a combination of government subsidy and the payment of a licence fee by members of the public. This had been introduced under the Wireless Telegraphy Act of 1923.

22 The BBC's Royal Charter lasted ten years and expired at the end of 1936.

Meanwhile the MU continued to be pragmatic and cautious in its relations with the BBC. In line with its strategy of the 1920s to control – rather than oppose – music broadcasting, the Union spent much of the 1930s negotiating with the Corporation over a vast and complex array of issues around musical employment. Relations were generally cordial and an article in the MU *Report* commented on the 'good relationship that exists between the Corporation and the Musicians' Union', noting its 'relatively good terms and conditions' (July 1936: 3).

The same article calculated that the Corporation employed 6 per cent of London musicians, and it became a priority to recruit 'the few remaining members' of the BBC's orchestras not already in the Union (July 1936: 3). Achieving a density of membership within the BBC orchestras, combined with the BBC's sense of obligation towards propagating musical employment, became central to the MU's subsequent negotiating successes. A BBC memo to Dambman in 1935 highlighted the sensitivity with which the Corporation had to proceed, recognising that 'there would be a public outcry against the cutting down of employment at the present time when musicians and artists are so very heavily hit' (WAC, R8/123/1).

Initial negotiations between the Union and the BBC saw concerns around conditions of employment in the various types of work offered by the BBC, and the Corporation's uses of music assume more importance than pay. Issues included work on BBC premises, outside broadcasts and relays,[23] and the reproduction or repeat recordings of performances.[24] The negotiations were further complicated by technological advances (notably in recording), different rates for staff musicians and casual appearances,[25] the location of the performances,[26] and even the type of music being performed. Much to the BBC's annoyance, the Union viewed television as distinct from other broadcasts and insisted on new agreements for it. Having reached satisfactory agreements in many of these areas, the goal posts moved again with the commencement of television broadcasts and the outbreak of war.

[23] Details of the Union's definitions of outside broadcasts and relays, as well as the various fees it sought, can be found in MU, 2/3/5.

[24] The BBC initially used Blattnerphone devices to record audio and distribute recordings to its Empire stations overseas. In 1942 the BBC reached an agreement with the MU on recording its musicians; a later agreement made in 1946 was more restrictive, reflecting the MU's view that the previous agreement was an emergency one made under wartime conditions (WAC, R8/123/8).

[25] The MU was always insistent that deals covered *all* (UK) musicians used by the BBC, regardless of whether or not they were MU members. In November 1935 the BBC took the view that all professional musicians were in the MU, with only solo artists (who were classed differently) remaining outside (WAC, R8/123/1).

[26] Broadcasts from the provinces were usually paid at a lower rate than those from London.

The MU and BBC archives offer great detail on the negotiations, showing them to be largely convivial[27] but intractably slow. While the BBC was not entirely blameless here, for the Union delaying was often a tactic. The speed of negotiations was often hampered by the Union insisting on consulting a full EC, which only met four times a year. Less complex negotiations were often resolved by the BBC offering to contribute to the Union's benevolent fund.[28] By the 1940s, the scale of the BBC's musical enterprise was apparent[29] along with the scope of the agreements that it had reached with the Union.[30] As the Union built its membership within the BBC it achieved an unprecedented degree of leverage with this employer, which was playing a significant part in improving the profession's fortunes.

These, however, were not the only arrangements involving the Union in the 1930s and 1940s that were to shape its future. The other, connected, area with which it became more concerned was directly related to the growth of broadcasting (and the public performance of records). This involved the rights of performers in recorded music. While it negotiated with the record companies via PPL, this was a matter that affected a number of parties, including musicians, record companies, broadcasters, and other users of recorded music.

The result was a complex, interdependent, tripartite relationship among the MU, the BBC, and PPL. To simplify, the Union needed the BBC to create employment for its members, while the BBC was reliant on MU members for the musical content of its broadcasts. For PPL the BBC was to become its biggest single source of income via payments for the use of recordings controlled by its members. Meanwhile the Union had the potential to disrupt the recording practices that PPL members (i.e. the record companies) were reliant on. This resulted in agreements not only between the Union and the BBC over pay and working conditions for 'live' musicians, but also a separate set of negotiations between the BBC and PPL over payments to those musicians featured on recorded music used by the Corporation. As noted above, the first such payment was made in 1935 and allowed the BBC to broadcast fourteen hours of music a week for an annual payment to PPL of £20,000. This increased to £30,000 in 1938 and by a further £10,000 per annum in

27 For example in June 1935 the BBC agreed that it would not build up a library of recordings as a means of replacing live musicians (WAC, R8/123/1).

28 In the initial granting of permission to use Blattnerphone recordings for broadcast to the Empire, the BBC made an annual donation to the fund (WAC, R8/123/1).

29 In 1943, the eleven orchestras employed 388 musicians for a minimum of twenty hours a week (MU, 2/3/5).

30 The MU archive has copies of seventeen agreements on issues such as employing musicians after midnight and 'Trailer Records', dated between 1938 and 1943. This does not necessarily account for all the agreements reached in the period, nor for those signed before but still operational.

1941, albeit with an increased allowance of twenty-one hours' 'needletime'.[31] At this point these agreements did not directly involve the Union, but this was to change as the amount of money involved multiplied alongside the number of Union members involved in recording.

Performers' rights and PPL

The relationship among the Union, broadcasters, and record companies was directly connected to another area that was a matter of mutual concern: copyright and the related rights of performers. The potential of this to affect Union members was first recognised in the claims made by the MPPA in the late 1920s. However, it was a combination of the Carwardine ruling, and the record companies' attempts to act on it, that forced dialogue between them and musicians' organisations over payments to performers. Initially these discussions were tentative and the stakes involved relatively small. However, their outcomes came to be of huge importance as both the broadcasting and recording industries grew in subsequent decades. In order to reveal the importance of Carwardine, it is important to see it from the perspective of both the record companies and musicians.

In pursuit of new forms of revenue, the major record companies had conferred throughout the first part of the 1930s on the matter of controlling public performance of their records. This initially involved a number of record companies imposing a ban on the public performance of their records in 1932, though this was legally unenforceable and opposed by both the National Council of Music Users (NCMU) and the Cinematograph Exhibitors' Association (CEA). A compromise was reached with the former the following year that allowed 'bona fide gramophone societies' to continue playing records in public places 'on the understanding that permission to do so is revocable at any time after members of the industry have definitively formulated their policy with regards to the performance in public of gramophone records' (*Yorkshire Evening Post*, 10 April 1933: 8).

Faced with the difficulties of imposing such a ban, the phonographic industry (as it then billed itself) met regularly to co-operate on such matters, setting up a Public Performance Committee, which included representatives of the major record companies and manufacturers of the time under the banner of the British Phonographic Industry (BPI).[32] The committee took legal

31 This term was used to describe the number of hours of recorded music owned by PPL member companies that the BBC could play across its radio networks. The 1941 agreement was eventually extended until after the end of the war.

32 This moniker was to be revived by a record companies' trade organisation that formed in 1973 – but, while the logics were similar, the organisations were entirely separate.

soundings and contributions from each of its members to fund the test case against Carwardine. Following the ruling it moved quickly, in January, to constitute PPL as a limited company. With directors drawn from the record companies, PPL's purpose was to control the use of recorded music via the rights to do so being assigned to them by its members. It spent its first year reaching agreements with a range of major users of recorded music in public places.

Although it was inevitably unpopular with the various music users, PPL soon established itself and began to generate new streams of income for its members. However, it was particularly wary of any opposition posed not only by recorded music users but by other interested parties in such usage – musicians, composers, and the music publishers representing them. With the Carwardine ruling open to legal challenge, PPL moved quickly to assuage both groups and offer them a stake in its new-found gains.

For PPL, providing compensation for musicians was a tactical move: accepting that they had some interest in the use of their recordings, but being careful not to acknowledge any legal performers' rights to payment. Initially the MU had a relatively minor part in discussions with the record companies, with the ISM's Frank Eames at the forefront of the negotiations between PPL and representatives of musicians who had appeared on recordings. Some of this was conducted via the letters pages of *The Times*. Aware of the record companies' machinations, Eames wrote highlighting the mutual interests of the record companies and musicians in limiting the public performance of records. He linked the decline in income of the record companies to 'the daily public performances of records, either through broadcasting or other reproducing mechanism', and supported 'the claim of the solo-performer that his interests in the public performance of his records constitutes [*sic*] a right which can be defined and made statutory' (27 March 1934: 10).

In response, shortly after its first meeting on 6 April 1934, PPL's Chair, S. J. Humphries, acknowledged Eames' claim and set out the new company's position on performers' rights. The right of the performer to remuneration from the use of their work was to become a major issue for the Union as the recording industry grew in size, and is covered in detail by Williamson (2014, 2015). The performer's right to such an income would not become statutory until 1996, but PPL went some way to recognising it when Humphries stated that, though the record companies did not admit a 'legal right of the performing artist', they accepted that 'recognition should in some way be given' to such artists (*The Times*, 13 April 1934: 10). Phonographic Performance Ltd then established a committee to discuss the issues with representatives of recording artists, including the ISM, the MU, Actors' Equity, and the VAF.

A meeting in May 1934 saw PPL offer to make an *ex gratia*[33] payment to the societies for subsequent discussion about how this would be distributed. Eventually the parties settled on 20 per cent of PPL's net income. The next problem was how such income would be distributed to both the recipient organisations and their members.

PPL had asked the organisations to come forward with a proposal for discussion, which they duly did only to be 'astounded to find out [that] ... the directors had in the meantime decided to distribute the monies through their own Company, and therefore it would not be necessary to establish a special Company for this purpose' (*MU Report*, July 1935: 4). This was a blow to the MU, which had hoped to use the MPPA as a vehicle for distributing funds and had held discussions with PPL about how the monies might be used. Of crucial importance for the Union was their insistence that the *ex gratia* payment should *not* be 'intended solely for those musicians who had actually had their performances recorded in gramophone records' (MU, 2/1/6) but should be paid to the organisations' benevolent funds and used for *all* their members. As ever, the Union saw itself as representing *all* musicians, regardless of whether or not they were members.

While important precedents were set by this arrangement, it was to remain relatively low on the MU's list of priorities until the growth of the recording industry meant that the implications of the agreement had potentially greater ramifications in the post-war period. Meanwhile it advised the small number of its members who were to receive payments from PPL to be cautious in what they were signing up to. It suggested that they reject the PPL's initial terms – that the rights performers were assigning were 'not revocable and might be held to bind the signatory for all time' – and suggested that while members might accept PPL payments they should insist on the addition to their terms of the words 'subject to its being terminable by either party giving the other six months' notice' (*MU Report*, July 1935: 4).

The Union reiterated its commitment to establishing the legal right of performers to prevent the public use of their recordings independently of the record companies. It continued to work and negotiate with PPL as, in the absence of a legally enforceable performers' right, the deal offered by the record companies was the best it could hope for. While changes in the profession and the recording industry meant that the Union's interest in the establishment of a performers' right and negotiations with PPL were to become much bigger issues in the post-war period, the opening of a dialogue in the 1930s was the starting point of a lengthy journey towards establishing performers' rights.

33 'For favour' – PPL made it clear that this was a voluntary arrangement and that the payment did not constitute an acceptance of the principle of a performers' right.

As time progressed a combination of increased union membership (especially in the Corporation's orchestras), the growth of the recording industry, and the demands of broadcasters and the public for more recorded music combined to extend the Union's power in negotiations with the recording industry. Perhaps even more influential was the American musicians' recording strike of 1942–44 when James Petrillo, the AFM's leader, withdrew his members' labour from recordings until a settlement was reached. Despite coming under considerable pressure from the US Government and record companies, the AFM held out and achieved its aims – namely that 'the record manufacturers contribute a fixed fee from every recording to a union fund for unemployed musicians' (DeVeaux 1988: 128). Decca settled first in September 1943, with the other labels finally doing the same in November 1944.[34]

Unsurprisingly, the American strike made the record companies nervous that a similar one could take place in the UK. In reality, this was unlikely, as the MU could not replicate the situation in the USA where 'virtually every professional instrumentalist, popular and classical, belonged to the AFM ... effectively creating a "closed shop" of union members' (DeVeaux 1988: 128). Nonetheless, the strike threat came to underpin industrial relations in the British recording industry for many years, its likelihood increased by the AFM's success and the MU's revitalised membership.

War again

The final and not inconsiderable outside disruption to the Union's activities during the period was the outbreak of war in September 1939. Initially its impact was felt more by musicians than employers. Although many musicians were called up for service, an over-supply of musicians meant that they were normally replaced in their workplaces. Generally the entertainment industry was not affected, and theatres, music halls, and cinemas continued to operate as normal. But the war was to present specific problems for the BBC. Its role during wartime involved not only a propaganda function but also the boosting of public morale.[35] Here music – in particular popular music – played a large part. For the BBC music was 'central to its mission of cultural uplift' (Baade 2012: 4) and so it sought to retain as many of its orchestral musicians as possible.[36]

[34] For accounts of the AFM strike see Gorman (1983), Lunde (1948), and Roberts (2014).

[35] The MU also made much of musicians' ability to boost morale. See Baade (2012: 88–9).

[36] Baade (2012: 89) suggests that 'straight' musicians fared better than dance musicians here. After the war the MU argued that agreements made during the war with the BBC and other organisations were emergency ones that needed to be revisited once hostilities ceased (WAC, R8/123/8).

Dambman's main priority on the outbreak of war was to ensure that musicians were not forced into the type of pay cuts that Williams had agreed in 1914. In the lead-up to the war, the LDC had already rejected proposals by some managers to reduce salaries in the event of hostilities. This stance was echoed in the first edition of the *MU Monthly Report* following the declaration of war. Here Dambman stressed the lessons of 1914, noting that:

> It is often declared that history repeats itself. Shortly after the War had been declared in 1914, an attack was made on musicians' wages. Employers insisted that the number of those who patronised theatres, music halls and cinemas would be seriously reduced; and that only by 'all concerned' making 'sacrifices', could the business be saved and employment preserved. (1939: 1)

The Union was banking on a repeat of the experience of the First World War, when the demand for entertainment increased and created opportunities for those musicians still in the country. It also sought to clarify the position both of those musicians who were still working and of those called up for military service. For the former, this centred around what would happen in the event of their contracts being terminated at short notice, for the latter, 'whether musicians called up under the Military Training Act (1939) would, in certain specified cases, be permitted to have the date of commencement of training postponed' (letter from Dambman to Ministry of Labour, 15 June 1939).[37] This was partly a contractual issue, as the Union was worried that members would be in breach of contract if they had to leave their positions to serve.

In this hypothetical situation, it was perhaps not surprising that the Government was not overly sympathetic. A reply from W. Nicholls of the Ministry of Labour on 6 July merely reiterated the contingencies of the Act, which he said 'empowers the Minister to make regulations for the purpose of securing the fair adjustment of contracts of service in force between employers and employees when the latter are called up'. Individual musicians who could show good cause for deferment were asked to apply to the Ministry as per the existing rules.

By 1940, the Ministry had established an Entertainments National Service Committee (ENSC), which in turn engendered a Music National Service Committee (MNSC) under the Chairmanship of Sir Hugh Allen.[38] Dambman served on both, and short deferments were agreed for, among others, members

37 This, and the reply from W. Nicholls of the Ministry of Labour, were both published in the *Musicians' Monthly Report*, August 1939: 2.

38 Allen was a former director of the Royal College of Music and a distinguished musician/conductor.

of the LPO. In 1941 the BBC wrote to the MNSC seeking indefinite deferment for all its musicians, arguing their importance to its output and that they could not find replacements of an equal standard. Rather than agreeing to indefinite deferments, the Committee offered short-term ones for the BBC musicians. These were renewed, often subject to musicians 'giving a certain period of their time each year to the entertainment of the Services and factory workers' (MU, 1/7/1943). By the last two years of the war equilibrium had been reached between the employment situation within the profession and demand for additional personnel for the armed forces, meaning that the Committee served little meaningful purpose. Baade reports that the Ministry 'regularly dismissed Musicians' Union pleas for more extensive deferrals' (2012: 88), and in 1944 Dambman offered to resign from the Committee, as he was rarely able to attend the meetings in London owing to the MU's General Office being temporarily operated from 11 Byram Arcade in Huddersfield. Though Allen rejected his resignation, Dambman attended no further meetings until the restoration of Union activities from its London office at 7 Sicilian Avenue in May 1945, shortly after the end of the war in Europe.

If Dambman's influence on Government policy was limited, the London District Branch played an arguably more significant role in defending the profession's status. This was evident in their rapid response to the launch of German air raids on London in September 1940, which had resulted in some entertainment venues closing[39] and employment in others becoming vulnerable because of both the air strikes and the possible imposition of a curfew.

Within a few weeks, the LDC had produced a pamphlet setting out their concerns about, and aspirations for, the profession,[40] met with the Ministry of Labour, and organised a mass meeting of musicians on 8 October at which the VAF and the National Association of Theatrical and Kinematograph Employees were also represented. Billed by *Melody Maker* as 'the most important meeting in the whole history of the musical profession' (12 October 1940: 1), it was attended by over 600 musicians and further highlighted both the insecurity and importance of their work during the war. When meeting the Ministry, the LDC demanded 'weekly compensation in keeping with their standard of living and their abilities as trained musicians', and called on the Government to provide *musical* employment (such as playing in munitions factories and air-raid shelters) rather than assimilating musicians into the general wartime workforce. The Ministry's response was to suggest that the

39 Including such major employers as the Chiswick, Holborn, Wood Green, and Shepherd's Bush Empires; the Hippodrome; and the Palladium.

40 Entitled 'The present crisis in the music profession', a copy can be found in MRC, MS 292/91M/184.

musicians work in munitions factories and to state that the Government considered 'the present unemployment pay sufficient' (MRC, MS 292/91M/184).

If the anxiety in the aftermath of the start of the Blitz was understandable then, as Dambman had predicted in 1939, 'when the country settles into its War stride, entertainment will more and more become a necessity' (Dambman 1939: 1). As a result, the outcome for the profession and the Union was similar to that experienced during the 1914–18 war, where a period of uncertainty was followed by what Mackerness describes as 'phenomenal demand for all kinds of musical enterprise' (1964: 267). Accordingly, Union membership rose and it was broadly supportive of both the war and the Government's attitude towards musicians. The Delegate Conference held in 1943[41] passed a motion that affirmed the Union's 'desire to see this war fought to a successful conclusion' (*Monthly Report*, January 1944: 1). It also highlighted the role of the State in bringing about acceptable wartime conditions for the profession, noting that 'it cannot be stressed too strongly that the present flourishing of the Entertainment Industry is due to the Ministry of Labour being in favour of providing entertainment to the civilian population to maintain their morale' (*Monthly Report*, January 1944: 1).

This may not have represented the views of all the Union's members at the start of the war, as many of those involved in both the Union and the CPGB – notably Ben Frankel and Charles Kahn – were supportive of the People's Convention, a Communist-inspired gathering held in London on 12 January 1941 with over 2,000 delegates. The latter's involvement saw him dismissed from the BBC on the grounds that he constituted a threat to national security, but after the involvement of the National Council for Civil Liberties, the Prime Minister announced that 'artists who attended the People's Convention should not be debarred from giving broadcast performances in the normal way' (*The Times*, 21 March 1941: 4). The MU was not officially represented at the People's Convention, with an EC meeting on 10–11 December narrowly voting against a London motion to appoint delegates.

By the end of the year, the invasion of the USSR by Nazi Germany led to the Convention's collapse as Britain and the USSR became allies against Germany. Nonetheless, its brief existence highlighted divisions within the Union and the inherently political nature of much musical work during wartime. At the 1940 meeting at Victory House, Alex Mitchell argued that as 'private enterprise was no longer supporting the industry it was only to governments that musicians could turn' (*Melody Maker*, 12 October 1940: 1). By

41 The 1943 Delegate Conference marked the start of the Union's modern-era gatherings. Hereafter we refer to these as Conference.

the war's end, the growing music profession and Union membership were in a large part down to public sector support and the direct or indirect subsidy of musical labour. As well as work in the BBC and entertaining the forces, both local authorities and the Committee for the Encouragement of Music and the Arts (CEMA)[42] were increasingly involved in the employment of musicians, giving the Union new types of employers to engage with.

Conclusion

In the aftermath of the unemployment caused by the displacement of cinema orchestras, the perilous situation in which the Union found itself was remedied by people and circumstances over which its leadership had little control but that were to combine both fundamentally to change the British music profession and to reinvigorate the Union. A combination of politically driven activism within the Union, and the intervention of both the public sector (via the BBC and the Entertainments National Service Association) and the private sector (via the record companies) brought in new types of employers, employment, and income for musicians over which the Union was able to establish considerable influence. Both the number of working musicians in the UK and the Union's membership increased, and by 1945 the latter had reached 12,415 – its highest level since 1931.

Internally, a relatively small group of predominantly London-based musicians were, via the VOCs, a starting point for a revival in Union membership, causing hundreds of dance musicians to join in the mid-1930s. In doing so, they were responsible for a shift in both the Union's musical emphasis (away from pit musicians to dance musicians) and politics. Under Dambman the Union's leadership remained somewhat removed from the VOC members, many of whom were actively involved with the CPGB. Some of the latter – notably Mitchell, Van Phillips, and Jack Dearlove – became involved in official capacities within the Union where Dambman's lack of attention to internal matters left them a degree of autonomy and influence. This helped the Union in terms of growing its membership, but also created divisions among musicians from different social and musical backgrounds. The well-organised CPGB faction was able to operate successfully within what was a small and, at the time, relatively weak Union.

This was exacerbated by growing inequality across the profession, caused by changing musical tastes and the growth of the broadcasting and recording industries. Initially this inequality was more visible in the popularity of dance

42 The forerunner of the Arts Council, CEMA was set up by Royal Charter in 1940.

music and the higher fees its musicians could attract, but the permanent positions in BBC orchestras for the most talented musicians created more inequality in both job security and income. In addition, the quantity and type of work in London meant a growing divide between the lot of a typical musician in the capital and beyond, while the recording industry re-emerged in the 1930s as a serious threat to the (live) work of some musicians while being a source of wealth for others.

These changes – and the restrictions on foreign musicians that were largely formalised during 1934 and 1935 – were to lay the foundations of the modern British music industries. For the second time, the Union had emerged from a period of war in a more powerful position than it entered it – this time with an array of possibilities opened up by both the public demand for music of all types and the range of new employers and organisations with which to negotiate.

5

Worlds of possibilities: 1946–1955

The ten years following the end of the war were characterised by unprecedented change in both the Union and the industries with which it was negotiating. Fortunately for the Union it was able to do this from a position of some strength. Membership grew rapidly during and after the war and reached its highest level to date in 1948,[1] when Alex Mitchell reported that 'the profession appears reasonably busy' with 'hopeful' prospects (MU, 2/5/3/2).[2] For Mitchell and others in the Union's leadership this was measured largely in terms of employment in the cafés, hotels, theatres, and halls in London at a time when both the recording and broadcasting industries were becoming not only large-scale employers of musicians but also more important in terms of economic value, power, and international influence.

This chapter examines how these changes played out externally and their impact on the Union. Starting with an overview of the state of the music profession in Britain at the end of the war, it then considers the structural and organisational issues facing the Union as it doubled in size over the space of ten years. Internal problems revolved around musical, geographical, and political differences, and we examine each before contemplating the Union's position in the wider music industries. Here we investigate the Union's relations with the recording and broadcasting industries and the overlapping importance of copyright in the wake of technological developments. Our contention is that these negotiations were to shape the British music industries for the next forty years or more.

We end by returning to the continuing problem of foreign musicians and the end of the 1935 restrictions on visiting musicians, which coincides with another point of major industrial, legal, and musical change (see Peterson

[1] This reached 25,600 in 1948 and grew every year until 1954 when it reached 28,960.
[2] A series of regular reports submitted to the EC between 1946 and 1953 gives a fascinating insight into the mechanics of the profession in London during this period.

1990). This time, the growth of the recording industry, greater international trade, pending copyright legislation, and the public demand for new forms of music all combined to present a range of threats and opportunities for the MU that we examine in the remainder of the book.

A survey

A useful starting point for any study of post-war change in the Union can be found in a survey Mitchell conducted for the Union in 1946 to establish where members were working and to measure the density of Union membership in each of the main fields of employment (MU, 2/5/3/2). Although the methodology is unclear and the results not entirely surprising, it is a useful document that highlights the huge shift in British musical employment since the demise of the cinema orchestras and the growth of standing orchestras from the late 1920s.

The headline figures from Mitchell's survey[3] (see Figure 8) showed that just over 2,000 musicians were still working in theatres and music halls, but nearly 3,000 were engaged (full-time) in ballrooms, and the largest segment – 'casual dance musicians' – consisted of over 8,000 workers. Symphony and large orchestras – bolstered by not only the BBC orchestras but also the formation of a permanent orchestra at the Royal Opera House in 1945 and the Royal Philharmonic Orchestra (RPO) the following year – accounted for around 1,600 musicians. Substantial numbers of musicians were working in the somewhat arbitrary groupings of 'touring-stage, BBC and recording' (just under 1,000), and 'hotels, restaurants and cafes' (around 1,200) and miscellaneous[4] (about 500).

While the survey did not account for all working musicians, its groupings are not always helpful, and the boundaries among them are porous, a number of its findings were important. The first was that, across the UK, the range and quality of musical work had improved dramatically in the post-war years. Second, pay and conditions had improved, in at least some quarters. These provided both opportunities and challenges for the Union. The survey showed the strength and weakness of its own organisation: it was well-represented where there were large groups of musicians with relatively secure employment and less well where musicians were working casually, often self-employed, across a number of workplaces.

[3] Dated 1 December 1946.

[4] This listed 'ice rinks, night clubs, etc.' as other places of employment, with holiday camps and shipping companies being the other main employers.

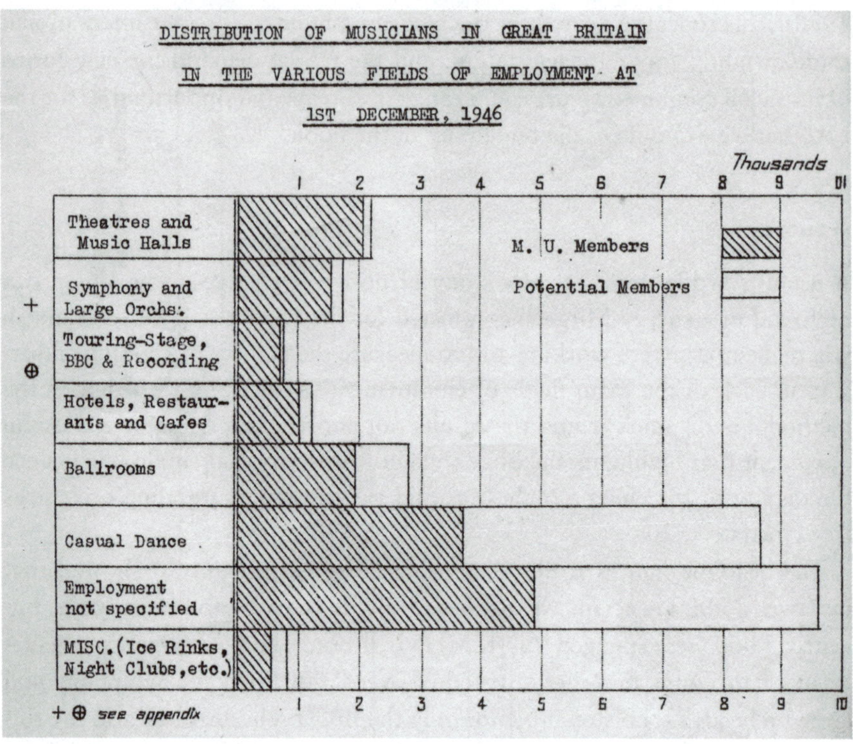

Figure 8 A snapshot of Alex Mitchell's survey of musical employment conducted in 1946.

Mitchell's priority was to recruit among those musicians who worked in ballrooms. In December 1948 he reported a solid density of membership in theatres, music halls, and symphony orchestras but noted that 'considerable concentrated efforts will be required to establish a similar position with Messrs J. Lyons and Co. and with the Mecca Ballroom circuit' (MU, 2/5/3/2).[5] These disparities across the profession meant that those musicians with steady employment had very different views of the Union from those working on a self-employed or freelance basis.

For example, Tschaikov (*2014*) told us that when he joined the RPO, Sir Thomas Beecham was known as 'a good payer. The Union rate was £2 per session for the sub principals and £3 for principals. He paid £4.20 and £5.25.' Moreover, the orchestra was doing 'an enormous amount of recording', and 'in 1947 or '48, I would be earning £45 a week. And that was a lot of money then.'

[5] Lyons and Mecca were the largest employers of musicians, in restaurants and ballrooms respectively.

In short, the Union's negotiations had been fruitful for those musicians with settled places in orchestras. In addition, both the BBC and the newly formed OEA provided an easy and obvious point of contact with which the Union could engage.[6] However, its attempts to achieve '100% organisation' were hindered by musicians in what Francis called 'the sphere of casual employment' (1949: 6). Here, the presence of self-employed and 'double-jobbing' musicians, along with the over-supply of labour and the absence of Union presence in the workplace, meant that organising was highly problematic.

Similarly, new styles of popular music were to present the Union with the challenge of trying to recruit among the plethora of small ensembles that emerged in jazz, skiffle, and rock 'n' roll. Typical of this was the trombone player Chris Barber, who decided to become serious about his musical endeavours and turn professional in 1953. He had been a member of the MU since his amateur band played for the BBC Jazz Club in 1949, but found the unionisation of jazz musicians particularly problematic, arguing that 'it made sense for musicians when, for many years, they were working in ballrooms. Playing certain hours, sometimes being asked to play longer, they were naturally organised and that was absolutely sensible. For us, it didn't make sense. We were creative artists, who made the thing up' (*Barber 2013*).

The Chris Barber Band was also one of the first groups for whom recording was as important as performing live, another problem for a Union organised around live performance.[7] Such was the dominance of the live performer in the Union's worldview its first reference to 'live' music as a distinct entity did not come until 1946 when it was trying to curtail the BBC's use of records (*Melody Maker*, 9 March 1946: 3). Within ten years the size and nature of the British music profession was to be transformed, creating a range of new issues for the Union to deal with.

Consequently, not only did the MU grow in size, but its membership became much less homogeneous. This meant that maintaining a united front was increasingly difficult, and for a period sectional interests fought their own corners. Furthermore, Dambman's retirement in 1948 (and the election of Van Phillips as Chair of the EC in 1949) were to reignite the political tensions of the war years, and it was to the Union's credit that it was able to maintain some degree of coherence when being pulled in different directions by specific interest-groups both inside and out.

[6] Formed in 1947, the OEA's original members comprised the BBC; five permanent orchestras (City of Birmingham, Liverpool Philharmonic, London Philharmonic, Hallé, and Scottish); and the Covent Garden, Sadler's Wells, and New London Orchestras.

[7] The first Chris Barber Band album, *New Orleans Joys*, was recorded and released in 1954.

Bandleaders, composers, and semi-professionals

At grassroots level, the most prominent signs of disunity came internally from bandleaders and composers and externally from semi-professionals. The bandleaders were particularly agitated by what they considered the poor fees paid by the BBC for outside broadcasts, and the Dance Band Directors' Association (DBDA) – which had been largely dormant after an initial burst of activity in 1937 – began to organise again after the war at the instigation of Lou Preager.[8] Attracting the support of many of the best-known bandleaders of the time,[9] it yielded significant power both within the Union and externally, and its reactivation might be seen as a reflection of frustration with the Union's leadership. Dambman reached retirement age in 1945, but was encouraged by the Executive to stay on as GS. However, having joined the Union in 1902, he represented an era that predated the emergence of dance bands and the changes they brought across the profession. For much of the preceding ten years, he had been involved in detailed negotiations with the BBC that brought considerable gains for both staff and casually employed musicians. Conversely, bandleaders, who were increasingly powerful in the wake of the Corporation reorganising its output at the end of the war,[10] were not only dissatisfied but able to wrench negotiating power away from the Union's leadership.

Remarkably, the DBDA were given autonomy to negotiate with the BBC, and it was not long before their demands were trumpeted across the pages of *Melody Maker* (25 January 1947: 1). These were largely economic, but they also sought control over the 'musical interpretations' that their bands performed (rather than ceding this to BBC producers) and made complaints about the BBC's engagement of foreign bandleaders, most notably the imminent visit of Jack Harris.[11] There was some evidence of success as the MU ensured that the Ministry of Labour duly rejected the proposed work permit for Harris (*Melody Maker*, 26 April 1947: 5), and a threatened strike at the BBC by studio dance musicians, due to begin on 1 May 1948, forced a 25 per cent pay increase out of the Corporation (*Melody Maker*, 24 April 1948: 1).

8 Preager was a well-known trumpet player and bandleader, best known for leading the orchestra at the Hammersmith Palais between 1942 and 1960. By the late 1950s he was also a well-known radio broadcaster.

9 Victor Silvester and Billy Cotton were both on the Committee.

10 This saw the introduction of the Light Programme (1945) and the Third Programme (1946), both of which were heavily reliant on live performances, with the former utilising a large number of dance bands.

11 Harris had actually lived and worked in the UK between 1927 and 1940, including a spell (with Ambrose) as owner of Ciro's Club in London. In 1947 the Union's rules were amended so that any 'alien' musician resident in the UK had to be in the country for twelve months before they could apply for membership, which needed EC approval (MRC, MSS 21/1537/MIS/1–19).

Besides the DBDA, the other significant grouping within the Union was the Arrangers, Composers and Copyists' Section, under the leadership of Phil Cardew.[12] This was politically important, as both Cardew and many of its members were also part of a Music Development Committee (MDC) and its successor, the Committee for the Promotion of New Music, which was set up in 1949. Both were set up ostensibly to campaign for the allocation of further funds for musical activity in the wake of the formation of CEMA in 1940 and its successor, the Arts Council of Great Britain (ACGB),[13] but it was something of an outpost for the CPGB faction within the Union.[14]

Semi-professional musicians offered a different type of challenge for the Union's leadership. If those with regular income and professional status tended to organise within the Union, the temptation for semi-pros to organise externally was much greater. Attempts to form a Semi-Pro Association of Great Britain, described by Mitchell in May 1947 as 'merely the latest attempt to get a foothold on the MU's organising territory' (MU, 2/5/3/2), were followed four years later by a group called the Semi Pro Musicians' Fellowship organising in East London but, like its predecessor, it failed to take off.

The immediate impact of the former group was to act as the catalyst for some reorganisation on the part of the Union's London District to recognise the difference between those professionals working in central London and the often semi-professional musical careers of those in its suburbs. This coincided with an application to the EC by a group of ninety part-time musicians, who were in the Union but organised their own social events in South-East London, to open a distinct Branch for the area.[15] By February 1948 this and four other suburban branches had opened,[16] while the former London Branch was rebranded as the Central London Branch.

A leadership election

The organisation among groups with distinct musical or geographic identities was often closely tied to their wider political outlooks, and the longstanding tensions between left and right in the Union came to the fore again in 1948. These focused around two elections: one to replace Dambman, which was

12 A prominent bandleader in the 1930s, Cardew spent his later career primarily as an arranger and agitator.

13 The ACGB was founded in 1946 and initially headed by John Maynard Keynes.

14 Members of the MDC included CPGB members Ben Frankel, Charles Kahn, and Ivor Mairants. The Committee for the Promotion of New Music was more broadly based and its committee included composers Vaughan Williams and Benjamin Britten.

15 For a history of the South-East London Branch by one of its Branch Secretaries, Gary Hyde, see Hyde (2001, 2013).

16 These were in South-East, East, North, South, and West London.

held in September, and another to appoint a Chair of the EC the following February. The GS election was between two candidates – Bertram Newton Brooke and Hardie Ratcliffe – who represented different generations and worldviews within the Union. The former was older, had been active in the Union for considerably longer,[17] and was from the straight and conservative end of the profession, while Ratcliffe was associated with dance musicians, the VOCs of the 1930s, and the DBDA.

Ratcliffe won by 5,561 votes to 3,800, his success as much a result of his high profile within the Union as his politics. Ten years as AGS had earned him a reputation as someone who had 'the ability, initiative and organising flair to carry out his new job worthily and well' (*Melody Maker*, 11 September 1948: 1), but his proximity to the CPGB members in the Union caused concern both externally and internally. According to a Special Branch report of 16 September, he was 'not known to be a member of the Communist Party' but he had 'friends among the Communists', although they also suggested that he was something of a 'mystery man' who was believed by some in the Union to have 'merely used the Communists for his own interests' (TNA, KV3/379).

Inside the Union, Ratcliffe's politics also caused some unease. Election material produced by the London Fellowship of Musicians (LFM) claimed that he represented the CPGB in the campaign, something he explicitly denied (*Melody Maker*, 14 August 1948: 4).[18] Nevertheless, his association with Communists was clear both before and after the election. His nomination forms were signed by Party members Francis and Mitchell. After his election, Ted Anstey[19] was appointed AGS and Francis Assistant Secretary, meaning that the national leadership of the Union was to the left of the EC and the London Branch – both of which were dominated by the more conservative parts of the profession. Somewhat prophetically, the same Special Branch report also predicted that Ratcliffe's reliance on support from the left meant his 'position may prove to be rather unenviable' (TNA, KV3/ 379).

Initial evidence of this came during the first major crisis of his leadership, when the ramifications of the first Executive meeting of 1949 became a major news story. This began with the election of Van Phillips to the post of Chair on 8 February, and was followed by a walk-out of nine of the

17 Newton Brooke had joined in 1909 and was appointed London Organiser in 1920. He was fifty-nine at the time of this election, seventeen years older than Ratcliffe.

18 The LFM was a largely anonymous organisation that campaigned against the Communists in London.

19 Despite being suspected of being a Communist and having an MI5 file, Anstey was at times in conflict with the Party and not a known member.

twenty-three-strong Committee two days later.[20] Phillips was a well-known CPGB member, whose background meant that he was treated with suspicion in both the Union and the Party.[21] Indeed, a Special Branch report in 1944 had claimed that he had 'for some time been suspected of being a police informant by members of both the Musicians' Union and the Communist Party' (TNA, KV 3/377). His election, and its aftermath, prompted considerable press coverage, under headlines such as 'Red coup in music' (*Daily Mail*, 15 February 1949) and 'Communist is now chairman of Musicians' Union Executive' *(Musical Express*, 11 February 1949: 1).

When Phillips defeated Batten, by 12 votes to 10, his opponents complained that as he was not a member of the EC at the time he was ineligible to chair it.[22] Although it was pointed out that this was not against Union precedent or rules,[23] it was used by supporters of the defeated Batten to leak stories to the press, putting both Ratcliffe and Phillips on the defensive. Ratcliffe responded by defending Phillips' record as a former member of the EC and argued in a letter to all Branch Secretaries that 'his election to the executive will make no difference to the union politically. He has no vote, except a casting vote, and he is one of the few Communists on the executive' (TNA, KV/3/380).[24] While this was true (there were only three other known party members on the EC at the time), less plausible was Ratcliffe's claim that he had 'never known Mr Phillips bring politics into union matters' (TNA, KV/3/380). His opponents pointed out numerous instances of this, not least a public meeting he hosted just a few months previously (organised by the Acton Branch of the CPGB), asking 'Can you mix music with your politics?'.

The second controversy at the EC meeting, which resulted in the walk out, was an attempt by the left to counteract the LFM's influence, with several branches and district councils, in the shape of a number of resolutions condemning its lack of transparency. When one of these was brought forward, nine members of the committee walked out at Batten's behest.[25] This brought further negative coverage for the Union in the following day's newspapers, with the *Daily Herald* quoting one of the nine dissenters as saying that 'Communists are in control of our Union and we protest against their

20 At the time the EC met four times a year for four days. This meeting ran between 8 and 11 February 1949. The post of chair was determined annually by a vote at the first meeting of each year.

21 He was a successful American bandleader who had moved to live and work in the UK.

22 He had lost his place in the previous round of EC elections.

23 J. B. Williams had chaired the EC in the 1920s without being an elected member of it.

24 He also mentioned the work Phillips had done as chair of the MDC and founder of the Musicians' Social and Benevolent Council, which had raised over £26,000 for the MU's Benevolent Fund.

25 All the London and East District delegates and some from the North-West joined the walkout.

tactics' (11 February 1949). This forced Ratcliffe to respond again, telling Branch Secretaries in a letter that Batten *et al.*'s protest was that of 'a disgruntled minority led by the defeated candidate for the chairmanship' (TNA, KV 3/379).

The matter did not end here and there were at least three further attempts to undermine or remove both Ratcliffe and Phillips from office. Just days later, the Sheffield Branch Secretary, G. Hallam, denounced Ratcliffe's circular as 'highly improper, being unauthorised by the EC and a very biased personal statement' (TNA, KV 3/379), and sought support for a motion of no confidence in the General Secretary and Chairman of the EC that called on them to resign immediately.

Vic Sullivan and London Branch Committee member Bill Richardson wrote on 28 February stating their opposition to Van Phillips as 'he represents Communism ... an ideology that is alien to the British way of living' (TNA, KV 3/379). They challenged Ratcliffe, imploring that 'if he is a Communist, or has Communist sympathies, let him have the courage to openly say so!', while accusing the MU delegates – with the exception of Sullivan – of following the CPGB line at the previous year's TUC conference. They also viewed the appointment of Harry Francis as Assistant Secretary as 'further infiltration [by the CPGB] into high office in the Union'. Finally, the remaining Communists were voted off the LDC at the end of 1948,[26] and a number of resolutions for the 1949 Conference tried to remove Phillips from office, notably a motion that precluded any non-naturalised British subject holding office in the Union.

Despite all this Phillips and Ratcliffe survived, and there were signs of some reconciliation in a statement issued after the next EC meeting in May. This downplayed the events of February and claimed that 'the occurrences referred to were exceptional, did not have the importance or significance attributed to them, and ... did not impede the Committee's work'. It also regretted that the events gave the impression that 'political issues and differences interfere with our discharging our duties' and claimed that 'there have been very few occasions ... when subjects of primarily political interest have been discussed' (*MU Report*, June 1949: 1).

This and the Conference of the same year marked some form of truce. Little more was heard from the LFM, and the CPGB's decline during the 1950s – especially following the Soviet invasion of Hungary in 1956[27] – meant that it no longer had the same degree of influence either in the MU or beyond. Nonetheless it is important to note that, despite the various divides within the

[26] Phillips, Frankel, and Kahn all lost their places on the Committee for 1949.

[27] Almost 7,000 members of the CPGB left (Beckett 1995: 138).

Union, it remained remarkably effective in industrial relations and at regulating the domestic labour market when faced with the perceived threat from foreign musicians. We now turn to such matters.

PPL, the BBC, and the post-war recording industry

In the immediate post-war period the most convincing evidence of the Union's external negotiating power came in the form of an agreement reached with PPL in 1946. This was to influence the way the Union operated for over forty years and had an equally large impact on the recording industry and broadcasting in the UK. It created a complex, but mutually dependent, relationship between the Union, the record companies (represented by PPL) and the BBC. This meant that the Union played an integral and undervalued role in shaping the UK's modern music and broadcasting industries. To unpack this, we begin by detailing the post-war position of the British record companies and the attitude of both the MU and the BBC towards them, before considering the immediate aftermath of the 1946 agreement for the interested parties.

To understand the strength of the Union's position in its post-war negotiations with the recording industry, it is important to note the relative weakness of the industry's position. Unlike the American record industry, where sales had more than doubled in value during the war,[28] 'the European record industry was in a depressed state' (Gronow and Saunio 1998: 95). This was accentuated in the post-war period when the American companies were quicker to adopt new formats (LPs and 45s) than their European counterparts.

One bright spot for the major British companies had been the modest success of PPL in generating some much-needed additional revenue. Since its formation in 1934, it had become a small but effective collective agency, drawing income from a range of music users and redistributing it among its members and performers. There are two things to note about the early years of PPL. The first is that the legal basis for its claim (the Carwardine ruling) was still disputed in some quarters and a cause of concern to its directors until the implementation of the 1956 Copyright Act. The second is that, as the biggest individual user of recorded music, the BBC did most to swell the coffers of PPL, paying £20,000 a year from 1935, an amount that had doubled when a third needletime agreement was reached in 1941.

With the recording industry still recovering from the war, the MU came to the table at the end of the war in a much stronger position than when PPL was formed, seeking to control the public use of recorded music, in order to

28 From $44 million to $109 million (Barfe 2004: 138).

protect members' jobs. Not only was its membership growing rapidly, but the Union had, for the first time, clarity of vision on matters relating to the use of recorded music. This was almost certainly inspired by the AFM's experience, but still allowed it to take full advantage of a situation where PPL needed the MU's co-operation in order to develop the nascent British recording industry along American lines.

Such clarity on the MU's part was evident in the formation of a Special Recording Committee to examine the threat to live music from the use of records and, in 1945, a Conference motion set out the Union's policy on records. This set out the its priority as being to control and limit the use of records, rather than seeking any type of outright ban. Its three aims were to limit 'the extent to which gramophone records may be used for public entertainment ... to obtain payments to the Union from the users of any records reproduced publicly either directly or by radio broadcasting ... [and to] acquire some control over the issuing of licences, and the conditions upon which such licences are issued, by PPL, for the use of records for public entertainment' (MU, 1/7/1945).

Though this seemed ambitious, by the time of the Union's next conference two years later, it had achieved all of these aims. This achievement resulted from a complicated set of negotiations involving the three interested parties – the MU, PPL, and the BBC. The journey involved two sets of negotiations – those between the Union and PPL and the subsequent ones between PPL and the BBC with the Union as a clearly interested party.

Following the 1945 Conference, the Union instigated discussions with PPL seeking to limit the use of records on radio and television and in public places, while simultaneously seeking to monetise what uses were permitted. From the Union's perspective this was a relatively straightforward negotiation and agreement was reached within a year. There were three reasons why the Union was able to get what it wanted from PPL. First, from its inception PPL had accepted the right of performers to compensation from the public use of recorded music. It was also concerned that failure to reach an agreement would mean that the MU would embark on the type of industrial action taken by the AFM, with potentially disastrous consequences for the British recording industry. Finally, PPL was fearful of performers legally disputing its claim on the monies it was extracting from music users. To prevent the latter, it was willing to offer a share of its returns to performers, and the easiest way of doing this was to broker a deal with the body representing the largest number of British musicians – the MU. Thus, PPL was willing to negotiate with the MU as the representative of *all* musicians and not just those members involved in recording.

The 1946 agreement

Regardless of the obvious advantages to both sides, the deal struck between the MU and PPL – which became operational on 20 May 1946 – was still remarkable. It focused on three main areas – record broadcasting by the BBC, payments to the Union, and licences for public performance. We return to the last of these later in the chapter and concentrate here on the first two parts of the agreement. The first stipulated that, under the terms of its next agreement with the BBC,[29] PPL would impose a number of restrictions on the BBC's use of recorded music, limiting the Corporation's use of records on its three radio networks to twenty-eight hours a week.[30] More remarkably, the allocation of needletime would reduce over the course of the three years, with twenty-six hours a week in the second year of its operation and twenty-two by its third. The Union would receive 10 per cent of PPL's net distributable income for the first two years of the agreement[31] and 12.5 per cent thereafter.

If this seemed like a great deal for the MU, there was one major problem when it came to its implementation: the BBC. Given the proposed restrictions imposed on its output by the MU–PPL arrangement, it was perhaps surprising that it had played no part in the agreement. Indeed, PPL had been somewhat disingenuous when it came to informing the BBC of the nature of its discussions with the MU. While the BBC was negotiating with PPL an extension to their 1941 agreement in good faith,[32] PPL was prioritising its deal with the MU. When pursued by the Corporation, PPL attributed the delay to 'the parallel negotiations ... our industry is conducting with the Musicians' Union' (WAC, R8/88/2), but gave no detail of their nature. Only on conclusion of its deal with the MU did PPL return to negotiations with the BBC.

Acting in his capacity as copyright manager for EMI (rather than specifically for PPL), Brian Bramall ominously wrote to the BBC's Legal Adviser, E. C. Robbins, on 16 May 1946 to inform him that 'the position is changed somewhat as a result of the agreement which has recently – with some difficulty – been reached with the Musicians' Union and changed circumstances require a meeting rather than correspondence' (WAC, R8/88/2). When meetings eventually took place, the BBC was understandably disgruntled, but found itself to be relatively powerless. It needed PPL's permission to use

29 This was being negotiated simultaneously.

30 When originally drafted in 1946 this was for twenty-eight hours a week, shared between the Light Programme and the Home Service, with an extra two hours to be added for the Third Programme when it launched in September 1946.

31 Meaning from 1946 to 1948, though it was also agreed that it would be paid 10 per cent of such revenues backdated to 1 June 1945.

32 This allowed the BBC twenty-one hours of needletime per aerial, and was extended by agreement in 1943 until six months after the end of hostilities.

records, and PPL could now no longer grant this without regard to its own arrangement with the MU.

This did not prevent the BBC from at least trying to undermine and delay the implementation of the proposed new restrictions. It had already begun this by challenging the monopolistic nature of the record companies and would later argue that it was wrong for two third parties (the MU and PPL) to collude in frustrating the operations of another. To these ends, the Corporation had written to the Board of Trade raising concerns over the monopoly Decca and EMI enjoyed within the recording industry, only to be told that the BBC should itself attempt to break the monopoly (letter of T. Flett to Sir William Haley, 21 March 1946 (WAC, R8/88/1).[33] The Board noted that Herbert Morrison, the Lord President of the Council, was 'interested in the possibility of breaking the monopoly which EMI and Decca at present hold over the industry', and suggested that 'consideration ought to be given to the idea of empowering the BBC to produce and sell gramophone records, either of their own programmes or of performances by their orchestras etc., without their being broadcast' (Flett to Haley, 21 March 1946).

Although not an immediate aspiration of the BBC, this was of little help in dealing with its more practical concerns about the PPL–MU agreement. These were articulated by its Deputy Director General, Sir Noel Ashbridge, who questioned 'the propriety of two bodies making an agreement which so largely concerned the functioning of a third body working under Royal Charter' (WAC, R8/88/2). Dambman countered that the BBC had no right to intervene in the agreement made between it and PPL, and that it was 'irregular that the BBC should question any of the terms of the agreement made between the MU and Phonographic Performance Ltd' (WAC, R8/88/2). Such entrenched positions made significant progress unlikely, but it was now clear that the BBC saw the MU as the force behind the agreement – rather than PPL, with whom they were ostensibly negotiating. A further meeting of the Union's executive in December resulted in Dambman's writing to PPL intimating that the MU would make no concession on the terms of the agreement, and when the MU again refused to meet directly with the BBC in early 1947, the Corporation had little option but to agree the terms as they stood.[34]

The agreement was officially announced in a press release issued by PPL on 21 May, but had been operational since 1 May. It was pre-empted by a report

33 Flett was Secretary to the Lord President of the Council and Haley was Director-General of the BBC. In fact the BBC had agreed with the MU that it would only record its orchestras for broadcast and not for records for sale to the public (WAC, R8/88/2).

34 Otherwise its existing agreement would have expired, allowing it no right to play recorded music.

in *Variety* a month earlier, which had hailed the Union's 'victory against disk manufacturers' (16 April 1947: 37) and a *Melody Maker* story that described it as 'one of the Union's most sensational victories in its fifty years' history' (17 May 1947:1). The full implementation of the agreement between PPL and the MU – with the BBC's consent – was not only a measure of the Union's power over the other two parties but would also provide it with a new source of income, though it was keen to stress that control was more important than money. In 1953, Ratcliffe reflected on the deal as 'without doubt one of the most valuable ever made by the Union' but claimed that the financial rewards were 'looked upon as of minor importance' (MU, 4/3/1/2/5).

It also set the tone for future negotiations between the parties, and here the language used by PPL in its discussions with the BBC is highly revealing. For example, in October 1946 Bramall reported that needletime was 'one of the essential terms on which the MU was *prepared to allow* the Gramophone Companies to make records' (WAC, R8/88/2, emphasis ours), and in July 1948 he wrote to the BBC that its relations with the Union governed 'the *possibility* of future recording' (WAC, R8/88/3, emphasis ours). Such language is typical and gives the impression that recordings were only possible thanks to MU consent. Though in subsequent years the BBC, independent broadcasters, and politicians challenged this view, it was to provide the framework for broadcasting of recorded music and the base of the MU's power in the music industries until 1989.

Broadcasting after 1947

Notwithstanding the importance of the agreement reached in 1947 for all parties, the relationship between the BBC and the MU was still defined more by live music than it was by recordings. There remained a vast array of other agreements between the two parties relating to the employment and use of both the staff orchestras and casual musicians. These included a recording agreement[35] as well as a range of restrictions on relays and outside broadcasts, and the fees for casual studio broadcasts and performances on television.

These were to result in various disputes – and even withdrawals of labour[36] – by MU members working for the BBC, and in 1948, the Corporation made a robust defence of its dealings with the Union in a statement in the *Radio*

35 This limited the number and use of orchestral recordings. Details can be found in WAC, R8/123/1–9, while WAC, BM61/54–85/54 contains a note from the Head of Programme Contracts of 5 April 1954 that outlines the history of the recording agreements.

36 A ban on relayed performances by members was imposed at the end of April and on television performances from the end of May.

Times. In doing so it emphasised the relatively good working conditions in BBC orchestras and noted that it had, 'since 1939, doubled its employment of outside musicians' and was 'at present paying to members of the Musicians' Union a total of approximately one million pounds a year' (cited in *MU Report*, July–August 1948: 1). However, the Union was quick to point out the recent doubling of the licence fee and its determination to ensure a share of this for its members.

The fractious nature of post-war industrial relations between the Union and the BBC was to have another outcome – Government intervention. With so many points of dispute between the two, in July 1948 the Ministry of Labour set up a committee of inquiry into relations between them. This had a remit to 'make an award on the question of minimum fees for casual studio broadcasts and to examine and make recommendations on other questions which the BBC desired to be included in a comprehensive settlement' (WAC, R8/88/3). While the committee's establishment ended the immediate dispute over casual studio broadcasts, its report was not published until the following year and it was unable to change the MU's stance on needletime. In their evidence to the committee, PPL had shown a willingness to increase the amount of needletime given to the BBC,[37] but such flexibility was met with a hardening of attitudes on the Union's part and it threatened to oppose all needletime when the agreement with PPL came up for renegotiation in 1950.

The BBC's evidence showed that it accepted the principle of needletime – if not its extent. However, when the inquiry supported PPL's view that between twenty-eight and thirty-five hours might be permitted 'without undue prejudice to the Union' (WAC, R8/88/1) the Union refused to change its position. Dambman had claimed in his evidence that restricting the use of records would benefit musicians, while also arguing that it was opposed to the BBC using records at all (Forster 1948). When the 1947 needletime agreement eventually expired in 1950, it was allowed to continue until being finally renewed for another three years – on essentially the same terms[38] – in 1952, following further painstaking negotiations. There is insufficient space here to detail these, but it is worth noting that the MU's tactics in dealing with the BBC and PPL generally consisted of a combination of delays,[39] obfuscation, and the cross-collateralisation of issues.

[37] It was willing to increase it to thirty-five hours a week; the BBC sought fifty-two hours a week. The Committee's recommendation of thirty-five was later blocked by the MU.

[38] The twenty-two hours of needletime for the three radio networks remained; some concessions were made for overseas, regional, and local broadcasting and the fee payable by the BBC increased from £65,000 a year to £70,000.

[39] BBC files show a number of letters from PPL to the BBC expressing concern at how long the MU took to respond (WAC, R8/88/4).

A final outcome of the inquiry was the establishment of a joint consultative committee (JCC) between the BBC and the MU in an attempt to help soothe industrial relations,[40] though this met infrequently before falling into abeyance and did not prevent the BBC having to go to the Industrial Court arbitration service in 1953 in order to resolve a long-running dispute with the MU over staff pay.[41]

Given that the Union's power over broadcasting was achieved as a consequence of the BBC and PPL's respective monopolies, the prospect of any weakening of such monopolies greatly concerned the Union.[42] When the Conservative Government elected in 1951 decided to override the opposition of the Beveridge Report to commercial broadcasting and introduce an element of competition into the television (though not radio) market, the BBC's broadcasting monopoly was under threat, with important implications for the Union.[43]

When the Television Act (1954) paved the way for commercial television to launch in 1955, the Union was torn between viewing this as a threat or an opportunity. However, after being approached by one of the independent contractors (Associated-Rediffusion), the Union reached agreement on fees for live performances, delayed and repeated transmissions, and overseas broadcasts just days before Independent Television (ITV) launched, ensuring that musicians involved were handsomely rewarded.[44]

Public performance

While the MU's terms surrounding broadcasting were the most headline-worthy and economically significant part of the 1946 agreement, the cultural and industrial impact of the restrictions placed on the use of records in public places was equally important. The reach of these was vast and – at least notionally – covered *all* public spaces. Of most concern for the MU were

40 Details can be found in WAC, R8/111/1 and 2.

41 The ruling, made in February 1953, increased pay and cut standard working hours, but also established the BBC's right to use musicians in both television and radio, thus denying the Union the separation it sought (WAC, R8/111/1). The Union was also involved in Industrial Court cases with the OEA in 1952 (OEA minutes, 17 November 1952) and a long-running dispute with the SWETM was settled with help from the Ministry of Labour in 1955 (SWETM minutes, 1 December 1955).

42 From 1950, the MU instructed its members not to record for non-PPL companies and printed a blacklist of non-PPL record companies in the *Musician*.

43 The Broadcasting Commission under Lord Beveridge was set up by the Attlee Government to examine broadcasting in the UK in 1949. In its evidence to the Commission the MU argued for 'the continued state ownership and management of broadcasting' (cited in Briggs 1979: 347).

44 ITV launched in September 1955. The basic fee agreed was £6 for each appearance of less than four hours, with repeat fees and additional fees for overseas broadcasts.

those places of entertainment where musicians were employed and that used recorded music as either a whole or a partial replacement for live musicians.

At the MU's prompting, the licences issued by PPL, which allowed the playing of records in return for a fee, were further limited. No records were permitted to be 'played, used or performed or permitted to be played at any theatres, music hall, dance hall or other place of entertainment' where one of four conditions applied: if the venue was subject to 'a trade dispute directly affecting the rights or interests of musicians', if records were played 'in complete or partial substitution for musicians employed', if musicians would have been employed 'but for the exigencies of war or national emergency', and if 'musicians could, having regard to the size and nature of theatre, music hall, dance hall or other place of entertainment be employed' (MU, 1/7/1949). If the first three were relatively straightforward and finite, the final provision could effectively be used as a blanket to cover almost any public use of records.

Two major issues emerged that hindered the operation of the agreement. First, creating a situation where PPL could refuse licences could be seen as engaging in the type of restrictive practices that would attract the attention of legislators. By way of contrast, provided the appropriate fees were paid, PRS – which collected royalties for public performances on the part of the music publishers and songwriters – never refused to grant a licence for public performance. The issue became prominent in the deliberations leading up to the publication of the report of the 1952 Copyright Committee, which was established with a view to reforming copyright legislation. Both PPL and the Union saw the Committee's recommendations and pending legislation as a potentially serious threat to their agreement. Ratcliffe described the potential dissolution as 'a most disastrous occurrence' (MU, 2/1/14). Both parties submitted extensive written and oral evidence, but faced considerable opposition from an assortment of recorded music users. In addition, the Labour peer, Lord Burden, used examples of PPL licences for old-time dancing clubs as the basis for calling the MU–PPL agreement a 'travesty of trade unionism'[45] and a 'legalised racket' that 'denies opportunities for innocent recreational or cultural activities, except on terms prescribed by the Musicians' Union' (cited in McFarlane 1980: 115).

Second came practical aspects. These were raised both at the Union's 1947 Conference and at EC meetings around the same period. At this point PPL was still a small, London-based operation that was trying to manage and

[45] See http://hansard.millbanksystems.com/lords/1953/jan/21/copyright-and-television#S5LV0179P0_19530121_HOL_4 for the full transcript.

monetise the use of gramophone records in thousands of locations across the whole country. Its inability to do so was unsurprising. Consequently, the Union's head office received a barrage of complaints from local branches about PPL's failure adequately to police the agreement. Furthermore, the imprecise nature of its wording meant that inconsistencies were easily found in how PPL applied the rules and how ballroom owners interpreted their licences. An EC meeting in June 1948 saw many members expressing 'grave concern about the increased use of gramophone records and the failure of PPL to restrain its licensees from using records in substitution for bands and orchestras' (MU, 2/1/10). A series of meetings between the Union and PPL followed seeking to clarify what the 1946 agreement meant and how it could be better policed.

Compromise followed on both sides. The MU recognised that PPL could not stop all uses of records, while PPL assured the Union that it would 'do everything possible to ensure records will not be used in substitution for a band or orchestra' (MU, 2/1/1949). The terms of the agreement were changed to replace the 'with regard to the size and nature of the theatre' clause to a guiding principle that 'records should not be licensed by the Company [PPL] for use in substitution for the employment of musicians'. However, implementation of the agreement remained a problem, and the Union was still receiving complaints about PPL's failure to act in instances where records were seen as having replaced live musicians well into the 1970s.

Here it is important to consider what may appear parochial and regressive views held by parts of the Union's membership in a wider context. By the late 1940s and early 1950s, it was already apparent to at least some in the Union's leadership that the stance of its Broadcasting and Recording Sub-Committee, which 'remained opposed in principle to the (secondary) use of records for public entertainment' (MU, 2/1/1949), was no longer sustainable and that a more international outlook on matters related to copyright might be the best route to achieving some form of legal recognition of performers' rights in UK law.

Internationalism

The post-war period saw the Union becoming more engaged with and aware of the work of other musicians' unions, in both the USA and Europe. The success of the AFM's 1942–44 strike and the payments it won from the record companies in respect of individual recording musicians to a fund for unemployed musicians clearly influenced the MU's thinking when it came to its own negotiations with the record companies in 1946. This alarmed some within the BBC. According to an internal memo, written by Programme Contracts Director Bill Streeton, the MU and AFM had been in frequent contact since the advent of the talkies, while during the war, Dambman and Petrillo 'maintained a regular correspondence in which they discuss [*sic*] professional, economic and political developments likely to affect the interests of either body'. Streeton pointed out that the MU was unlikely to adopt the militant tactics employed by the AFM, but that 'they are on the alert for every development that might be applied to conditions in this country' (WAC, R8/123/8).

Relations with European unions also grew closer, along with an acceptance that – while the MU was the largest musicians' union in Europe[46] – it could still learn from other unions. The 1947 Conference was visited by Sven Wassmouth from the Swedish Musicians' Union, and the promptings of the Swiss Union were to be of even greater significance as the catalyst for the formation of the Fédération Internationale des Musicians (FIM). This was constituted following a meeting of various musicians' unions in Zürich in August 1948. A draft constitution was agreed that included the provision that the British Union would nominate a President, a post that was held by Bill Batten until the first FIM congress the following year. Although the largest musicians' union (the AFM) did not join, FIM was to play an important part in future negotiations surrounding the performers' right, with the MU maintaining its place at the head of the organisation.

Challenging licensing

The biggest threat to the 1946 agreement and its provisions for the use of recordings in public came from some of the largest employers in the ballroom dancing industry. In 1948, following a meeting of the Mecca-dominated Association of Ballrooms, it was decided to set up a record label that would circumnavigate the restrictions incorporated within the MU–PPL agreement.

Danceland Recordings, which was set up by Danceland Publications,[47] wrote to the MU intimating that it would 'produce records which will require no licence from any dictatorial or monopolistic body' and that could 'be played in public, as desired, without the need of making any returns' (MU, 2/1/10). They then proceeded to produce hundreds of 'ballroom numbers in standard arrangements' (Thornton 1995: 39) by generically named acts like the Danceland Old Time Orchestra, the Danceland Samba Orchestra, and the

[46] This was partly due to the number of musicians working in Britain, but also a consequence of the restricted membership of the French and German unions, which consisted almost entirely of musicians playing classical music in permanent orchestras.

[47] A publisher that produced magazines and sheet music for ballroom dancing enthusiasts.

Danceland Salon Orchestra. Their records were recorded surreptitiously in Mecca-owned premises in London and sold to businesses such as 'broadcasting companies, theatres, ballrooms, hotels and others in the fields of entertainment where live musicians are normally employed' (*Musician*, October 1951: 8).

The MU's response mostly focused on threatening members who took part in the sessions with expulsion.[48] An article entitled 'They're after your jobs' described how participating musicians who were working for 'less than £20' were involved in making 'scab' records that 'would be used over and over again to keep Union members out of work'. For the Union, this was seen as 'a far more serious offence than having acted as a blackleg in an individual dispute' (*Musician*, October 1951: 8). The Union also published a monthly list in the *Musician* of PPL member companies for whom it was permitted to record, and expelled three members for having participated in Danceland sessions.

Although the sessions continued and Danceland Records appeared for a few more years, the Union and PPL managed to curb their effectiveness, something assisted by the generally poor quality of the recordings. Nevertheless, this brief disruption to the MU–PPL 1946 agreement was the first serious instance of commercial operators attempting to override an agreement that had its roots in notions of what was for the good of the music profession. While the BBC's commitment to the music profession made it susceptible to pressure from the MU and PPL, the private sector had little cause to worry about the wellbeing of musicians who were in plentiful supply. Danceland's intervention served further to align the interests of the record companies and the Union: with shared financial stakes and common opponents in the broadcasters,[49] they were frequently found lobbying together on matters concerning copyright.

This closeness was further solidified when the Union received its first payment from PPL in 1951.[50] Initially uncertain what to do with the money, it continued to negotiate with PPL over the conditions attached to what became known as the 'phonographic funds'. Negotiations finally reached a conclusion in 1955 when it was determined that the bulk of the money should go to a Special Account, with 5 per cent allocated to the Union's General Purposes account and a further 5 per cent to pay the MU's affiliation fees to FIM. It

48 In 1950 the MU barred members from recording for non-PPL labels (*Melody Maker*, 4 November 1950: 1–3) and in 1952 it fined five members who had made non-PPL records for the Oriole and Vogue labels (*Melody Maker*, 26 July 1952: 1 and 8).

49 PPL still considered an abundance of recorded music on the radio as detrimental to the sales of their records, though this belief gradually waned.

50 Initially the payments were extremely irregular (and poorly documented). By January 1958 over £100,000 had been paid to the Union covering the period from 1945 to 1956.

was agreed that PPL would be consulted and that 'no part of the funds in the Special Account shall be used for the purposes of furthering any trade dispute or for any purpose which may be contrary to or adversely affect the interests of PPL or its member companies' (MU, 1/7/1957).

While the exact use of the funds was to be determined at subsequent conferences, by this juncture it was taken as read that they would be used collectively and for the benefit of *all* musicians, rather than being redistributed to those who had played on the records that generated the income. This understanding was in line with the MU's view that its represented all musicians, but it was to have considerable ramifications in subsequent years.

Pending copyright reform accelerated the co-operation between the Union and the record companies. In the run-up to the 1956 Copyright Act, the Union's executive noted that PPL had shown 'a marked reluctance to take action, except on a few occasions, either to withhold or withdraw licences'. However, it was keen to stress to members that the agreements with PPL were 'still of enormous value' and that 'records controlled by PPL are still withheld from most theatres' (MU, 1/7/1955).

In fact, in the years since the end of the war the Union had considerably broadened its outlook when it came to the secondary use of recordings. Faced with the growth of both the recording and broadcasting industries, it decided that control of the broadcasters could only be achieved with the co-operation of the record companies and worked with them both to generate income and to protect the employment of live musicians, who remained the Union's primary focus.

Aliens, orchestras, and jazz

If the expanding market for recordings was a relatively new threat to such employment, the issue of the presence of foreign musicians in the UK remained prominent. Indeed, as the recording industry grew in the 1950s, the Union was faced with an ever-greater demand among both its members and the general public to hear foreign musicians, forcing it into more nuanced and progressive policies than had previously been in operation. These were evident in two main areas – visits by (mostly European) orchestras and (mostly American) jazz musicians.

The Union's position had long appeared to be an intransigent one of opposition to the visit of *all* foreign orchestras despite the normally specific nature of their visits. While the MU argued that such musicians were displacing their British counterparts, in many instances it could not be reasonably argued that the visiting orchestras were putting British ones out of work. However, this merely resulted in variations in the Union's rationale for opposing their visits. For example, the visit of the Vienna Philharmonic to Covent Garden in 1947 was met with an MU protest (see Figure 9), described by Mitchell as 'undoubtedly the greatest MU demonstration ever' involving 'between three and five hundred members' (MU, 2/5/3/2). In this case, the Union's complaint was that the Ministry of Labour had issued work permits for the orchestra

BRITISH MUSICIANS PROTEST

First-class British Symphony Musicians are ignored while the Vienna Philharmonic Orchestra plays in the Orchestral Pit at the Royal Opera House, Covent Garden

The Facts :—

The Vienna Philharmonic Orchestra obtained visas and permits to perform in this country without the Ministry of Labour having any consultation with the British Musicians' Union. Next, the Musicians' Union learned that the Covent Garden Opera Trust had engaged the Vienna Philharmonic Orchestra to appear in the orchestral pit at Covent Garden for a season.

On August 25, the Musicians' Union protested, only to be informed that the Ministry of Labour had granted the requisite permits for the engagement.

The London Trades Council, representing 650,000 Trade Unionists, has passed this resolution :—

"That this London Trades Council views with alarm the decisions of the Ministry of Labour in issuing labour permits and the Home Office in issuing visas to members of the Vienna Philharmonic Orchestra to perform as an accompanying medium at the Covent Garden Opera House without prior consultation with the Union concerned.

"We, therefore, demand that the Ministry of Labour and the Home Office cancel immediately, the permits and visas issued for this specific purpose; and that in future no foreign workers be given permits to work in this country without prior consultation with the Trade Unions concerned."

The Trades Union Congress backs the Musicians' Union and has made representations to the Ministry of Labour

WE DEMAND THE MINISTRY OF LABOUR UPHOLDS THE RIGHTS OF BRITISH MUSICIANS

London Caledonian Press Ltd. (T.U. all depts.), 74 Swinton St., London, W.C.1—W27911

Figure 9 Handbill for the MU's protest against the visit of the Vienna Philharmonic in 1947 (MU, 1/9).

without consulting them. A year later, it opposed the appearance of the Berlin Philharmonic at Earls Court as part of a number of reconciliation events following the war because of the minimal payments involved. Ratcliffe told the *Manchester Guardian* that 'they have come here to play only for pocket money. If the musicians are good enough to come here, they should be paid, not encouraged to scab' (3 November 1948: 5).

Such matters became somewhat easier to manage after the formation of the OEA in 1947 at the instigation of the Arts Council. Although constituted as a 'consultative and advisory body' to be used as a sounding board by the ACGB, its priorities were rapidly established, with the 'conditions of engagement of foreign orchestral players' at the top of its list (ACGB minutes, 12 March 1948). The OEA became both an ally and an opponent for the Union. By supporting restrictions on foreign orchestras it added weight to the Union's protestations to the Government, but it also became a powerful opponent when it came to negotiating pay for orchestral musicians and attempts to impose closed shops.

Minutes of the BBC, OEA, and the Socity of West End Theatre Managers (SWETM) are full of references to MU attempts to institute closed shops. For example, a memo from the Head of Programme Contracts of 7 October 1954 commented that he couldn't see why the MU was pushing on this as 'there are very few quarters outside which a MU "shop" does not exist in practice' (WAC, R8/111/2). In the early 1950s the Union also sought to impose minimum sizes for orchestras, which were generally resisted by employers. For example, in 1949 it refused to allow BBC broadcasts from music halls with orchestras of fewer than twelve members (WAC, R8/111/1) and the BBC was unable to produce such shows. Meanwhile SWETM Executive minutes from March 1953 reveal disputes about minimum orchestras at a production of *The Redheaded Blonde* at the Vaudeville Theatre following a similar dispute at the Croydon Empire during the 1952/53 pantomime season.

With the financial positions of most orchestras insecure, and dependent on subsidy of some form, disputes soon emerged as to whether they could afford the types of pay rises routinely pursued by the Union.[51] This resulted in the MU trying to break ranks by attempting to negotiate separately with the management of individual orchestras, something the OEA 'deplored' (OEA minutes, 23 November 1952), while it sought reassurances from its members that they wanted it to conduct negotiations on their behalf.

51 An example of the Union's effectiveness in negotiating pay rises came in 1950 when a six-week strike by members employed by the Bournemouth Corporation forced it to increase fees for the Bournemouth Military Band, who were being paid less than Union rates. Initially the Corporation refused to recognise the Union, but faced with major disruption to entertainment in the town during the summer season was forced to negotiate.

Nevertheless, the Union and the OEA shared similar views about visiting orchestras. Both made representations to the Ministry of Labour over orchestras visiting for the Festival of Britain in 1951, and OEA minutes of the period indicate common purpose with the Union over the question of visits by foreign orchestras. The OEA's position was that it was not against foreign visits per se but that any such orchestras should be 'of international standard' (OEA minutes, 2 April 1952). In essence, like the Union, they believed that such visits should be tightly controlled.

In an attempt to address this question, in 1952 the Ministry of Labour set up a consultative body, the Visiting Orchestras Consultative Association (VOCA). This was established after solicitations from the Union and the OEA, who both argued for involvement in decisions regarding visits by foreign orchestras. As well as the Union and the OEA, it included agents and representatives of the British Council, the ACGB, and local authorities. Ratcliffe recognised that VOCA meant that 'information about plans to present foreign orchestras in Britain is now available much further ahead than formerly' (MU, 1/7/1955).

The Union's records suggest that its stance did not change and that it continued to oppose most visits, including those of the Danish State Radio Orchestra in 1953 and a Yugoslav orchestra the following year. But Ratcliffe still complained about the Union's lack of power over such visits, writing to VOCA in 1954 suggesting, somewhat disingenuously, that 'the Union's attitude had been very liberal towards the appearance of foreign orchestras in Britain, since ... every such appearance was economically of disadvantage to the Union' (MU, 2/1/13). Frustrated by its limited influence, at the end of 1955 the Union's General Purposes Committee voted on a motion suggesting that the Union withdraw from VOCA.[52]

It was not only in the classical world that the Union's embedded attitudes to visits by non-British musicians were being challenged, and it soon began to appear anachronistic and difficult to maintain. A key factor here was the growing number of Union members who dissented from the view that *all* foreign musicians should be excluded from the UK. In particular jazz musicians were frustrated that they were denied the chance to see era-defining American musicians whose appearances in Paris and Dublin were being enthusiastically reported on in the press. Some deep-rooted, anti-American feeling among some of its leadership further influenced the

[52] This was defeated and the MU remained a member of VOCA until it dissolved in 1992. Meanwhile VOCA introduced a quota system that operated for a number of years until it came under increasing scrutiny from the Government for being anti-competitive and against audiences' interests.

Union's thinking. Nevertheless, its position gradually shifted to one that at least allowed the possibility of more foreign musicians performing in Britain. Its concern was now what *type* of foreign musicians were allowed and on *what terms*.

In 1947 it was reported that 'the "closed shop" in reciprocal agreements between English and continental dance orchestras is about to be opened' (*Melody Maker*, 29 March 1947: 1) with a proposal that the bands of Harry Gold and Bernard Hilda play in Paris and London respectively. Hilda's financial demands, which he blamed on high UK taxes, ensured that this did not happen immediately. However, two years later he appeared with his band at Ciro's Club in London, with Nat Allen and His Orchestra playing the Club des Champs-Elysées in exchange. *Melody Maker* described this as 'a very historic occasion' (8 January 1949: 1), as Hilda's was the first foreign dance band to hold a London residency since 1935.

The MU used this as a template for future arrangements. Importantly, Hilda had visited the MU and addressed its EC in 1948, highlighting the need for international unity among musicians. Ratcliffe told *Melody Maker* that 'it was possible to relax the normal opposition to the entry into Britain of a foreign band because I was consulted at a very early stage'. He also announced what amounted to a substantial change in the Union's policy, writing that 'we have been trying to make arrangements with the unions of musicians involved, under which there could be properly controlled exchanges of bands' (*Melody Maker*, 8 January 1949: 3). Seemingly, the Union's concern was now more about controlling the decision-making than it was the actual presence of the foreign musicians.

While Hilda's visit – and a number of similar exchanges with the Dutch union – indicated that the MU was not going to try to stop all foreign musicians, it is important to recognise that in both instances the demand for British jazz in these countries was greater than the reciprocal demand. However, the number of established and renowned American jazz musicians for whom there was a demand in the UK was far greater than the number of British acts for whom there was a similar audience in the USA. This presented a different kind of problem for the Union, and one it could not easily control via reciprocal exchanges. The result was that its approach to American jazz was a strange mixture of ideological and practical concerns.

As noted in Chapter 4, some critics have viewed the Union's policies as discriminatory against jazz and black musicians specifically. Far more evident was a mixture of anti-Americanism and some fundamental misunderstandings about the nature of jazz. The former is best viewed in the context of the CPGB's 1951 publication *The British Road to Socialism*, which articulated what Evan Smith calls 'a wider hostility to American popular culture and the influence of the United States in Western Europe' (2011: 90).[53]

This antagonism may help explain the Union's continued denial of the uniqueness of American talent, something that was clearly being demonstrated in jazz. During our research we heard many variations of the same quote, which former MU official Brian Blain (*2012*) attributed to Harry Francis: 'What do we want Louis Armstrong for? We've got Kenny Baker.'[54] Chris Barber recalled a meeting with Ratcliffe in the 1950s to discuss a possible visit by Louis Armstrong when he explained that 'we need inspiration from the leaders of this music' only to be met with the response 'why do you always want an American musician? Why don't you get a Russian trumpeter?' (*Barber 2013*).[55] For Barber this showed that all that mattered to the Union was that both played the same instrument. For Blain it was evidence of a 'cultural lag' within the Union whereby 'keeping out American jazz musicians was about keeping out dance bands from the Dorchester and other big hotels. It was a 1930s concept'. The EC had failed to recognise the artistic development of jazz and still saw it as being about 'shuffling about dancing to a bastard form of it in West End hotels' (*Blain 2012*).

Thus, while there was considerable resistance to both jazz and American musicians among parts of the Union's leadership, this was not necessarily reflective of the membership as a whole. In addition, the proximity of the great jazz acts – and the growing awareness of their work among British audiences and musicians – caused further resentment at not being able to witness them live. Particularly frustrating were the reports of the many visits to the UK of such acts when they were able to perform in restricted circumstances. Some found their way on to variety bills as a means of circumventing the restrictions on instrumentalists, while others visited surreptitiously. The most famous instances of the former were the visits of Duke Ellington and Benny Goodman to play at the London Palladium in 1948 and 1949 respectively.

Both played short sets alongside various vocal acts,[56] dancers, and comedians to some disappointment. *Melody Maker* reported of Ellington that 'without his magnificent orchestra to interpret the artistic sophistication of his music, Duke is just a pleasant, smoothly spoken personality' (26 June 1948: 1), and such sentiments were echoed in their reporting of Goodman's

53 The CPGB influence on the Union was still significant, given Ratcliffe's proximity to the CPGB faction and the prominent positions still held by Party members Phillips and Francis.

54 As does Godbolt (1976: 55).

55 In 1957, Chris Barber's Band organised tours for and backed a number of American blues musicians, using a loophole in the regulations to bring them in as variety artists.

56 Vocalists, who were not members of the MU or AFM in their respective countries, were not subject to any Ministry of Labour or union restrictions.

visit the following year. However, the Goodman shows more clearly highlighted the Union's continued influence over live music in the UK and, when required, the speed of their operation. Just three months before his eventual appearance, *Melody Maker* optimistically reported that Goodman was being lined up to play in Britain and claimed 'it is understood that the educational value to the music life of this country … is so great as to enable the Musicians' Union to view favourably a limited number of appearances' (16 April 1948: 1). The following week it was revealed that promoter Harold Fielding was in negotiations for him to play with the Philadelphia Orchestra and that Goodman was willing to employ British 'stand-by' musicians if permitted to play with them (23 April 1948: 1). However, by the following month such lofty ambitions had been curtailed. Realising the lack of Union support for such a venture, the plan for Goodman's visit was scaled down to his appearing at the Palladium as a variety act with his Sextet backed by the venue's resident Skyrockets band.

This too was vetoed by the Union's EC at a meeting in May, resulting in a series of negotiations between the Palladium, the MU, and Goodman to rescue the engagement. Rumours initially circulated about Goodman fronting a hand-picked group of leading British musicians.[57] However, despite approaches by Goodman to Bert Ambrose, this too was vetoed by the Union. The shows finally went ahead in July with Goodman accompanied by his own pianist (Buddy Greco) and the Skyrockets. Despite all this, Francis was quoted as saying that 'The MU is anxious to make it clear that there is no personal animosity towards Benny Goodman, and we have never been opposed to his visit here' (*Melody Maker*, 9 July 1948: 1).

Goodman's performances disappointed because of the context that had been largely imposed by the Union. However, there were some signs that the arguments that some of the American jazz performers were unique, could not be adequately substituted by inferior British players, and could offer something of an education for British musicians had become part of the press and public discourse – something that the MU could not resist forever. Over the next few years any ambitions the MU may have harboured to maintain a complete exclusion of American jazz musicians were eroded by a combination of pressure from the growing number of commercially powerful agents and concert promoters, musicians themselves (especially those wishing to play in the USA), and the general public.

57 Among them Kenny Baker, Johnny Dankworth, Jack Parnell, Laurie Morgan, and Harry Roche.

Some promoters took the law into their own hands. By arranging for Sidney Bechet and Coleman Hawkins to play, unannounced, in London in 1949, the London Jazz Club and the Willesden Music Makers' Club respectively not only broke the law, but directly challenged the Union's position. The two performances were lauded by journalists – Bechet's appearance was described as 'the most exciting and dramatic occasion in the history of British jazz for the last fifteen years' (*Melody Maker*, 26 November 1949: 1) – but those responsible were subsequently found guilty of contravening the Aliens' Order (1920) and fined (*Melody Maker*, 20 May 1950: 1). It was not long, however, before larger and more powerful organisations attempted to bring American jazz musicians to the UK.

In 1952 the National Federation of Jazz Organisations (NFJO) booked two American musicians, Lonnie Johnson and Ralph Sutton, as part of the Royal Festival Hall Jazz Festival. Despite the Ministry granting them work permits, subsequent accounts from disgruntled fans in *Melody Maker* (5 July 1952) described how the Union had 'sabotaged the event by insisting that their members did not appear on the same bill, resulting in the withdrawal of (among others) Johnny Dankworth, Geraldo and Humphrey Lyttelton'.[58] According to Mitchell, 'the NFJO scraped the bottom of the pot for blacklegs and with difficulty found them' (MU, 2/5/3/2), allowing the festival to go ahead. When the MU expelled the eleven members who had taken part,[59] there was a considerable backlash against its actions.

From the Union's perspective, the most alarming consequence was probably a letter from Owen Bryce in *Melody Maker* suggesting that the NFJO could become a 'new jazzman's union'[60] and commending them on their efforts with the festival despite what he called 'the lack of co-operation, cowardice and deliberate sabotage they encountered' (12 July 1952: 3). Other correspondence in *Melody Maker* following the festival suggested petitions and mass demonstrations against the MU's stance, with one writer, Eric Townley, noting that 'the mills of the MU grind slowly, but always produce the same rotten flour' (21 June 1952: 3).

The first American promoter to present a problem for the MU was Norman Granz, who offered to bring his Jazz at the Phil package tour[61] to London to play for MU funds (or a charity of its choice) in 1952. The Union's rejection

58 Johnson did nevertheless join an informal session with Lyttelton in Golders Green during his trip.

59 From fifty 'blackleg' musicians used by the NFJO.

60 This did not happen. Following the festival debacle, the NFJO split internally and disbanded in 1953, being reconstituted as the National Jazz Federation.

61 This included the likes of Ella Fitzgerald, Lester Young, and Oscar Peterson and was on tour in Europe at the time.

of this brought further focus on its position. Anstey was quoted as saying that 'we appreciate that the public – including our own members – would like an opportunity of hearing in person this orchestra and groups of specialists' (*Melody Maker*, 12 April 1952:1) but rejected the possibility of the package performing without an equivalent British package going to the USA. If the lack of movement by the AFM made the Union's position tenable, its motives were again called into question when an unnamed Union official, echoing Ratcliffe's comments to Barber, asked *Melody Maker* 'Why are you fellows so keen to have American bands in this country?', and suggested that they should show more interest in Russian ones (19 April 1952: 3).

Overall the Union's leadership was unable to quell the growing demand for American musicians, an appetite that was further whetted in March 1953 when, at the second attempt, Granz was able to bring Jazz at the Phil to London. Two shows at the Gaumont State Cinema in Kilburn took place in aid of the Lord Mayor's National Flood and Tempest Distress Fund. In order to expedite the presence of the musicians, the Ministry relaxed entry conditions, with the Home Office issuing special entry notes to allow them in. The press response to what was the first appearance by an American *band* in eighteen years followed a familiar pattern: lauding the American musicians and demanding further visits from their peers.

The MU did not oppose Jazz at the Phil but faced increasing pressure from its own members. Johnny Dankworth, who later signed to the American record label Capitol while still unable to perform in the USA, was one of those who put forward a motion to the London Branch in 1952 in favour of a limited number of visits each year by American acts for educational purposes. Two years later Ted Heath – one of the few British bandleaders for whom there was any demand in the USA – wrote to Petrillo, offering to perform for four weeks in the States on a trial basis in an effort to break the impasse on British bands visiting the USA (*Melody Maker*, 16 October 1954: 1).[62]

Unsurprisingly, Petrillo rejected the offer, on the grounds that any such arrangement could not be made 'between this organisation [AFM] and any particular band or bandleader' (*Melody Maker*, 13 November 1954: 1). Instead, he insisted that any such agreement should be reached between the respective unions. However, pressure from star musicians on both sides was an additional factor in forcing the two unions into further dialogue.

This had begun with a meeting of Ratcliffe and Petrillo in Paris in July 1953 (see Figure 10), where the American suggested a completely free exchange of bands between the two countries for a year's trial period. Reporting a month

[62] He copied his plea to British and American newspapers and trade publications.

Figure 10 James Petrillo (left) of the AFM meets Hardie Ratcliffe in Paris in 1953 to discuss reciprocal exchanges of musicians (MU, 5/1/106).

later to the EC, Ratcliffe explained that he had rejected this on the grounds that 'American bands would completely dominate the employment opportunities in London', but added that Petrillo had agreed to 'put to his International Board and recommend the adoption of a plan to permit reciprocal exchange' (MU, 2/1/13). In his next correspondence with the Union, Petrillo, apparently on the direction of his Executive Board, merely repeated the previously rejected offer of a one-year exchange with no restrictions. A further two years of occasional correspondence followed, with little progress made.

At the start of 1955, Granz was quoted as saying that 'I don't think the ban on American musicians playing in Britain will ever be lifted' (*New Musical Express* (*NME*), 25 February 1955: 6), making the rapid moves towards the first reciprocal exchanges a few months later all the more surprising. The *NME* and its publisher, the former agent and promoter Maurice Kinn, played a major part in brokering the first exchanges. Initially, they reported the desire of both Woody Herman and Stan Kenton to play to British audiences, quoting Kenton as saying 'I am willing to do a straight swap with Ted Heath on a strictly reciprocal basis ... we would cross the Atlantic with our orchestras and play the same number of dates, with the same number of musicians'

(*NME*, 11 March 1955: 6). Kinn then sought to make this happen via a number of meetings with Heath, Kenton, and the two Unions. In May Harry Francis wrote to Heath indicating that if the AFM agreed to the exchange, 'the MU is likely to agree, assuming it is for a similar period at approximately the same time' (*NME*, 20 May 1955: 7).

Meanwhile Kenton met Petrillo to argue his case, reporting that he was 'confident of successful developments' (*NME*, 17 June 1955: 7). However, a further four months were to pass before Petrillo made his decision. When the exchange was finally approved, *NME* hailed it as 'a great day for the *NME* and a great day for the music profession as a whole' (14 October 1955: 6), but celebrations among the musicians involved were fairly muted, especially when Heath considered the restrictions placed by the AFM. Owing to the insistence that he could only play concerts, and not do more lucrative 'dance' gigs in hotels, the bandleader and Harold Davison – who was promoting the British shows – were left pondering the economics of the situation and were forced to recognise that, in Jack Payne's words, 'the odds pile up in favour of the Americans' (*Melody Maker*, 22 October 1955: 3). Nevertheless, Kenton's British shows were largely announced by the end of the year and took place in March and April 1956,[63] while Heath's Carnegie Hall appearance was announced as the start of his US venture.

Conclusion

The Kenton and Heath arrangement was merely one of a number of momentous events in the Union's history, which were condensed into a decade during which it was able to take full advantage of favourable external conditions to consolidate its own power. The period 1945–55 marked a high point in terms of its industrial leverage, but also left a formidable legacy in terms of the working practices that emerged and that the recording and broadcasting industries would find almost impossible to alter for decades to come. The successes were largely derived from the huge increase in membership in the period, which in turn resulted from the huge demand for musicians from live music venues, record companies, and broadcasters.

This allowed it to make what would have been previously inconceivable advances on behalf of its members and to consolidate its power. Despite pressure from Government, politicians, and major employers, the Union had managed to boost its income and increase wages across large parts of the

[63] His first show at the Royal Albert Hall on 11 March 1956 had already been announced. Further shows around England were announced at the end of the year, with Scottish shows (and another at the Royal Albert Hall) added subsequently.

profession, most notably in the orchestras and for those involved in recording. In addition, the agreement with PPL ensured that it was well positioned to exert control over the use of recorded music in both broadcasting and public places, while similar manoeuvring allowed it to maintain substantial leverage over visits by foreign musicians.

The most remarkable aspect of such advances was that they were achieved by a Union that was frequently divided on both musical and political lines and that seemed, at times, bereft of visionary leadership. Much of its success was achieved as a result of favourable external conditions and attitudes – the healthy state of the entertainment economy; the precedents set by the AFM; and the willingness of the Government to become involved in pay negotiations, regulation of the employment market, and funding of the arts. Even those threats to what Thornton calls the Union's 'ideology of liveness' (1995: 42) from public performance of recordings and television were turned to some form of financial advantage for either the Union or its individual members.

As the MU was in the right place at the right time to capitalise on the musical and socio-political shifts in the aftermath of the war, its future was secure and the pace of subsequent change was much slower. With little movement in the Union's leadership, the next part of its history was to be characterised by an even greater sense of cultural lag as it stood relatively still while the UK's musical culture changed around it. If dance bands and jazz had posed problems for the Union's ageing leadership, officials, and members, then skiffle, rock 'n' roll, and what Union publications referred to as 'beat groups' were to show an even greater disconnect.

6

The beat generation: 1956–1970

This chapter spans the interval between two landmark years in the MU's history, arguing that the intervening period marked a time of relative stability within the Union while the music profession, music industries, and broadcasting were all subject to a further series of major changes. At the same time, the Union began to reap the benefits of the considerable advances it had made in the post-war years but found itself increasingly adrift from the changing nature of its constituency.

Bookending the period were a number of important events. Its outset saw the start of the reciprocal exchanges with American artists, the passing of the Copyright Act and the start of the Union's redistribution of the PPL income. Outside the Union – but equally important – was the weakening of the BBC's broadcasting monopoly with the expansion of the ITV network beyond London and developments in popular music.[1]

By 1970, the musical landscape had changed somewhat, but the Union's preoccupations remained largely the same. A feature in *Melody Maker* (4 July 1970: 22) focused on the age-old issues of needletime and foreign exchanges, but also new ones closely tied to the General Election campaign of the same year. Britain's potential membership of the (European) Common Market and the proposed introduction of commercial radio were to have a huge impact on the Union in the 1970s, but the most telling questions centred on the Union's attitude to new forms of pop.

This chapter explains the connected and often tortuous negotiations and decision-making processes that shaped the MU's response to changes in both the music profession and music industries. It begins with the music profession and an examination of the Union's interactions with the many emergent,

[1] The first ITV franchise (Associated-Rediffusion) that covered London launched in 1955; services for the Midlands and the North of England launched in 1956.

smaller ensembles working in jazz, skiffle, rock 'n' roll, and the 'beat' scene of the mid-sixties, before considering the issues surrounding orchestral employment. We then discuss the Union's internal machinations, looking at its leadership and organisation during the period, with particular emphasis on the impact of the 'phonographic funds'. The chapter concludes with a return to some recurring issues, concentrating on broadcasting, copyright, and foreign musicians.

Skiffle and records

The substantial changes in the production and consumption of popular music in the UK and beyond after 1955 have been extensively covered elsewhere (see Cohn 2004; Frame 2007; Melly 1970; Peterson 1990). However, the MU's attitude towards them has rarely been discussed.

The previous chapter used the example of Chris Barber to highlight that it was not only the new types of music that the Union found difficult to respond to, but the wider cultures and practices that accompanied them. For the Union, the new musical forms of skiffle and rock 'n' roll that emerged in the mid-1950s presented both musical and ideological problems. Its approach largely consisted of criticising the musical competence of the practitioners and claiming that they were depriving *real* musicians of work.

Such responses generally reflected the views of those already working in the profession. This was perhaps most famously articulated by Steve Race[2] in *Melody Maker* when he argued that 'viewed as a social phenomenon, the current craze for rock and roll is one of the most terrifying things to have ever happened to popular music'. He lamented the American influence and the paucity of playing, claiming that rock 'n' roll was a 'monstrous threat' to jazz that should be opposed 'to the end' (5 May 1956: 5). The MU's stance became apparent when the leadership was forced to respond to complaints from members about the loss of employment, initially caused by the proliferation of skiffle contests taking place in late 1957 and 1958. These were again viewed as taking work from MU members. It is telling that the Union's first pronouncements on the subject came nearly four years after Lonnie Donegan,[3] as part of Chris Barber's Band, recorded two skiffle tracks, including 'Rock Island Line'[4] for Barber's *New Orleans Joy* album.

2 Race was a known journalist, musician and broadcaster.
3 Donegan began playing and recording skiffle songs while a member of Barber's band, before leaving to launch a solo career.
4 'Rock Island Line' and 'John Henry' were released as a single in 1955, reaching number eight in the UK charts.

Skiffle was a relatively short-lived phenomenon (McDevitt 1997),[5] but one that caused considerable disruption to the Union's mindset. The low cost and home-made nature of the instruments – including washboards and tea-chest basses – and lack of musical training required to play it made skiffle an extremely popular, participatory form of music. According to the Union, ballroom owners were coerced by public demand to accommodate such events. The participants were largely amateur or semi-professionals and not Union members. While the contests usually offered prize money for the winners, no fees were paid for the musicians involved – a practice that riled the Union. Additionally, such contests frequently replaced nights where MU members had played, and the Union's concern was as much about loss of income for its members as it was over the welfare of those participating in the contests.

Nevertheless, Harry Francis identified what he called 'the exploitation of skiffle groups' as a prime concern, although this betrayed the Union's actual thinking, which was perhaps better encapsulated in his assertion that 'in other trades and professions, the unskilled man is often a liability to his fellows and is rejected by them for that reason'. Equally revealing was his remark that within skiffle the 'audience can make a star out of an absolute phoney' (*Melody Maker*, 25 January 1958: 3).

The Union's General Purposes Sub-Committee went as far as to discuss whether those playing skiffle were actually musicians.[6] A policy statement in February 1958 declared that 'members of skiffle groups are to be regarded as musicians, irrespective of their standard of performance, and should therefore be enrolled as members' (*Bulletin to Branches*, 6 February 1958). Recruiting skiffle musicians would, it was hoped, bind them to Union rules that prevented them from playing with non-members. As many of the contests offered as prizes appearances with groups who were Union members, this policy had two notional effects: both control to the contests and to increase Union membership.

However, skiffle was not the only threat to employment in the ballrooms. One of the Union's first concerns arising from the rock 'n' roll era was, by the late 1950s, the rise of the disc jockey (DJ). With only a handful of American bands visiting the UK as a result of the reciprocal exchange scheme, the only way audiences could hear American rock 'n' roll music

[5] Donegan, Barber, Alexis Korner, and Bill and Ken Colyer were widely accepted as being the first to play skiffle in the UK on Ken Colyer's return from New Orleans in late 1952. By 1958, the front cover of *Melody Maker* was proclaiming 'Skiffle on the skids' (17 May 1958: 1).

[6] The EC had a number of sub-committees to deal with matters in more detail that could not be dealt with at routine meetings.

was when records were broadcast or played in public places. Subsequently, ballroom owners could see growing demand for record hops and dancing to records. In this scenario, the Union had multiple safeguards built into their agreement with PPL preventing the use of recorded music where it would threaten work opportunities for live musicians. But this was subject to public pressure, commercial concerns, and frequent flouting of the rules.[7]

For the musicians the essence of the problem was that, in many instances, records were substantially more popular than live bands (as illustrated by the cover of the *Musician*, Figure 11). One unnamed musician told *Melody Maker* that 'we can play a beat, but not *the* beat' (9 March 1957: 3), increasingly making live bands a secondary attraction to the records that were played when the players were taking a break. Aware of this, dance hall proprietors were keen to exploit the loopholes in the restrictions to maximise the amount of time given over to records. Infamously, Jimmy Savile, a General Manager for Mecca across Lancashire and Yorkshire in the late 1950s, simply paid the bands not to appear, explaining that 'I was taking fifty times more without them than I was taking with them' (Brewster and Broughton 2012: 14). Tony Prince, a singer with the Johnny Francis Orchestra, told us how, a few years later, he began playing records when the band took breaks at the Top Rank in Oldham, with similar results: 'The floor would be twice as full as it had been for the band. It must have been really heart-breaking for the musicians and Johnny because every time I finished and introduced Johnny they just booed … they wanted the records more' (*Prince 2012*).

The records to which he refers were increasingly ubiquitous elsewhere – on radio,[8] television, jukeboxes, and in those public places with licences to play them. With demands for records increasing within the ballrooms, the Union engaged in lengthy negotiations with Mecca over musicians' employment terms (MU, 4/1/3/27). Mecca represented a new challenge for the Union, being a major employer determined to erode musicians' terms and conditions, while simultaneously using its patrons' demand for dancing to records as a means of reducing its own reliance on live musicians. It could also now threaten to take cases to the newly formed Performing Right Tribunal (PRT, see below) and claimed as well to have a large stockpile of non-British records – which were exempt from the PPL–MU agreement – ready to use should its PPL

7 In interview, Jack Stoddart (*2015*), a former AGS with responsibility for live music, suggested that how this agreement was actually policed at a local level was 'anybody's guess'.

8 While needletime restricted the number of records the BBC could play, some stations outside the UK, like Radio Luxembourg, were already broadcasting 'non-stop pop'.

Figure 11 As the record industry grew in size the Union grew increasingly concerned about the replacement of live musicians, as illustrated by this cover of the *Musician*, December 1957 (MU, 1/5).

licence be withdrawn. While a new agreement was reached with the Circuits Management Association (CMA), which included both the Mecca and Rank chains, in August 1962 (*The Stage*, 4 September 1962: 3) it was clear that Mecca was not alone in disapproving of the MU's influence in the ballrooms.

By now, the Union seemed out of touch among both audiences and some musicians. This sense was accentuated by the next major shift in the production of popular music: the sudden explosion of self-contained British pop bands after the breakthrough success of the Beatles in 1962. Though young British musicians had been forming bands and performing American rock 'n' roll and rhythm-and-blues since the late 1950s, the significance of the Beatles' success industrially was the group's songwriters and the way in which they came to prominence. They were also emblematic of a new type of musical ensemble.

Beat groups and session musicians

The rise of skiffle and jazz and the emergence of 'beat groups' engendered a new world of small-scale live music activity that often lay beyond the reach of the MU. This took place in working men's clubs, jazz clubs, town halls, and other small venues operated by entrepreneurial music fans. Based in Sunderland, John Reed[9] bought a drum kit in 1962 and joined a band playing cover versions of chart hits in working men's clubs. For such semi-professional musicians, work was plentiful and reasonably well remunerated. Reed (*2013*) told us:

> I was making £25 a week in the band, doing Working Men's Clubs. We were working five or six nights a week. I mean every week. There were 200 Working Men's Clubs in Sunderland alone – shipbuilding clubs, boilermakers' clubs, miners' welfare clubs ... they all had entertainment on seven nights a week.

Within a year of Reed's first ventures into playing, the demand for beat groups playing at least some original material had increased to a point where many became a viable concern. Mike Evans, who later worked for the MU, was a member of the Clayton Squares, a Liverpool group who released two singles for Decca in 1965 and 1966. He recalled that 'when we played the Cavern in the early sixties, and other clubs in Liverpool, we got paid, and you'd have eight bands a night who got paid' (*Evans, 2013*). Notably, the payment was not based on MU rates. In 1962, the MU introduced a National Gig Rate (*Bulletin to Branches*, 8 June) but the logic determining this was to increase the rates for casually employed musicians playing as part of large ensembles in the dance halls and ballrooms. This bore little resemblance to the way groups like the Clayton Squares operated:

[9] Reed was later a member of British psych-pop group Toby Twirl, who released several singles for Decca. He went on to work for a number of British record companies (*Reed 2013*).

> I think we used to get £15 for playing the Cavern, but this was in 1964 … when £15 was not insignificant … and if you did two or three of them a night, which we did, then you were OK. On a Saturday, we'd do the Cavern early slot, some kind of regional dance hall, maybe in Warrington or somewhere, and then we would travel to Manchester and do the Twisted Wheel all-nighter and then we would get back to the Cavern and do the last slot there. Four gigs on a Saturday night … Never thought anything of it. (*Evans 2013*)

For the Union, the burgeoning beat scene around the country presented numerous problems. The working practices described by Reed and Evans were far removed from those of most Union members and their activities were often under the MU's radar. Where they did come into contact with such groups, MU officials often found themselves with little understanding of these musicians' working lives and were unable to apply the leverage that they could with those working for larger employers. It is also significant that, as shown, much of this activity was happening outside London, while the Union's centralised bureaucracy remained slow and inflexible in its response to such changes.

Initially, most beat musicians would only join the Union when they had to, and would frequently flout its rules. Evans joined because he came from a family of trade unionists, whereas Reed (*2013*) recalls that 'you just paid your annual fee. There was no advantage at all in joining, but in fairness, what could a local branch representative of the MU do for musicians in Sunderland?'. Reed's assessment was correct – several years would pass before the MU was able to offer a service that would persuade musicians outside the orchestras and dance bands to join voluntarily.[10]

The attitude of beat musicians towards the Union was not helped by the regular pronouncements from Union officials about newly popular forms of music being either a threat to existing musical employment and/or a short-lived fad. Numerous examples of this can be given. An unnamed official addressed the Music Group of the CPGB on 23 November 1964 and compared contemporary pop music unfavourably with the music of thirty years prior, focusing on the lack of technical proficiency as well as exploitation and corruption in the music industries. He was particularly keen to point out the economics of the recording industry, noting that 'recording companies could make more out of recording a "small" group than by employing a proper

[10] Many musicians found that they had to join when they reached a certain point in their careers: for example, when playing with Union members, recording for the BBC, or taking part in a reciprocal exchange.

dance band or an orchestra' before concluding that beat music 'would soon follow skiffle into oblivion' (*Music and Life*, January 1965: 4).

These themes – that beat groups were unskilled, put superior musicians out of work, and were being exploited by big business – were to recur. The following year, Ratcliffe told the PRT that 'pop music bears as much resemblance to real music as bingo to higher mathematics' (*Spokesman-Review*, 5 May 1965: 24). Harry Francis used the *Musician* to overplay the fears of exploitation, suggesting that the 'beat sound is dying ... and there are, of course, mixed opinions about whether its death would be a matter for regret or for celebration' (January 1965: 7). However, his article did not seek the sort of solutions that might have been possible via the MU's close relationships with many record companies that had been engendered during its negotiations with PPL.

With rare exceptions,[11] the Union hierarchy had decided that the changes in popular music were short-term and would be reversed. But, as the decade progressed, the Union's position on pop music was challenged in the press and by the growing number of members involved in making it. Not long after he joined the Union in 1965, Brian Blain was interviewed by *Melody Maker* to answer accusations that the Union was 'anti-pop'.[12] His response justified the opposition to unrestricted use of recordings, but argued that a greater number of pop musicians in the Union would change its stance. He also noted that 'even pop stars require the services of musicians who have gained their experience in theatres and palais' (*Melody Maker*, 22 July 1966: 8). Around the same time, the Union produced its first flyers (see Figure 12) using existing members from the pop world to appeal to their contemporaries.[13]

Blain was referring to the expanding number of session musicians who carved out a living by playing on records (Thompson 2008). These professional musicians were seen by the Union as vital to the success of the records, but the development of this new cadre of musicians caused it further problems. These related to its live music ethos, inequality, and authenticity.

Tellingly, those members working as session musicians were the first significant grouping of musicians that did not need to play live to earn a living, and word of the potential rewards spread quickly. In 1965 Mike Leander of Decca Records told *Melody Maker* that supply of session musicians in London could not meet demand, and urged 'the better musicians' to become

11 John Morton's work in Birmingham and the subsequent efforts of Brian Blain are important here.

12 The same issue was raised in an interview with Harry Francis in the same publication two years later (*Melody Maker*, 8 April 1968: 17).

13 Among those who appeared on later Union recruitment adverts were Sting, Nik Kershaw, Simon Rattle, The Farm, and Jimmy Page.

Figure 12 By 1966, the Union began to extend its appeal to the type of pop groups with which it had an uneasy relationship (MU, 1/9).

aware of the 'great career there is waiting for them' (6 November 1965: 7). By 1968 *Melody Maker* was reporting that 'the session boys do better than groups', and Manfred Mann told the paper that 'they earn much more money. I know one guy who earns £150 a week. He can live at home and work in town, whereas the guy in a group has to share the money and go on the road' (24 February 1968: 13).

In some respects the session player's lot was one that the Union could understand – its members in dance bands and orchestras had been providing a backing to stars and singers in music halls and ballrooms for decades. Yet this became more problematic when the recording industry practice of using session musicians to play the parts of group members became public. Matters came to a head when members of The Love Affair told a prime television show that, with the exception of singer Steve Ellis, they had not performed on their chart-topping single 'Everlasting Love'.[14] The confession caused consternation in some parts of the press, forcing Ratcliffe and Francis into commenting. The former told the *Daily Mail* that 'recordings should not be based on deception. For too long groups with minimum talent have climbed to prominence on the backs of really talented musicians' (quoted in *Melody Maker*, 17 February 1968: 4). Francis added that 'this thing should be stopped where people that can't play have to call on real musicians' (*Melody Maker*, 24 February 1968: 4).

Despite headlines in the music press suggesting an imminent MU ban on the practice referred to as 'ghosting', there is no evidence of this materialising. Ratcliffe announced that a 'code of practice' would be drawn up and presented to the record companies. However, a year later, this had been repeatedly deferred. The truth was that implementing such a ban would most probably have had a negative effect on both relations with the record companies and some MU members. Record producer Mickey Most argued that if the Union implemented such a ban it would 'be putting its own members out of work' (*Melody Maker*, 9 March 1968: 16). Instead, echoing previous negotiations with the BBC, it used the controversy as a bargaining tool in its subsequent attempts to increase both fees and rights for such performers.

Orchestras

Initially the rapid expansion of the recording industry and the emergence of new musical forms had little obvious impact within the part of the music world with which the Union was most comfortable. Despite a number of periodic claims from the Union and beyond of a crisis in the British music profession, the post-war world of the established orchestras had been largely uninterrupted by either technology or changing public demand. In addition, public subsidy of orchestras via the BBC, Arts Council, and local authorities had increased, with the Labour Government of 1964 particularly keen to increase support for the arts.[15]

14 For a more detailed account of this story see Williamson (2013).

15 This was evidenced by the appointment of Jennie Lee as Minister for the Arts and the publication of the first ever White Paper on cultural funding – 'A policy for the arts' – in 1965 (see Hewison 1995: 121).

Despite the perilous position of some individual orchestras throughout the 1960s, orchestral musicians were arguably more secure and well remunerated than at any previous point.[16] There are several examples of this. In 1962, after the threat of a strike, rank-and-file musicians in the provincial (and Scottish) orchestras received a pay rise from £15 to £20 per week.[17] This was supported by the employers, the OEA, even though they were unable to afford it and had to embark on a series of negotiations with the Arts Council and local authorities to fund the rise. Only after the Arts Council made representations to the Treasury were funds released, thus averting a strike (*Guardian*, 26 October 1962: 1). Two years later, the BBC, MU, Arts Council, OEA, and the Association of Municipal Corporations formed a Standing Committee on the Employment of Musicians, while BBC staff musicians were awarded a pay rise of between 2.4 and 3.8 per cent annually for the next eight years, beginning on 1 January 1965 (MU, 1/7/1965).

However, all this served further to increase the costs of orchestras, many of which struggled to make ends meet.[18] For example, in 1962, Eric Bravington of the LPO told the *Guardian* that it 'just about broke even' (7 July 1962: 3). The same year, the Royal Liverpool Philharmonic had to apply to the City Council to make up a shortfall. In Manchester – where the council was less supportive – the Chair of the Hallé Concerts Society, Alan Duckworth, appealed, in 1965, for a national inquiry into the British orchestral situation, citing both financial and recruitment problems (*Guardian*, 12 January 1965: 4). There was clearly a tension between the Union's aspirations for orchestral musicians' pay and the commercial realities of running an orchestra that had been partially masked by its experience of the largesse and public-sector ethos of the BBC. Outside the Corporation it was apparent that many within the OEA were increasingly relying on ever-larger public subsidies to match the Union's pay demands and other operating costs with no corresponding uplift in income.

The Union had limited sympathy for the orchestral employers and effectively used its pay claims and strike threats as a means of extracting more public support for the music profession. It had also, for some time, been painting a picture of a crisis in the music profession and appealing for the intervention of the BBC and the Arts Council – with some successes. In 1960

16 The MU saw off proposed cuts to BBC orchestras in 1957 (Briggs 1995: 230).

17 Sub-principals got £22 and principals £25.

18 In 1957 the MU and OEA had appeared before an industrial disputes tribunal in order to settle a pay dispute. One result was the establishment of a Joint Interpretation Committee to intervene in disputes (OEA, Box 58).

the *Guardian* reported that 'the employment position in "serious" music is probably as good as it ever was, but it is far from enough to absorb even the products of the leading music schools' (6 February 1960: 2). Later the same year, a four-day conference[19] gave the Union a platform to bemoan what Michael Moynihan described as 'the bleak outlook for professional musicians in Britain' (1960: 11). Here Ratcliffe described State patronage of the arts in the UK as 'totally inadequate' and local authority support as 'little short of contemptible', arguing that 'there is little incentive for talented young musicians to make music their profession' (cited in Moynihan 1960: 11). At this point, the estimated number of regularly employed orchestral musicians was only 1,500,[20] highlighting the growing problem of over-supply.

The Union also made great play of the BBC's willingness to accept its responsibilities to the music profession to create more work and opportunities. It successfully used the Corporation's requests for more needletime to extract substantial concessions in terms of commitments to employing musicians. The 1964 needletime agreement, which gave the BBC an extra forty-seven hours a week, came at a considerable price for the Corporation. A joint statement issued by the Union and the BBC included commitments to 'maintaining for the foreseeable future the present level of employment of musicians in established BBC orchestras', the formation of the Standing Committee on Employment, and – most remarkably – the formation of a sixty-five-member Training Orchestra 'to give young players in Great Britain an opportunity to acquire the skill necessary to qualify for incorporation into BBC and other orchestras'. Furthermore, the BBC guaranteed to spend a further £500,000 per year on the employment of musicians, and a total of at least £2 million on musicians performing in domestic radio each year, while promising to assist the Union in making 'the problems of the profession known' (WAC, R104/184/2).

This was another peak in the Union's influence. Remarkably, at a point when the costs of orchestral musicians were rising and the economics of both the BBC and individual orchestras coming under closer scrutiny, it had managed to secure concessions that would not only preserve and improve the working conditions of existing employees, but opened the possibility of actually expanding orchestral provision at a point where demand for it was weakened by records, broadcasts, and the greater variety and quality of both home and live entertainment.

19 This was organised by the National Music Council, and supported by the International Music Council of UNESCO.

20 Including those in the BBC orchestras.

Nevertheless, by the late 1960s, the economics of both the BBC and non-BBC orchestras were being seriously questioned and 1969 saw two major challenges. These were: first, a BBC review of its (radio) costs (in the light of political pressure not to increase the licence fee), and second, an Arts Council-commissioned 'Orchestral Resources Enquiry' conducted by the economist Alan Peacock, which examined both the funding and regional variances in orchestral provision across the UK. The results of both were contentious and triggered the first serious debates about levels of employment in, and funding of, British orchestras. These changed the Union's position: where it had once been on the front foot in negotiations, it was now increasingly trying to hold what it had.

Internally, there was evidence that the BBC was increasingly frustrated by the apparent hold that the MU had over needletime. In early 1968, as the existing agreement neared termination, the Corporation employed the consultants McKinsey and Co. to produce a report called 'Tactics for PPL negotiations'. This calculated the cost to the BBC of the needletime agreement as being £2.5 million per year in addition to the cost of employing 500 musicians. It noted that 'the BBC has accepted that it must take a firm stand against the MU and make major changes in the agreements. However, this step must be taken in the context of all the issues between the BBC and the MU.' It criticised the Union, claiming that discussions were hampered by its 'being increasingly out of touch with the realities of today ... and with the needs of musicians themselves'. Here it specifically highlighted what it saw as the Union's sole objective as being the maximising of employment with no regard for the cost or quality of the resulting music and its 'out-dated attitude that recording is evil' (WAC, R101/226/1).

Thus not only was the BBC thinking about further changes to its broadcasting output, but it was also considering how best to tackle and gain an advantage over the Union in future negotiations. Prior to the publication of its policy booklet *Broadcasting in the Seventies* (BBC 1969), newspaper stories began to emerge about its contents. The *Guardian* reported proposals to reduce the number of musicians employed by the BBC from 500 to 400, suggesting that the orchestras most likely be affected were the BBC Northern Symphony Orchestra (BBCNSO) the BBC Scottish Symphony Orchestra (BBCSSO), the Northern Dance Orchestra (NDO), and the Scottish Radio Orchestra (SRO), which all had local competitors who could realistically take over some or all of their work (28 May 1969: 18).

Broadcasting in the Seventies was published in July 1969 and set out to 'adapt our service to a changing world to meet changing tastes and needs', with the emphasis being on being able to 'live within our prospective income

... in the next five years' (BBC 1969: 1). Most importantly for the Union was the way in which it broached the issue of the BBC's patronage of live music and musicians over and beyond its broadcasting needs. Recognising that it had been cajoled into a position of employing more musicians than it needed, its stated intention was to reduce 'our employment of musicians, including our own standing orchestras, to nearer the level we need for broadcasting purposes' (12).

To do this it proposed the retention of five orchestras: BBCSO, BBCNSO, the Radio Orchestra, the Midland Light Orchestra, and the SRO, accounting for some 279 permanent employees. Concurrently, it sought to absolve itself from financial responsibility for the BBCSSO, the NDO, the London Studio Players and the BBC Chorus – the combined strength of which was 132 mostly full-time players – while seeking negotiations with the ACGB, the Welsh Arts Council, and the Arts Council of Northern Ireland over solutions to save the BBC Concert Orchestra and the Welsh and Northern Irish orchestras. Ominously, it noted that the MU had asked for 'an urgent and complete review of their relationship with the BBC' (BBC 1969: 12) after it got wind of its plans.

Ratcliffe labelled the plans 'the greatest threat to the music profession in half a century' (*Musician*, October 1969: 10–11). Importantly, support for the threatened orchestras came from prominent musical figures and politicians. Sir Adrian Boult and Yehudi Menuhin supported the Union and there was qualified support from William Mann, the music critic of *The Times* (6 June 1969: 13), while Sir Arthur Bliss, the Master of the Queen's Music, accused the BBC of replacing serious music with the 'aural hashish' of pop (*The Times*, 30 June 1969: 3). However, the most important interventions came from Parliament, with MPs across the House opposing the BBC's proposals.[21] The (Labour) Postmaster General,[22] John Stonehouse, supported Menuhin's view that the orchestras should play a greater part in the cultural activities of their towns and voiced his disagreement with the 'development of thought in the Corporation about patronage' (cited in *The Times*, 23 July 1969: 3). This was echoed by Conservative broadcasting spokesman Paul Bryan, who asked 'if the BBC is not going to continue in the role of patron to music, who would take it on?' (*The Times*, 23 July 1969: 3).

Politically, there were two Government interventions in the wake of the proposals that contributed ultimately to saving the threatened orchestras. The first was to tie the future of the BBC's orchestras to those orchestras that were

21 HC Debate 22 July 1969, http://hansard.millbanksystems.com/commons/1969/jul/22/broadcasting-in-the-seventies-bbc-plan.

22 The Cabinet Member responsible for broadcasting.

being investigated by Peacock. The *Guardian* reported that there would be no action on the BBC orchestras until the publication of Peacock's report (Woollacott 1969), to which the BBC and MU were asked to give evidence. The second came in August 1969 when it agreed to increase the cost of the TV licence,[23] thereby providing the BBC with additional funds that could be used to finance the orchestras. Two months later, Stonehouse announced that the BBC orchestras had been saved (Fiddick 1969).[24]

Despite the end of the immediate threat to the BBC orchestras, the state of orchestral music – described as 'rotten' in a *Times* leader (25 July 1970: 13) – remained a matter of considerable public discourse in the coming years. The publication of the Peacock Report (and a subsequent conference organised by the OEA in York) ensured that the divergent views of musicians, employers, politicians, and the Union remained in public view. The Report itself split members of Peacock's Commission, was criticised by musicians and the media, and was partially rejected by its funder, the Arts Council. The key, and most controversial, findings concerned the four London orchestras. Peacock recommended that the number of orchestras receiving subsidy and giving regular public concerts be halved,[25] with two having to survive on commercial film and recording work. It also criticised the lack of effort and imagination employed by orchestra management in promoting shows (especially those outside London) and predicted that by the mid-1970s, income from ticket sales would account for only 30 per cent of an orchestra's total expenditure.

These plans won no favour with Ratcliffe, who was a member of the committee, or Lord (Arnold) Goodman, who, as Chair of the Arts Council and a trusted fixer for a number of governments, was hugely influential in the eventual settlement. Ratcliffe issued a minority report and told *The Times* that the proposals for London orchestras would 'be unfair to some orchestras and have disadvantages for the public' (25 July 1970: 2). His disappointment stemmed from his belief that, with supply of musicians outstripping the demand of orchestras, orchestral employment should be increased. His minority report argued this, but seemed to fly in the face of the evidence of the previous decade. Realistically Ratcliffe was never likely to be able to increase orchestral employment and it was Goodman's intervention that prevented further erosion. According to Witts, 'Goodman sank his big bum on top of Peacock's Report' (1998: 197) by using its preface to reject two of its main

[23] The separate radio licence was scrapped at this stage, though neither was to become operational until 1971.

[24] The BBC's commitment to the Training Orchestra only lasted until 1971.

[25] Although not identified in the report, the Royal Philharmonic and New Philharmonia were seen as the most likely to be affected.

findings: the reformulation of London orchestras and a recommendation that pay scales for orchestras outside London be increased to match those in the capital.[26]

The two investigations had very different outcomes for the interested parties. For the Union it meant that, despite severe scrutiny, very little had changed in the employment of its orchestral members, while the BBC had to backtrack on its *Broadcasting in the Seventies* vision. In the aftermath of the Government intervention, the BBC's Director-General, Charles Curran, noted that 'the Government was accepting that the cost of maintaining the orchestras was a fair charge on the licence revenue' and that 'it would seem logical, too, that the formal involvement of the BBC in musical patronage as a national policy should lead to joint action with the Arts Council' (Curran 1970: 10). It was clear that Goodman had used his position as Chair of the Arts Council – and the broker in the BBC negotiations – to his impose his worldview despite the evidence generally being against his belief that the BBC and London could maintain the 1960s level of orchestral provision. Remarkably, all four of London's non-BBC orchestras still survive.[27]

Nonetheless, the issues that had been fermenting for the best part of a decade were unlikely to go away when the solution to the problems of over-supply, underfunding, and declining demand was simply a marginal increase in the supply of funds. The Union's strength, reinforced by threats of strike action, the record companies' support (Morris 1969), and Goodman's views meant that the BBC had little option but to back down. However, debates on the future of the orchestras continued, and for those musicians working at the BBC, a stay of execution was perhaps the best they could have hoped for.

Internal affairs

By way of contrast, an examination of the Union's operation during the period covered by this chapter offers some evidence of adaptability, but little change in organisation. To highlight this we briefly examine the Union's leadership and internal politics, describing two of the major conflicts and the eventual end of Ratcliffe's tenure, before returning to reflect on the biggest change in internal dynamics: the use of the PPL funds.

After the infighting in the aftermath of his election, Ratcliffe had settled into the GS job overseeing what was a period of relative consolidation. The

26 The background is entertainingly explored by Witts (1998: 188–206), who provides a short history of reports into orchestral provision in the UK and an unflattering comparative study of Goodman's 1965 Committee on the London Orchestras and Peacock's report five years later.

27 The New Philharmonia reacquired the name the Philharmonia in 1977.

officials who held the top posts – Ratcliffe, Anstey, and Francis as well as the London officials (Mitchell and Tom Barton) all remained in post for over twenty years, allowing them to cultivate relationships with Government bodies, politicians, and major employers while adapting little in terms of outlook. Politically, they were all identified with the left, though some of their most vocal opponents from previous decades, notably Vic Sullivan, remained on the EC.[28]

While the officials' personal politics were significant, they were arguably less important in shaping their attitudes than their age and musical backgrounds. Importantly, at least until 1970 the Union's key officials had all cut their teeth in the music profession prior to the war, and had been members of orchestras or dance bands. This was inevitably accompanied by a particular worldview, one that Brian Blain (*2012*) described to us as 'harking back to a previous golden age and to a degree trying to recreate it'. As noted above, one consequence of this was that a large percentage of the Union's energies was spent protecting those parts of the music profession its leaders knew best, while being generally suspicious of other musical developments. Thus, while the officials were politically to the left of many members, their musical instincts were deeply conservative. Their outlook also contributed to the two biggest internal issues during the 1960s – the difficult working relationship between officials and the EC, and managing the branches.

The most bizarre example of the former was when the Union's thirteen full-time officials went on strike for two days in March 1961,[29] while later tensions between Ratcliffe and the Executive saw him twice resign his position before being persuaded, on both occasions, to stay put. The officials' strike – previously unheard of in trade union history – was extensively reported in the press, with the *Guardian* detailing the history of the additional £2-per-week pay claim that caused it and the EC's reluctance to meet the claim. Ratcliffe lamented that the dispute was 'for the sake of a paltry £300, which the Union can well afford' (*Guardian*, 13 March 1961: 1), but quickly played down the dispute after agreement was reached two days later (*Guardian*, 16 March 1961: 15). He later penned an article in the *Musician*, which conceded that the officials' strike was 'unprecedented in our Union or any other' but went on to brand it 'a minor scuffle' and, in a generally conciliatory tone, concluded with the hope that 'normal good relations, now happily established may be maintained' (March 1961: 10).

[28] Sullivan, who was chair of the EC at the time, died in a car crash in April 1964.

[29] The pay claim referred specifically to the full-time District and Branch officials. They were joined on strike by National Office officials and three members of the Union's office staff.

This was not, however, borne out by subsequent events, and just over a year later tensions between the officials and Executive culminated in Ratcliffe tendering his resignation. This time he was careful to stress his general agreement with Union policy, but argued that 'he found his views too frequently differed from those of the executive on *internal* matters' (*Guardian*, 16 August 1962: 2, emphasis ours). His second resignation, at an EC meeting on 20–22 August 1968, was over a more specific matter – the proposed use of the 'phonographic funds' to pay the premium for the Union's Staff Pensions and Life Insurance scheme. Ratcliffe described this as 'contrary to his principles' (MU, 2/1/18) and the EC quickly decided to revert to the previous system of taking the premiums from the Union's General Fund, thus ensuring that Ratcliffe remained *in situ*. Conflicts between the EC and GS could be viewed as an inevitable consequence of the Union's power structure whereby its nominal leader was tied to representing policy positions decided by a Conference and delivered by an elected Executive. However, Ratcliffe's resignations were a direct challenge to the EC's power and, on both occasions, ended with it backing down.

Such conflict also resulted partly from the composition of the EC and the types of representative elected to it. Each district of the Union elected a number of members to the EC (determined by number of members) with those elected frequently being Branch Secretaries. The difference in attitude and outlook of these part-time functionaries and the salaried officials had been an underlying source of rancour for many years, but surfaced for the first time towards the end of the 1960s. At the heart of this were questions surrounding both the competence and the accountability of the Union's local-level administration. By 1965 the MU had 150 branches, with only a handful of the larger ones having a full-time branch official. Elsewhere, Branch Secretaries were elected annually and were charged with organising Branch meetings, collecting subscriptions[30] and submitting a share of these (along with accounts) centrally at the end of each quarter. In return, the Union's rules stated that 'the salary of the Branch Secretary shall be 25% of all entrance fees and subscriptions of admitted members' (MU 1962: 15). In larger branches this could amount to sizeable sums for modest amounts of work. Branch Secretaries were also entitled to an annual bonus. The complexity of its calculation and a lack of transparency surrounding it caused further suspicion. Inevitably, when relying on a remote and part-time workforce (many of whom had full-time jobs elsewhere), the quality and diligence of the Branch Secretaries varied considerably.

30 The Union operated a stamp system where members paid subscriptions to Branch Secretaries at the end of each quarter.

Some rumblings of open discontent about the arrangements came at the 1967 Conference when it was noted that the salaries paid to Branch Secretaries were 'greater than those of comparable voluntary officers of other unions' (MU, 1/7/1967). An EC meeting the following year highlighted examples of what was described as 'unsatisfactory administration', centred around 'certain disturbing features about the present ballot arrangements made by some branches' and a more general complaint from Ratcliffe that 'there were a number of branches where administration, contact with the National Office and branch accounting had practically broken down … at least ten branches scarcely existed' (MU, 2/1/18).

In response to these concerns, a meeting of the Union's officials in July 1968 resolved that they could demand access to branch accounts and report any reluctance on the part of a Branch Secretary to Ratcliffe. This upset some branch officials and resulted in the formation of an Association of District and Branch Officials, instigated by the South West District Organiser, Howard Rudge, and Tom Barton, who took positions as Chair and Secretary respectively. When the latter wrote to Ratcliffe announcing its existence, the matter was referred to the EC, which voted not to recognise it. However, the Association acted as temporary lightning rod for some disaffected officials.

A new leader

With Ratcliffe warning about the increased public scrutiny of trade union ballots and operations, it was obvious that his successor would be left with a number of festering organisational problems. Ratcliffe's announcement of his intention to retire at the end of 1970 sparked the first GS election in twenty-two years. This was contested among Morton, Rudge, and Francis in July 1970. Morton's success resulted from widespread support across the country and a modernising approach.

Though the candidates' positions were broadly similar in opposition to commercial radio, Britain joining the Common Market, relaxation of needletime restrictions,[31] and the continuation of the foreign exchanges, the key differences between Morton and the others came in his approach to pop musicians, the Union's internal workings, and external communications. Unlike Rudge and Francis, who defended the Union's handling of the emergence of new types of popular music, Morton forthrightly asserted that the MU 'hadn't responded to the changed patterns of the popular music business'

[31] Francis wanted to abolish needletime altogether, Rudge wanted not to increase it, and Morton wanted to reduce it (*Melody Maker*, 4 July 1970: 22).

and pointed to his own efforts in attempting to organise pop groups during the previous decade. He also set out his ambition for the Union to 'modify the structure of the Union and develop our skills to meet the 70s and 80s. Basically our structure belongs to an out-dated profession, I think we've got to build up a really first-class, streamlined, professional organisation' (*Melody Maker*, 4 July 1970: 22).

More recently Morton (2011) attributed his success to his outsider status and his approach to the changing nature of the music profession.[32] 'I had two advantages over the other two: one was being somebody new and the other was that I had some idea about how to go about being elected. Both of the others, I am sorry to say, had thought that they would automatically get elected and I didn't think that.' He also pointed to his experience of dealing with new types of musicians while working in Birmingham in the mid-1960s as assisting his electoral success: 'I was very conscious of the coming of Elvis and The Beatles and the general rock 'n' roll scene, before it was called that – and it was my view that the Union had to really cater for the new type of musician' (Morton 2011). Indeed, Morton had produced some of the first publicity material aimed at pop bands and used the proliferation of battle-of-the-bands competitions in the Midlands to recruit new members.

Officially taking over from Ratcliffe at the start of 1971, Morton had a number of things in his favour in his quest to reorganise the Union. Barton, Mitchell, and Anstey all retired around this time, allowing a younger generation to take some key positions. In 1968, John Patrick, a Midlands contemporary of Morton's, was elected Chair of the EC, and when Anstey retired in 1969 Francis was promoted to AGS with Jack Stoddart and Ben Norris appointed as Assistant Secretaries. This left Francis as the only pre-war official still in position and greatly reduced the likely internal resistance to change. Significantly, Blain (*2012*) reflected that when he began working for the Union 'the calibre of officials at that time to me was not very high. The people I ended up working with as colleagues were of a far higher standard than the people who were there when I started in the mid-sixties.'

Keeping music live

Blain's appointment was one of the few major internal changes during Ratcliffe's leadership.[33] Employing him to run the Keep Music Live campaign

32 See Chapter 7 for more on Morton's background.
33 Blain was initially appointed for one year in 1965, and given a permanent position as a Union official in 1966.

was the culmination of almost twenty years of deliberation as to how exactly the Union would use its 12.5 per cent share of PPL's net income. This speed shows both the Union's inherently cautious nature and the potential problems it envisaged in allocating the funds. Collecting the monies from PPL on behalf of all musicians (including non-MU members) presented a number of issues. Having decided that the funds should be used collectively rather than in individual payments to performers, the next issue was what to do with the money.

The first payment from PPL came in 1951 and the funds were largely untouched for the first five years, collecting interest while the Union sought to clarify whether the monies were taxable and to determine a spending plan. By the 1957 and 1959 Conferences pressure to develop a coherent policy had grown and a plethora of motions suggested how the funds should be allocated. A discussion of the funds took place at the 1957 Conference and laid the foundations for future policy. While it was noted that 'owing to the large sums involved, extreme care should be exercised in the making of decisions that might entail long-term commitments' (MU, 1/7/1957) a number of suggestions were put forward, including the payment of retirement and death benefits for those with thirty-five years' continuous membership, the formation of musicians' centres, and an agency – all of which were ultimately rejected. The most ambitious proposal suggested that '£10,000 per annum should be allocated for three years to finance a project to provide or promote employment for members', while a subsequently important emphasis on public relations was also evident in a proposal to publicise 'the Union's live music policy and the Union itself' (MU, 1/7/1957).

Meanwhile the scale of the payments increased. For example, in 1958 the Union received £59,482 from PPL, covering a two-year period up to 31 May 1957. Initial outgoings were largely administrative. Between the 1957 and 1959 Conferences, the largest amounts were transferred to the Union's main account[34] and to the National Council of Labour Colleges in affiliation fees (MU, 1/7/1959). The interest gathered was paid to the Union's Benevolent Fund and a proportionate amount was paid to the Northern Ireland Music Association (NIMA).[35]

However, it was two other payments that stood out in the Conference report of 1959 – a grant of £500 to the Welsh National Opera Company and a payment of just over £1,500 to various branches to subsidise May Day

[34] The agreement with PPL allowed 5 per cent of the total to be used for general purposes.

[35] The MU did not then have an operation or members in Northern Ireland, but the PPL funds were for Great Britain and Northern Ireland. The MU therefore sent a proportion of the PPL funds to the NIMA based on the number of members it had in relation to the number of MU members. The NIMA disbanded in 2001, at which point the MU began to recruit and organise in Northern Ireland.

Dances. In different ways both were significant pointers to the future use of the funds. The grant to an existing employer of musicians saw the Union's first action as a patron of music-making. The allocation of funds for May Day Dances was another statement, not just about solidarity with the labour movement, but also about live music. Branches had to use their allocation of money to employ live musicians, thus creating work.[36] Both contributions involved the direct or indirect subsidy of live music – something that was to become central to the allocation of the money from PPL.

In May 1959, the EC accepted the principle that 'a large proportion of the phonographic funds should be utilised in the direct promotion of employment for members' (MU, 2/1/15), but that year's Conference revealed some dissent about this plan. As articulated by Rudge, the issue was still centred around the ability of the funds to make donations to individual members, something that the EC and Ratcliffe strongly opposed, fearing that it might be 'said or alleged that the Union depended on the recording industry in any way' (MU, 2/1/15). Instead, the Union placed the emphasis on supporting live music in a number of ways, under the banner Keep Music Live – a slogan that was to become iconic. It was initially used on the cover of the Union's members' diary and turned into a stamp by the Manchester Branch in 1959, before the EC decided to issue similar ones to all branches (MU, 2/1/16).

Slowly, a system to apply for funding emerged through the district councils.[37] This created a barrage of applications and inevitable disgruntlement when proposals were rejected. Nevertheless, as well as further funding for producing diaries, organising May Day Dances,[38] and a range of Keep Music Live badges and stickers, the key development of the early 1960s was the awarding of further, more substantial grants to existing employers of musicians. For example, the RPO received £2,000 in 1963 and a further £3,000 in 1964, Scottish Opera received £2,000 in both 1963 and 1964, and the New Philharmonia received £2,000 in 1964. These set precedents in allowing organisations in financial crisis to approach the Union, but also created a level of administration, decision-making, and publicity for which it was ill equipped.

To deal with this it advertised in the June 1964 edition of the *Musician* for a new official to conduct the Keep Music Live campaign, and duly appointed Blain in January 1965. He represented a new type of official – considerably younger than the others and paid directly from the PPL funds – giving him a degree of autonomy within the Union. Blain reflected that 'I was never part

36 For more on the May Day Dances see www.muhistory.com/why-are-we-dancing-tonight/.

37 In exceptional circumstances national organisations could approach the EC directly.

38 The MU also supported an annual May Day Concert organised by the Labour Party at the Royal Festival Hall.

of mainstream MU activity. I was not involved in negotiations ... My job was to be ... running a committee that acted in a sense like a very, very mini Arts Council, recycling money to musical activity of all kinds' (*Blain 2012*).

Blain's arrival, to set up what became known as the Campaign for the Advance of Live Music (CALM) and what the *Musician* proclaimed as the Union's Live Music Year in 1966 (see Figure 13) was politically timely. It came at around the same time as the formation of the Standing Committee on the Employment of Musicians, Goodman's report on orchestral provision in London, and the Labour Government's *A policy for the arts* White Paper, all of which meant that debates around the employment of musicians and the subsidy of the arts were prominent in public discourse. In addition, the MU was supportive of – and connected with – the ruling Labour Government. It remained affiliated with the Labour Party and had close relations with Brian O'Malley, the Labour MP for Rotherham, who spoke on the Union's behalf in the House of Commons and briefly edited the *Musician*.[39]

Shortly after taking up the post, Blain described his aims as being 'to improve the quantity and quality of situations where the work of musicians may be heard' (*Musician*, January 1966: 11). He proceeded to lobby trades councils, local authorities, and other Unions to promote the cause of employing live musicians. This was partly a belated response to 'record dances', which Blain believed were now 'waning a little'. But he was also keen to ensure that the Campaign was a positive one and not just a continuation of the Union's gripes about recordings – 'there must be an expansionist side to our work'. At the heart of this was what he labelled 'propaganda and publicity to encourage the expansion of live music and entertainment' (*Musician*, January 1966: 11) and it was this, along with the patronage aspect of his activities, that made Blain an important and progressive force within the Union.[40]

The Campaign's launch highlighted two things internally. The first was that the growing importance of recorded music had done little to weaken the Union's view of the primacy of live music, the second that the Union was not fully united in such matters. Rudge, in particular, continued to snipe, telling *Melody Maker* in 1970 that the Campaign had deviated from its original aims, which he considered to be lobbying local authorities and dealing with the problem of recorded music (4 July 1970: 22). Despite such complaints, the Campaign and Blain remained integral parts of the Union's activities until the 1990s.

39 O'Malley was a part-time musician and had been an MU member prior to election. The Union contributed £1,000 to his election campaign from its political fund in 1963. It subsequently paid him for editing the *Musician* and contributed to his constituency party.

40 This was evident in Blain's frequent contributions to *Melody Maker* to reiterate the Union's stance that it was not 'anti-pop'. See, for example, *Melody Maker* (23 July: 8).

Figure 13 The *Musician* of January 1966 proclaims the year 'Live Music Year' to coincide with the launch of the Keep Music Live campaign and its Year of Live Music (MU, 1/5).

We now turn to the major challenges facing the Union during this period. Most of these are familiar and represent the consequences of the gains made by the Union in the post-war period. These can be seen in the connected areas of broadcasting, copyright, and competition.

Broadcasting

Despite the introduction of commercial television and much media discussion of commercial radio in other countries, the BBC retained its monopoly on radio broadcasting in the UK, while the relationship between it and the Union became increasingly complex. This mainly concerned the connected matters of employment for musicians and the use of recorded music in a context of mutual dependency. The connection between allocation of needletime and the employment of musicians[41] – and the ways in which the two were traded – is crucial to understanding the relationship between the Union and the Corporation.

The full story of the BBC–MU relationship is impossible to tell here. Much of it consisted of detailed and technical negotiations over pay and employment conditions. Occasionally disputes broke out that impacted on programmes and entered public consciousness. One example came in 1956, when the Union prevented members from taking part in any casual work in television or radio shows that were relayed or otherwise recorded during a dispute about fees for casually employed musicians.[42] This arose at a time when higher fees were being offered by ITV.

However, industrial relations were generally good. MU interviewees who had represented the Union in negotiations with the BBC all recalled the civilised manner in which they were conducted. Tschaikov (*2014*) noted that 'the catering arrangements were somewhat more salubrious than he had been [used to] and courteous; niceties were observed'. Patrick also told us that beyond formal negotiations, Ratcliffe had frequent informal contact with key BBC officials, something that is backed up by various documents in the BBC's WAC. He told us 'Hardie could ring up Arkell[43] and say "I think this is disgusting" and Arkell would say "OK, let's have a meeting about it." There was no heckling or shouting' (*Patrick 2014*).

The generally cordial relations were perhaps down to both necessity and the influence of a number of third parties to which each could attribute blame when things went astray. The MU and PPL routinely blamed each other whenever needletime negotiations stalled. But in the period after 1956 there were two important interventions by the Government that weakened the Union's negotiating position with the BBC in the longer term – the 1956 Copyright Act and, later, moves towards establishing commercial radio.

41 As early as 1957 Ratcliffe told PPL that the Union would allow the BBC more needletime if it gave guarantees about the number of musicians it would employ (MU, 2/1/14). A joint MU–PPL leaflet explaining the system for the public performance of records can be found in MRC, MS 271/t/27/1.

42 See WAC, R34/1222/1 for BBC preparations for the strike.

43 John Arkell, the BBC's Head of Administration.

Copyright

Ratcliffe expended considerable efforts in lobbying MPs over the proposed copyright legislation, but on its implementation admitted that 'although some amendments of the Bill were obtained, the representations of the Union did not in general succeed' (MU, 1/7/1957) and warned that 'some of the clauses in the new Act will adversely affect ... employment opportunities' (*Musician*, January 1957: 3). Two things in the Act particularly rankled the Union and the record companies. The first was its failure to 'create a copyright in records ... or in broadcast or television transmission as such' (MU, 1/7/1957) and the second was the formation of the PRT. While Ratcliffe conceded that the Act did formalise the right of the record companies to authorise or prohibit the public use of records, he worried that its implementation would make international lobbying for performers' rights more difficult and would make PPL less likely to act against those using records in public. Ratcliffe was the only Union official actively to address copyright matters at the time and, via FIM, was involved in the discussions organised by the International Labour Organization (ILO) that led to the Rome Convention of 1961. This recognised performers' rights to payment for the use of their recorded work in public, but allowed signatories to deal with this in different ways and was not enshrined in UK law until 1996 (see Chapter 8).

Following the 1956 Copyright Act there were numerous complaints from branches about the use of records in venues that had previously employed live bands. This forced Ratcliffe to admit in the early 1960s that the agreement was 'not working'. He blamed the PRT for this, arguing that they had placed PPL in a situation where 'they were no longer the deciding factor about the issuing of licences', meaning that 'they were no longer able to help the Union to the same extent' (*Musician*, January 1961: 17). These frustrations continued and Francis subsequently claimed that 'there have been many instances where PPL have been unable to operate their agreement with the Union by preventing the use of their members' records for public performance' (*Musician*, November 1962: 12).[44]

By the end of 1962 there had still been no referrals to the Tribunal. Nevertheless, PPL trod warily and employers – notably Mecca – used the threat of a referral as a means of deterring PPL from being too aggressive in their opposition to records being played. Importantly, PPL was a relatively small organisation with few resources to pursue the ever-expanding number of venues that were playing recorded music on their premises, but the

[44] PPL minutes from 1966 indicate that by then each complaint to the company was treated on its own merits.

record companies that owned it were highly aware of the commercial benefits of wider public exposure of their records, especially in respect of the youth market.

The PRT's real effects did not become evident until 1964 when the BBC threatened to use it in the deadlocked negotiations over increased needletime. A year later the Tribunal was called into action for the first time to rule on the needletime allocation for the UK's first legal commercial station, Manx Radio (see below, 172). This showed, first, the restraints that the PRT's existence placed on the Union's power apropos the BBC and, second, the threat that came via the weakening of the BBC's broadcasting monopoly – initially by pirate radio stations and eventually by the establishment of official commercial stations.

The story of pirate radio – the unregulated broadcast of pop music from offshore sites in the 1960s[45] – is told in much more detail by, among others, Chapman (1992), Johns (2009, 2011) and Stoller (2010a). Importantly, the availability (at least in some parts of the country[46]) of pop music on the radio presented a challenge to both the BBC and the Union. The lack of pop music on the BBC was partly responsible for the initial success of the pirates,[47] but more important was the shared belief of the Union and the BBC that the pirates were a precursor to the weakening of the BBC's radio monopoly. For the Union, Brian Blain acknowledged that 'a broadcasting system that makes no contribution to the existence of musicians cannot in any long term sense be in the interests of musicians' (1967: 14) and made a robust defence of the BBC, arguing that the best solution for all was more pop music on BBC radio.

Throughout this period, the Union's relationship with the BBC has to be viewed in the wider context of the needletime agreements reached in the post-war period. New agreements between PPL and the BBC in 1952 and 1958 had both increased the amount that BBC paid, but any concessions in terms of the number of hours of records allocated were minimal and hard-fought, with the Union remaining committed to limiting needletime and linking its use to guaranteed employment. When the 1958 agreement expired in 1963, PPL wrote to the BBC informing them that 'the representatives of the Musicians' Union are resolutely opposed to any increase in needletime' and suggesting that ignoring the Unions could precipitate 'an industrial dispute between the record industry and the MU' (WAC, R1014/184/2). Subsequently the new agreement saw a further increase in the fees the BBC paid for recorded music, with no addition to its needletime.

45 The first, Radio Caroline, launched in 1964.

46 Reception varied widely in different parts of the country.

47 In 1966, the Young Liberals had launched a 'Save Pop Radio' campaign and stickers appeared around the country declaring 'Hands off the pirates' and 'I want my Caroline' when the stations were threatened with closure.

This agreement was signed in November 1963, but was almost immediately challenged when the BBC applied to the PRT in January 1964 seeking an additional ninety-four hours per week. This was driven by two major considerations. The first was the Government's agreement to extend the number of hours that the Light and Third Programmes were permitted to broadcast.[48] The second was the pirates, whose emergence instigated wider political debates around the BBC's monopoly and the role of the commercial sector in broadcasting. For some time there had been increasing pressure to break the BBC monopoly, with the arguments first being made by R. H. Coase (1950) and enthusiastically picked up by the Institute of Economic Affairs (IEA),[49] which produced a number of reports throughout the 1960s. Pirate radio was central to this debate, and was a cause of tension within the new Conservative Government. Industry Secretary Edward Heath saw them as a 'fine piece of free enterprise', but the Postmaster General, Reginald Bevins, thought that action should be taken against them (Walker 1964). The latter view prevailed, but the forthcoming election campaign highlighted the Conservatives' enthusiasm for local radio broadcasting by the BBC and in the commercial sector.

In this context, the MU moved uncharacteristically quickly to reach agreement with the BBC. Fearful of the consequences of leaving any ruling to the Tribunal, it began the process of revising the needletime agreement it had achieved just a few months previously. With the Tribunal due to meet in June, the BBC withdrew its referral at the last minute and a new agreement was reached in November 1964. This granted the BBC the extra forty-seven hours a week noted above and was used for the Home Service.[50] While this was less than the BBC had sought, it still represented the Union's first considerable concession on needletime since 1947.

This enforced rethink by the Union was a strategic one brought about by the possibility of the Tribunal loosening all needletime restrictions. In agreeing to the forty-seven hours, it had made explicit the connection between needletime and employment opportunities, and used the BBC's commitment to live musicians to achieve a number of concessions. These were detailed in a lengthy press statement issued by the BBC and MU when the extra allocation was announced. They included the guarantees from the BBC noted above, including the formation of the Training Orchestra and establishing

48 The Third Programme had previously only broadcast in the evenings.

49 A free-market think-tank. Meanwhile the MU wrote to the Government in 1966 supporting the BBC's monopoly (WAC, R78/2, 563/1).

50 It also granted an extra five hours of needletime for BBC Television (now eight hours) in return for an extra £172,000.

the Standing Committee on the Employment of Musicians alongside other orchestral employers and the MU.[51]

When the Isle of Man Government gave permission for Manx Radio to become the first commercial radio station in the UK in May 1964, the station had to begin negotiations with PPL for a licence to play records.[52] This was a unique station, limited to the Isle of Man, and not covered under previous PPL licences. The Tribunal was asked to rule on its application. Its decision would set precedents not only for PPL, but also for the BBC and MU, both of which were represented at the hearing as interested parties. The BBC wanted to ensure that Manx Radio did not get proportionately more needletime than it had, while the MU was reportedly 'opposed on principle to any extension of broadcasting on records as damaging to the livelihood and ultimately to the existence of a sound musical profession' (*Edinburgh Gazette*, 11 June 1965: 401). However, the Tribunal awarded the station forty-two hours needletime a week and ordered PPL and the BBC to pay the majority of the station's legal costs.[53]

The Tribunal's ruling meant that the Union's protestations were ignored and that the BBC and PPL had to be cautious in future situations involving it. However, the next big issue in broadcasting – how to deal with the pirate stations – was largely negotiated between the Union, the Government, and the BBC with relatively little involvement from PPL and none from the PRT. The Labour Government elected in 1964[54] had moved towards Bevins' stance that legislation had to be introduced, effectively to outlaw the pirate stations.

This was duly delivered via the Marine &c. Broadcasting (Offences) Act of 1967, which made supplying or financially supporting the offshore stations illegal. The consequent loss of advertising revenues put most of them out of business.[55] However, there was political recognition that their audiences – who had turned to the pirate stations to hear the pop records that were in scarce supply on the BBC because of needletime – needed to be catered for. The settlement involved a rearranging of the BBC's radio output, with the launch of Radio 1 (a pop station) and Radio 2 (the successor to the Light Programme) on 30 September 1967.

The Union, PPL, and BBC had to reach a further agreement that would allow the new station sufficient needletime to play, if not 'continuous pop',

51 Initially PPL provided funds for this. When it withdrew this funding in 1967 it noted that it had no objection to the MU using the 'phonographic funds' for this purpose.

52 The Isle of Man Government had separate broadcasting laws from the rest of the UK, but the station had to be approved by the UK Post Office to be allowed to broadcast.

53 In its submission PPL had offered twenty-four hours. See Stoller (2010a: 183) for more.

54 It was re-elected in 1966.

55 Some, like Radio Caroline, continued to broadcast.

then at least enough to compensate audiences for losing the pirates.[56] As ever, the Union drove a hard bargain that did little to assist the BBC's attempts to provide a viable alternative pop station. With the Union's approval, PPL agreed to an extra seven hours of needletime for the proposed Radio 1. However, in addition to PPL securing extra fees, the Union made the BBC commit to various things, including spending an extra £250,000 on the employment of musicians, introducing a five-day week for all BBC orchestras, and increased fees for casually employed musicians should the licence fee rise (WAC, R101/226/1).[57]

While the new hours were sufficient to get the new stations up and running, the fix was unsatisfactory for the BBC, and acceptable to the MU only as part of its attempts to delay the onset of commercial radio. The launch of Radio 1 received a tepid response. The *NME* called it 'better than we'd dare hope for' and 'good in patches' (7 October 1967: 7), while the new BBC DJs Tony Blackburn, Kenny Everett, and John Peel all went into print condemning the needletime restrictions – much to Ratcliffe's annoyance.[58]

Blain attempted to explain the MU's stance towards both pirate radio and the BBC's involvement with pop music. While accepting that certain MU members owed some of their success to exposure on the pirates, he nevertheless condemned them, arguing that 'a broadcasting system that makes no contribution to the existence of musicians cannot in any long-term sense be in the interest of musicians'. Blain suggested that the BBC had 'opened up opportunities for a wide range of popular music to be performed' and that more pop music on the BBC 'would seem to me to be a very real gain for musicians, and in the long run, the public – a much more positive achievement than two hundred local radio stations equipped with a couple of turntables and a disc jockey' (*Musician*, January 1967: 14). Blain's article expounded both the ideological and practical reasons for the Union's continued alignment to the BBC and effectively set out its stall in the arguments over commercial radio that were to dominate the next two decades.

While the de facto end of pirate radio and the launch of Radio 1 further cemented the ties between the Union and the BBC,[59] tensions remained. Some

56 The *Radio Times* of 5 October 1966 carried an article entitled 'Why no continuous pop', which explained the limitations the Corporation was under. On 4 July 1968 it published an article called 'Record restraint', which again sought to explain the system.

57 The BBC took a case to the PRT over PRS rates for Radio 1 and considered doing the same for more needletime (WAC, R104/19/1). See Briggs (1995: 573) for more on the run-up to Radio 1.

58 See Cloonan (2013). The MU also objected to the station's use of jingles made overseas (WAC, R78/2, 563/1).

59 For example, in October 1967 Frank Gillard, the BBC's Director of Radio, wrote to the Union assuring it that 'We believe that broadcasting should do its utmost to promote the good health of those professions on which it heavily depends. We believe that the excessive use of commercial gramophone records in broadcasting is a trend which is injurious to the music profession and must be resisted' (WAC, R78/2, 536/1).

of these were along musical lines, and in both organisations there were moves to separate classical and non-classical musicians. In the MU, this became more of an issue after the VAF merged with Equity in 1967, at a time when the MU was still perceived as being anti-pop by many involved in the pop scene. With Francis claiming that 'many of the young musicians in the pop field are quite irresponsible people' (*Melody Maker*, 6 April 1968: 17), the Union did not seem like their natural home. However, the most visible signs of discontent came from the other side of the profession when members of the English Chamber Orchestra led some short-lived moves, involving the ISM, to split the Union into classical and non-classical sections, having been called out on strike against their wishes. The *Observer* reported dissatisfaction with the 'Union's closed shop policy for orchestras' and a sense among classical musicians that 'the rules which govern the employment of the majority of musicians are often incompatible with the artistic interests of the minority' (21 December 1969: 3).

In the BBC, the split was among senior managers dealing with the Union's continued influence. Discussions immediately prior to the formation of Radio 1 saw the BBC's Head of Copyright, R. G. Walford,[60] arguing both that the Corporation should return to the PRT to increase its needletime allocation and that it should 'make a case for two separate allocations of needletime – serious and pop'. He also suggested that the BBC had never recognised the MU for pop musicians many of whom, he had been told, previously joined the VAF as entertainers (WAC, R126/394/1). In 1969 the BBC's Managing Director of Radio, Frank Gillard, complained of the MU's 'iron hold' on needletime (WAC, R126/394/1).

However, prior to the publication of *Broadcasting in the Seventies* the MU had done a remarkable job in shaping the discourse around orchestral provision in the UK. It had also created a protected, well-paid, and in some instances under-utilised group of orchestral musicians, especially in the BBC orchestras. But by linking orchestral employment to needletime, continuing its endorsement of live performance over the routinely dismissed 'canned music', and tying itself to the BBC while opposing commercial radio, the Union had distanced itself from the needs of many musicians.

Competition and exchanging musicians

The last of the Union's breakthroughs in 1955 was the establishment of reciprocal exchanges with the AFM. This was agreed from a relatively weak

60 Walford would later write an influential BBC memo called 'Radio's bridle: A plain man's guide to needletime' (1971).

position, as the demand for British musicians in the USA was considerably less than the demand for American stars in the UK. It was therefore seemingly inevitable that the operation of the exchange scheme would be one that was peppered with problems, especially as it struggled to adapt to the changes in the musical world and audience demands in both countries.

The issues were initially logistic rather than conceptual. The terms of the exchanges meant that the touring bands had to play an equivalent number of shows and over-zealous promoters sought to maximise the opportunities afforded to them. When Kenton and Heath each duly visited the other's home country with their respective bands in 1956, the workload, travel, and pay and conditions for individual band members were all highlighted in subsequent reports. In the UK, Kenton's band played sixty-two shows in thirty-three days, resulting in complaints from the musicians and an over-saturation of the market for the promoters. In the USA, Heath had the further problems of distance and demand. Longer journeys and having to share bills with Nat 'King' Cole, led some to believe that the British bands were getting a raw deal in the exchanges.

Following the Kenton–Heath exchange, six further exchanges were organised in 1956.[61] But before the year was out, Leonard Feather, Payne, and others had lined up in the press to criticise what they saw as the inequity in the conditions for British bands touring the USA. Those involved in promoting the shows on both sides of the Atlantic were quick to respond. Harold Davison, the impresario behind many of the exchanges, argued that 'the demand for concert tours of America – even by top [British] names – is virtually non-existent' and asked for the exchange scheme to be given a chance. Joe Glaser, the agent behind the some of the US shows, was more forceful, saying that the MU 'should be grateful' for Ted Heath's Band being afforded the chance to tour with Cole and stating that the problem with a later exchange between Freddy Randall and Louis Armstrong was that 'it's trying to put a boy like Randall on an equal footing with Louis Armstrong' (*Melody Maker*, 27 October 1956: 7).

The domination of the early exchanges by large ensembles saw some American acts[62] circumnavigating the rules by visiting as variety artists (rather than as musicians) and being accompanied by British musicians. By the time Chris Barber's Band visited the USA in 1959,[63] the number of exchanges had decreased, with only three taking place in 1958. This was attributed to

[61] These included a second exchange for Ted Heath's Orchestra, this time with Count Basie's Orchestra coming to the UK. While these were mainly based around jazz and big bands, Bill Haley and the Comets were paired with Lonnie Donegan's band.

[62] Such as Sister Rosetta Tharpe, Sonny Terry, and Brownie McGhee, who toured in 1957/58 at the instigation of Harold Pendleton and Chris Barber.

[63] In exchange for the Woody Herman Band and George Lewis touring in Britain.

the lack of demand for British bands in the USA and the fact that the most in-demand American ones could earn far more at home than they could by touring abroad (*Melody Maker*, 6 June 1959: 6). Though Barber's tour was a success,[64] this was largely a result of a relaxation of the rules on the types of venues that could be used by exchange artists. Barber (*2013*) told us that some previous tours by British bands had consisted of 'sitting in a hotel in New York for four weeks and then returning home and saying what a great tour they'd had', but that connections between Harold Pendleton and Woody Herman's agent, Abe Turchan, had ensured worthwhile and properly remunerated tours for both acts.

If the addition of non-concert-hall venues had helped small jazz groups like Barber's to contemplate exchanges, it also opened up a potential market in other types of tours. Also in 1959, *Melody Maker* announced that 'America opens its show palace doors' (31 January 1959: 1) and that Frankie Vaughan was to appear at the Copacabana Club in New York. This facilitated exchanges by popular acts of all musical genres, something that was later to tilt the balance of power in the exchange relationship away from the AFM.

This happened around 1963/64 when the demand for British pop bands in the USA began to exceed that for American musicians in the UK. With such a threat to its power, the AFM made strenuous attempts to block tours by British acts because of what Roberts describes as 'two overlapping issues, an economic one and a cultural one' (2010: 7). Roberts (2010, 2014) details how the AFM lobbied the US Government to refuse visas to incoming acts that were, in its view, of insufficient cultural merit and whose sole justification for being in the country was commercial. Echoing some of the language used by the MU a decade earlier, a report in *Billboard* in March 1964 noted that 'an invasion of British musical groups on the US personal appearance scene' was 'disturbing' the AFM and that they were 'mulling some sort of action to halt the "Redcoat" invasion, or at least bring about a more equitable arrangement by sending more Yankee musicians to Great Britain' (28 March 1964: 10).

The British Union were marginally more pragmatic in its approach to pop musicians than their US counterparts. Despite AFM President Herman Kenin's protestations to the US Department of Labor that the Beatles and their peers were not unique and that their appearances in the USA should therefore be opposed, the AFM was unable to secure a blanket ban on British groups. Increasingly, package tours of three or four British groups visited the USA in return for American orchestras (or large ensembles) playing the UK. The AFM was still able to obstruct individual tours, however, with 1965

64 Barber enjoyed a hit single, 'Petite Feur', and later appeared on the Ed Sullivan Show.

marking something of a nadir in this regard. The year started with the *NME* announcing that 'the US government is putting an end to American tours by British groups – and this time their action is official' (1 January 1965: 6). It cited problems with tours by the Zombies, the Hullaballoos, and the Nashville Teens[65] as the US authorities – under AFM pressure – ruled that various British bands were not of sufficient artistic merit to warrant the necessary work visas to tour.

On their return the Nashville Teens urged the MU to impose a ban on all American bands visiting the UK until matters were sorted out with the AFM and the US authorities. The band's John Hawken protested that 'the Americans have had a monopoly here for so long, and now when British groups get popular over there, they don't like it' (*Melody Maker*, 6 March 1965: 13). The MU did little to support the groups, and although the exchanges were stopped for a week later in the year, this was the result of conditions imposed by the US promoters rather than the refusal of visas to British bands.

However, the music papers remained full of instances of both UK and US acts whose touring plans had been adversely affected by the various regulations imposed on live shows or broadcast appearances.[66] Importantly for the MU, the exchange system ensured that they retained a stake in the decision-making process. When challenged in 1968 about its continued suitability, Harry Francis argued that not only should it remain in place but 'it needs to be operated much more rigidly than it is, it has become much too fluid in recent times' (*Melody Maker*, 30 March 1968: 12). A year later, the MU's executive reviewed its policy in this area, something that served to highlight the number of exchanges now taking place and resulted in a further bureaucratisation of the scheme.[67] This included new rules that future exchanges should 'consist of groups of similar size and generally similar type and of similar number of man engagements' (MU, 1/7/1971). In addition, broadcast appearances were excluded, members of the bands taking part had to be members of the MU for six months, and applicants (usually agents or promoters) had to pay the Union a £50 administration fee.

Despite such problems, the exchange scheme survived, with various amendments, into the 1980s. However, the gradual internationalisation of the

65 These bands had travelled to the USA on H2 visas to allow them to do promotional work in New York. It was expected that upon arrival these would be upgraded to H1 visas allowing them to tour, but these were rejected.

66 Sandie Shaw, the Byrds, the Kinks, Sammy Davis Jr, and Wilson Pickett were among those reported at various points between 1964 and 1969 as having problems.

67 The year 1969 saw seventy-two separate exchanges with the USA, with the British bands generating $2.8 million in fees. In 1970 there were eighty-four exchanges and $3.9 million in fees (MU, 1/7/1971).

music industries (especially with the success of British bands abroad) ensured that discourse around the problem of foreign musicians working in the UK decreased in volume during the period of its operation.

Conclusion

In examining the changes in the music profession in parallel with those in the Union, this chapter has shown significant change in the music profession, juxtaposed with relative stagnation in the Union. Notably, new musical styles found an increasingly wide range of musicians entering the profession, many of them operating in small groups or ensembles, distinct from the orchestras and big bands that had been the Union's traditional backbone. In addition, many of them were to become reliant on both the recording industry and an international marketplace to build their careers, putting them at odds with the MU, whose efforts had focused on limiting both activities. However, it was not only the new types of music and their commercial and industrial exploitation that concerned the Union during this period. For the first time, questions were being asked about the sustainability of orchestras. Having enjoyed the benefits of near continuous growth since the 1920s, and the patronage of the BBC, the Arts Council and local authorities, such an interrogation, even in the wider context of increased Government support for the arts, caused considerable concern within the Union.

When faced with having to respond to such dramatic changes it is easy to portray the Union's response in a largely negative light – especially given the frequently reactionary utterings from its ageing leaders, the perception that it had been a barrier to technological and industrial progress, and its efforts to restrict the free international movement of musicians. However, it would be remiss to ignore the context for the MU's policies.

Empowered by the agreements it bartered in the post-war period, the Union maintained orchestral employment (and increased pay) in the BBC and beyond. It also continued to act as an important restraint on the BBC (via needletime), the record companies and commercial operators in the ballroom and nightclub businesses (via the PPL agreement), and concert promoters and agents (via the reciprocal exchange scheme). With the election of a Labour Government in 1964, it was able to exert some influence over policy, particularly around moves to break the BBC's radio monopoly. So, while the Union sometimes appeared out of step with the times, it enjoyed considerable power despite repeated challenges by bodies such as the PRT and BBC management. Its ability to resist was partly a result of steady membership levels, dogmatic negotiation backed up by strike threats, and the strategic use of the 'phonographic funds'.

Nevertheless, Ratcliffe bequeathed John Morton a number of daunting challenges following Morton's election as GS in June 1970. Aware that the Union had failed to deliver the same kind of benefits for its members working in popular music as it had for those in more traditional forms of musical employment, Morton recognised that the Union needed varying degrees of modernisation in outlook, personnel, and structure. These would happen gradually, but were often of secondary importance to pressing external issues. While a number of issues were familiar, the 1970 election of a Conservative Government committed to legislation to limit trade union power and advance commercial radio meant that Morton would face a different set of challenges.

7

The John Morton years: 1971–1990

When John Morton took over as General Secretary at the start of 1971, he had a number of advantages over his immediate predecessor.[1] Having convincingly defeated his two older opponents in the previous year's election, he arrived with a strong mandate for change and was the first leader to have worked outside the music profession. He began his trade union life as a sixteen-year-old printer, joining the Typographical Association during the war and the MU in 1946 as a semi-pro piano player working in the Midlands.

Morton progressed through various levels of Union work, serving as Branch Chairman and Secretary in Wolverhampton and a member of the Midlands District Council before being elected to the EC in the late 1950s. He continued to work as a musician before giving up playing professionally to become a paid MU official as Birmingham Branch Secretary.[2] In 1962 Morton began working in further education, teaching industrial relations at Solihull College, while remaining active within the Union. Significantly, his education work gave him a detailed insight into the way other unions operated and shaped his thinking about the MU's place in the wider world.

Morton reported that his aims on being elected were to achieve 'full organisation [within the profession], recognition and respect within the trade union movement, international involvement and respect and the ability to deal with the highly technical copyright issues' (*2014*). He also hoped to unite the MU with other performers' unions in order to strengthen it (a plan he subsequently had to abandon). However, the Union now had a leader who saw its place in a wider context and whose understanding of copyright was invaluable both during his tenure and beyond. Additionally, his time as a working

[1] He was elected in 1970 and took power on 1 January 1971.

[2] All full-time officials of the Union were required to stop playing professionally on taking up post.

musician, lecturer, and activist gave him greater insight into the working lives of contemporary musicians than his predecessors had held.

Coupled with personnel changes in the Union, this left Morton in a better position to effect internal restructuring. However, there remained a number of external threats to the Union's power. Morton was elected in the same month as a Conservative Government and was to spend all but five years of his twenty-year tenure working under one. The steady dissolution of the post-War political consensus was to have huge implications for the wider union movement and some very specific ones for the MU. Morton's period in office was dominated by four major, inter-connected challenges to the Union's existing sphere of influence: the arrival of commercial radio in 1973; a further threat to employment in the BBC orchestras, culminating in a strike in 1980; the referral by the Association of Independent Radio Contractors (AIRC) to the PRT in the same year; and an investigation into collective licensing by the Monopolies and Mergers Commission (MMC) in 1988. Significantly, all were connected to broadcasting.

The first part of this chapter concentrates on the developments within the Union, particularly with regard to its outlook and personnel. The second focuses on the aforementioned challenges to its power, placing them in the wider political context. We argue that a mixture of pragmatic negotiation and dogmatic defence of the belief in the primacy of live music enabled the Union to remain powerful throughout Morton's tenure. This was not an insignificant achievement.

The changing MU

Faced with major external changes the MU under Morton's leadership had to adjust internally to reflect both the changing nature of its membership and pressures from both the Government and employers. In both instances Morton's influence on the Union's agenda and tactics – rather than initiatives from members – was the single most important factor in ensuring some degree of institutional change. This was particularly the case in popular music, where members in pop groups had a very different relationship with their Union than those in orchestras and other ensembles.

We show how the MU became more outward-looking and how its officials adapted to the growth of the recording industry and the increasing number of its members who made the majority of their income from recording. In its attempts to modernise, the MU made a number of moves that could be seen as more inclusive and supportive of the increasing proportion of members who were involved in popular music,[3] particularly in appointing officials to deal with session musicians and to organise pop groups. While the Union's leaders no longer felt that that pop groups were either a passing fad or musically of less value than their orchestral counterparts, they still made for uncomfortable bedfellows, and a combination of residual musical snobbery and the fact that pop musicians were virtually unrepresented in the Union's hierarchy[4] meant that the tension between different types of musicians was an issue for much of the 1970s and 1980s.

Morton's ambition for the Union to be more influential across the British trade union movement and beyond was apparent from the start of his period as GS, and could be partially attributed to his views on the importance of copyright and performers' rights. Aware that, in terms of the law, performers were viewed as something of a homogeneous mass and that copyright regimes were shaped internationally rather than nationally, Morton sought to cultivate alliances with the other unions representing performers in the UK, while using his role as FIM's President[5] to become an influential voice for musicians within the deliberations of the World Intellectual Property Organization (WIPO) and the International Labour Organization (ILO).

Some moves towards wider co-operation among the entertainment unions pre-dated Morton's term, with the formation of a Confederation of Entertainment Unions in 1968. As one of nine unions involved, the MU played a relatively minor role, and the confederation's main concerns were films, broadcasting, and the theatre, rather than music per se. However, the Confederation highlighted the possibility of collaboration and was something of a tentative precursor of the trade union mergers that became characteristic of subsequent decades.

Having found himself as 'the main spokesman for [all] performers at the WIPO and ILO', Morton's instinct was that actors and musicians had 'so many interests in common' that a merger would be advantageous. He now admits that in the early 1970s he had 'a very ambitious notion … which I had to abandon, which was to get a performers' union, consisting of Equity and ourselves' (*2014*). Such a vision met with both internal and external opposition.

Both Equity and some MU members voiced their opposition to such suggestions, and when it became clear that merger was not an option, Morton used

[3] In 1975 Brian Blain estimated that around a third of Union members were involved in pop and rock music (*Melody Maker*, 1 March 1975: 36).

[4] There was an almost complete dearth of musicians from popular music backgrounds in Union positions during the period, partly resulting from their working practices, which did not mirror the members' committee system prevalent in orchestras. Put simply, orchestras had stewards, pop groups didn't.

[5] Morton was President of FIM between 1973 and 2002 and is now its President Emeritus.

his good relations with Equity's GS, Peter Plouviez, to form the Performers' Alliance in 1976. At its launch, both Morton and Plouviez stressed that it was not a merger and that both unions would retain their individual identities (*The Times*, 2 July 1976: 2). The Writers' Guild later joined the Alliance, and it remains a tripartite lobbying organisation, with an all-party group in Parliament. Morton became more involved with the TUC than his immediate predecessors, spending a number of years as a member of its GC, attempting both to make the problems of the music profession more widely known and to achieve greater political influence.

He was a natural alliance builder and the products of this resulted in some of the most fundamental changes under his leadership. These were evident in the internal restructuring of the Union and attempts, via new staff, to enfranchise those musicians with whom it had previously struggled to engage. Furthermore, once in office, he moved quickly to revitalise the Union through a mixture of enforced and calculated changes in personnel, which were to shape both perceptions of the MU and its future activities. After Ted Anstey retired in 1969, Harry Francis moved to AGS before retiring in 1973. Two new Assistant Secretaries, Jack Stoddart and Ben Norris (see Figure 14),[6] took over the responsibilities of Anstey and later Francis, while Brian Blain remained an important figure via his supervision of the Keep Music Live campaign's developing portfolio of patronage and music development activities. Overall, after 1973, the age profile of the Union's leadership was greatly reduced, though this did not always manifest itself in a greater sensitivity to the specific needs of the new type of musicians detailed above. The appointments of Don Smith and Mike Evans during the 1970s were also significant, as both played key roles in the Union's expanding range of activities. Their work was further evidence of the Union's attempts to adapt to the changing nature of the music profession.

Smith, a Canadian who had moved to the UK to study at the Royal College of Music (RCM) in 1956, became a full-time official for Central London in 1969 and was appointed Session Organiser in 1971. Apart from recognising the importance of recording and, in particular, looking after the session musicians working in the recording, film, and TV industries, Smith's position was as something of an enforcer of the Union's many rules surrounding recording sessions and their uses, a job he did until 1998. His work earned him a number of successes for musicians but the enmity of many employers and the press, where he was labelled 'Doctor Death'.

[6] Stan Hibbert was added as an Assistant Secretary in 1973 when Francis retired as AGS. He and Norris remained as Assistant Secretaries (with no AGS) until after Norris's departure in 1981, when Stoddart was promoted to AGS. Hibbert remained as Assistant Secretary.

Figure 14 The Union Secretariat in 1971 – from left: Harry Francis, John Morton, Ben Norris, and Jack Stoddart (MU, 5/2).

Smith's major spheres of influence were in broadcasting and film. At the BBC he was a regular at recordings of the *Top of the Pops* television programme,[7] ensuring that the ban on miming – which the Union imposed in 1966 (*NME*, 30 June 1966: 7) – was observed. Believing that miming to records on television put musicians out of work, the MU insisted that if they did so, it had to be to a re-recorded backing track, thus creating session fees for the musicians involved. Though this created employment, it also presented all kinds of practical problems, with record companies trying to circumvent the rules and Smith trying to figure out when they did so.

More controversially, later in his MU career, Smith was at the centre of interest from *The Sunday Times*, which investigated what it described as his 'awesome power' over recording practices in the film and television industries (Sutherland 1988). As well as citing examples of Union fees and conditions being considered prohibitive for production companies, the article emphasised Government ministers' concern about 'working practices in the Musicians' Union' (Sutherland 1988) and highlighted the growing use of Eastern European orchestras to record Hollywood film soundtracks that would have previously been recorded in the UK. While this partly reflected wider media and Government attacks on trade unions during this period, it also highlighted tensions among different groups of musicians within the Union.

Those musicians who earned most from recording became disgruntled, both with what they saw as the loss of work resulting from the Union's terms

[7] *Top of the Pops* was a chart-based BBC television show that ran weekly from 1964 to 2006 drawing large audiences.

and conditions and with the distribution of the funds that their recordings generated. The first rumblings of unrest came in 1987 when a number of recording musicians, under the leadership of Tristan Fry, organised under the banner of the Guild of Professional Musicians.[8] Fry stressed that 'in case it is thought that any "breakaway" union is intended, I wish to make it quite clear that it is understood between the guild and the Union's General Secretary, John Morton, that the guild continues to operate strictly in accordance with the Musicians' Union's guidelines' (*The Times*, 14 May 1987: 15). However, his supporters' rhetoric showed the scale of the MU's problems. Producer Mike Batt claimed that 'the Union is pledged to the slogan "Keep music live", but they are killing it off – they're keeping it dead' (Davison 1988). While the MU was eventually able to see the Guild off, it represented perhaps the most viable of the periodic threats to the Union's position as the largest and most powerful musicians' organisation in the UK. Morton clearly took it seriously, saying:

> They spent quite a bit of money. They got themselves an American lawyer and he asked for a meeting and came to see me. And it was obvious what he had done. He had looked at a previous split in the AFM and had looked at us carefully and the possibility of recreating that situation here. I tried to explain to him that it wasn't going to happen and we would always be able to see it off. (*2014*)

Despite gathering several hundred members among the top session players – and having generated what Morton described as 'quite a substantial sum' (*2014*) – the Guild floundered. But its presence foreshadowed the problems the MU would face in the 1990s. Morton attributes much of the MU's ability to resist the Guild to the good relationship Smith had built up with the more successful (and generally London-based) session musicians. However, its formation highlighted how, as the music profession had fragmented since the 1960s, the Union faced an increasingly difficult task in preserving itself as a unified body representing the needs of all musicians.

At the heart of this were the Union's efforts to organise effectively in what its documentation referred to as the 'Group' field. Since the late 1960s, attempts had been made to enhance the Union's reputation with musicians in genres, such as pop, rock, jazz, and reggae, where it was subject to regular criticism. Brian Blain was often the public face of the Union's interactions with jazz and popular music and faced robust criticism from musicians in

[8] A well-known session musician, Fry began as a percussionist in the LSO and played on a wide range of pop records and film and television soundtracks.

these fields via a music press that questioned the Union's relevance. In 1973, during controversy surrounding the work permit for the Faces' Japanese bassist, Tetsu Yamauchi, *NME* asked 'how long can Britain's vast number of rock musicians continue to allow themselves to be represented by a Union so ridiculously out of step with its contemporary needs?' (23 August 1973: 18). Two years later Blain had to defend the Union in *Melody Maker* over three pages of attack from an array of musicians including Edgar Broughton, Russ Ballard, and Barbara Thompson. Discontent focused on the exchange system, the Union's leftist politics and the sense that its officials had 'their hearts irrevocably locked in the era of the Palais band', that 'you pay and there's nothing done for you', and – most damningly – 'the Union didn't help me, it hindered me' (1 March 1975: 36–8).

Overall it was clear that many musicians saw the MU as an obstruction to their activities. Meanwhile the Union was just as suspicious about the more commercial end of the music industries and was, with some justification, perceived as resistant to popular musicians. For example, although the Union had complained about the nature of contracts offered by the recording companies and the exploitation of pop groups, it did not initially see it as part of its job to interfere on such musicians' behalf. But in the mid-1970s, music press criticism and the changing nature of the membership saw the Union take a number of proactive measures to address the situation.

These began tentatively with a number of 'Rock Workshops' that Blain organised (using the PPL funds) around various branches from 1973 onwards. If these were something of an uncomfortable clash of cultures, they at least illustrated that the previous genre hierarchies were finally being challenged in some parts of the Union. The workshops, and their associated bands, continued to be a feature of MU activity for a further two decades. During that time, the Union became much more interested in the industrial – rather than musical – aspects of popular music, and made another significant appointment when Evans joined as 'Rock Organiser' in 1977, holding the position for seven years. He had collaborated with the Union after forming an organisation called the Music Liberation Front in his native Liverpool, and had worked with Blain on a number of events including programming a tent featuring performances and demonstrations at the Bickershaw Festival in 1972.[9] Moving to London to work as a music journalist in 1976, he took the job at the Union after encouragement from Blain.

[9] This festival in the north-west of England featured the Grateful Dead, the Kinks, Captain Beefheart, and others.

Along with his most obvious allies in the Union (Blain and Smith), Evans made some progress in shifting perceptions. However, he now believes that he was in an invidious position. Though the workshops continued, he observes that they 'kind of suited the MU's idea of what a rock 'n' roll musician should be like – they didn't want any hairy-arsed blokes shouting and swearing' (*2013*). He concedes that they were of a high quality, and though the Union remained 'slightly out of touch it was certainly a lot nearer than it had been' (*2013*). As well as running the workshops, Evans generated good publicity for the MU on a number of campaigns – notably securing a fixed fee for support bands at the Marquee (*NME*, 21 September 1978: 3) – and offered advice to numerous musicians. For the first time, the MU showed an interest in recording contracts. Evans recalled:

> Half the problems with the rock musicians were the contracts. So I set up a contracts service where we got a showbiz lawyer onside and he was on a retainer and would look over all the contracts that hapless musicians brought to me. All sorts of people came in and went through this contract scheme. I remember Glen Matlock when he got kicked out of the Sex Pistols and Annie Lennox and Dave Stewart from the Tourists, before they formed Eurythmics … There were all these people from that scene coming along with their tales of woe. (*2013*)

If these represented successes, Evans was never a natural union official and found himself estranged from both former friends in bands and the music industries. His post included responsibility for the American exchange scheme, which was a continuing cause of problems for the very musicians Evans wanted to assist. He left in 1984 and around this time the EC proposed a review 'of the Union's arrangements in the Group Field', explaining that:

> The Committee now feels that further impetus needs to be given to the adaptation of the Union as a whole to changes in popular music and musicians. A substantial proportion of the Union's membership now performs in Groups of different kinds. Union organisation in certain areas of the music industry, the development of relevant Union services and the Union's public relations activities have all contributed to substantial recruitment of 'Group' musicians but there does not appear to be a corresponding degree of involvement of newer members in Union activity. (MU, 1/7/1983)

The solutions proffered were familiar ones, with mention of 'consultative arrangement', 'further information and advice to branches', and the provision of 'special workshops' (MU, 1/7/1983). Moves towards achieving these objectives were managed by a number of officials, including Blain and Jan Ford, the Union's first full-time female official, who was appointed Employment Promotion Officer in 1981.[10] Ultimately, it was Mark Melton – appointed Music Business Advisor in 1987 – who carried on and developed the work that Evans began, developing a Contract Advisory Scheme (CAS) and being given a regular platform in the *Musician* to write on issues surrounding the music industries that were likely to be of interest to pop musicians.

Melton (*2012*) saw his role as re-enfranchising 'a section of the membership that they would refer to as "the rock musicians" or "the young kids"', seeing this as a problem related to the Union's lingering attitude towards recorded music. He set about making the Union's work more inclusive and attractive to recording artists. Notably, Melton did not find the kind of problems that had hampered Evans, and said of his fellow officials 'I think they could see how things needed to be changed, because they were at the sharp end of it. Most of my colleagues were middle-aged. Some of them were reaching retirement and I was twenty-eight, but they made me feel welcome and did everything they could to help' (*2012*).

The Union also held a number of advice sessions in London and elsewhere, led by Melton, who was careful to include potential members who had been doubly disenfranchised – on the grounds of ethnicity or the type of music they made. He recalls holding packed sessions on negotiating contracts at the Union's headquarters in London, and the impact having so many young musicians in attendance had on the officials.

> It was absolutely packed and colleagues of mine who attended were absolutely stunned because they had never seen so many young people in the room. I remember John Morton, who is a man of real poise and dignity, getting up to address this group of musicians, and maybe 50 per cent of them were young black kids, and he was trembling. I'd never seen him like that before. He could command a room easily but … it was a real watershed. (*2012*)

If this offered evidence of the Union doing its best to adapt to changing musical cultures, there was further evidence of a desire to embrace a wider constituency of musicians. Melton recalls advising a number of DJs and producers, whose activities had previously been viewed with a mixture of hostility or suspicion, largely on the grounds that they were using technology (for example synthesisers, samplers, and turntables), which was regarded as reducing employment opportunities for live musicians. On occasion this

[10] Her job was largely to police the PPL agreement with unrecorded uses of recorded music in discos and to encourage employment of musicians.

could provide some humorous interludes. For example, Melton (*2012*) told us of how he and future colleague Horace Trubridge[11] attended a rave in the north-east: 'we were in our early thirties and no-one else there was over the age of nineteen. We were completely out of place. People were looking at us and I think Horace had a sheepskin coat on. I think they thought we were the Drug Squad.' Nevertheless, their attendance betrays some serious points. Not only was the Union finding ways of reaching new audiences and potential members, it was also employing new people and ways of doing so. Besides organising and participating in a number of music-industry-related workshops and events around the country,[12] Melton and Trubridge collaborated on the promotion of the Institute of Contemporary Arts (ICA) Rock Weeks in 1989 and 1991,[13] and were later involved in *Sound City*, a series of gigs and seminars held each year in different locations around the UK.[14]

Commercial radio broadcasting

Morton's attempts to change the Union internally were repeatedly disrupted by far larger external events. These challenges – both philosophical and specific – were evident from early in his tenure. His predecessor had benefited from serving during a period of post-war political consensus in which trade unions were widely regarded, by both governing parties, as being a positive force. This changed with the election of the Heath (1970–74) and Thatcher (1979–90) Governments, whose philosophies and trade union legislation represented a considerable challenge to the MU's organisation and modus operandi. This was particularly evident in broadcasting, and it was here that the MU came to fight its major battles during the 1970s and 1980s.

The abolition of the pirate stations and the launch of Radio 1 in 1967 had provided the Union with some relief in its opposition to the type of commercial radio stations that had increasingly been mooted as a solution to the problem of pop music and needletime. Faced with public demand for more records on the radio, the Union decided that it would prefer to deal with the BBC – over which it retained significant influence – than the commercial operators. Despite some concessions over needletime, the 1967 arrangements

11 Trubridge had been a member of various pop bands (most notably Darts) and was working for Hackney Council, running an agency called Hackney Agency for Music Marketing Action. He joined the MU as a consultant in late 1990 and as a full-time careers adviser the following year.

12 Importantly these were open to all – not just MU members – and Melton saw these as recruitment opportunities.

13 These were curated weeks of shows at the Institute of Contemporary Arts in London. The 1989 line-up famously included the Stone Roses and Jane's Addiction.

14 Sound City was a Radio 1 event, with various local authorities, BPI, and the MU as the main partners and sponsors.

that helped establish Radio 1 did not fundamentally change the Union's relationship with the BBC and, with the support of the Labour Government, it delayed the onset of the type of commercial radio stations that had prevailed in other countries, where they provided the kind of 'non-stop pop' that audiences demanded. However, the support of some Conservative MPs for the pirates and of others for commercial radio more generally continued to raise questions about the BBC's radio monopoly.

The Union remained resolutely opposed to commercial radio, believing that it would be bad for the employment of musicians, but the 1970 Conservative Party manifesto argued that 'people are entitled to an alternative radio service as much as they are entitled to alternative television service' and promised that 'we will permit local private enterprise radio' (www.politicsresources.net/area/uk/man/con70.htm). When the Party was elected in 1970, the MU found itself on the wrong side of public opinion and Ratcliffe (and subsequently Morton) had to devise strategies that made the best of a difficult situation.

Heath's Government was quick to act on matters pertaining to both trade unions[15] and broadcasting. The new Minister of Posts and Telecommunications, Christopher Chataway, hastily dissolved the proposed public inquiry into broadcasting under Lord Annan[16] before turning his attention to the introduction of commercial radio. Here it was immediately apparent that the MU was the major barrier to commercial stations being able to play the type and quantity of records that would sustain them, and Chataway opened discussions via meeting a Union delegation – including both Ratcliffe and Morton – on 6 October 1970. Ratcliffe told him that the Union was 'still opposed in principle' to commercial radio, but accepted that the 'government had been elected with a mandate to introduce it' and expressed a willingness to participate in negotiations with the Government, record companies, and broadcasters (TNA, HO 256/665).

Though the meetings appeared cordial, both sides had entrenched positions and, at a subsequent meeting on 6 July 1971, the Union told the Minister that as the new stations would be able to utilise non-PPL music the Union and PPL had little incentive to grant them extensive needletime. Civil servants consulted with the BBC and advised the Minister that audiences 'could not tolerate substantial doses' of non-PPL music, warning him that the MU's position was stronger than it had declared because, in the event of a dispute over needletime, it held significant power over the record companies because

15 With the Industrial Relations Act (1971).

16 This had been set up two days before the General Election by the previous (Labour) Government.

of the perennial threat of withdrawing members from recording (TNA, HO 256/665).

The Sound Broadcasting Act was passed in 1972, establishing the framework within which both BBC and independent local radio (ILR) would operate. The BBC was initially granted permission to operate twenty local radio stations,[17] with scope for up to sixty independent stations. The latter were to come under the auspices of the new Independent Broadcasting Authority (IBA), which would hold considerable control over what was still to be a highly regulated sector. The IBA invited interest in the initial franchises (Glasgow, Manchester, and Birmingham, plus two in London), and the two London stations, LBC and Capital Radio, launched in October 1973.[18]

With the arrival of the stations imminent, agreement on needletime was reached with remarkable alacrity between the IBA and PPL. With the agreement of the MU, PPL allowed the stations up to nine hours a day, a much higher proportion than the BBC. However, the stations had to pay a high price. Initially, this was 3 per cent of their annual advertising revenue, rising by 1 per cent per annum across the next four years (Stoller 2010a: 186–7). In addition, as a concession to the Union, the stations were obliged to spend at least a further 3 per cent of their revenues on live music performances. When these were added to the costs of the franchises and the separate royalties paid to PRS, it was clear that setting up an independent radio station in the UK was not the licence to print money that some had hoped for. Stoller argues that while the deal was punitive for the stations, it was the best the Authority could have done given the circumstances, wherein an agreement had to be reached quickly to allow for franchises to be awarded (Stoller 2010a: 187). As the preferred broadcasters were still to be chosen, John Thompson represented the IBA in negotiations with PPL. The result was that those who were eventually to run the stations were not party to the agreement that was to shape their future businesses. This was to underpin many future complaints about the costs of broadcasting from the AIRC, which formed in the wake of the first franchise awards in 1973. From the Union's perspective, John Morton (*2014*) reflected that 'the original agreement that was reached with the IBA was quite a good agreement, taking everything into consideration'.

For all the MU's opposition to independent radio, the deal struck with the IBA meant that, at least initially, it did not represent a substantial problem. Morton reflected that 'the original agreement that was reached with the IBA … was quite a good agreement, taking everything into consideration' (*2014*).

17 The first began in 1967, but the total of twenty had originally been agreed in 1970.

18 Radio Clyde (Glasgow) began broadcasting on 31 December 1973, and the Birmingham (BRMB) and Manchester (Piccadilly) stations launched in 1974.

The arrival of ILR meant that the sums paid from PPL to the Union increased substantially, the new stations offered some employment to musicians, and – perhaps most influentially – the wider economic circumstances prevented the proliferation of ILR stations to anything like the extent the Government initially envisaged. A lack of advertising revenue made these risky ventures and, by the end of 1976, there were only nineteen new stations.

Following two electoral defeats for the Conservatives in 1974, the new Labour Government revived the Annan Committee and simultaneously announced a limit on the number of new stations. Annan's report three years later called local radio provision in the UK 'a mess' (Annan Committee: 205), blaming this on a lack of planning. The report was generally positive about the existing ILR stations, but noted that a number of those who gave evidence to the Committee – including the MU – proposed that 'independent local radio should not develop further or [should] be closed down completely' (157). While the MU's submission did call for the abolition of the independent radio stations (*Stage and Television Today*, 19 June 1975: 12), it also highlighted its changed stance on ITV, which it now accepted.

Arguably the biggest issue for the Union during the introduction of ILR was the recalibration of its relationship with the BBC. With the new stations now able to play more pop music than Radio 1, executives within the BBC sought more needletime and began to ask more fundamental questions surrounding the nature of their agreement with PPL. The last needletime agreement dated back to 1968, with a few subsequent amendments,[19] and the MU proved reluctant to engage in further discussions unless they involved the issue of more guaranteed employment for musicians. The BBC was less and less willing to offer such guarantees as it was operating under greater financial restraints and also at the mercy of the findings of the Annan Report.

The Corporation's concerns were largely based around Radio 1, which was increasingly criticised for its lack of recorded music. For example, *Melody Maker* ran a front-page editorial headlined 'Radio One: Give the fans what they want' (23 June 1973: 1), condemning the needletime arrangements and highlighting what it saw as the hypocrisy of the record companies and the obstinacy of the Union. This seemed to match the frustrations of those working at Radio 1. Its Head, Derek Chinnery, wrote an internal memo on 21 October 1974 arguing that 'we pay over £500,000 to PPL and this should be cut' on the basis that 'the payment is based on an agreement made in a different

[19] Radio 2 was granted an extra fifteen hours a week in 1973.

era, dating back to the 1930s when records were regarded as an occasional alternative to live music' (WAC, R104/194/1). Particularly problematic for Radio 1 was that while it was being forced to pay PPL heavily for what was effectively promotion of its members' records,[20] ILR and Radio Luxembourg benefited from the same record companies buying advertising time.

Notwithstanding this, internal dissent did not appear to influence the Corporation's negotiators. For much of the 1970s, needletime negotiations proceeded at a glacial pace, and the five-year agreement signed in 1968 was continued until 1978. The points of stagnation were now less about the number of hours – wherein PPL usually offered a degree of flexibility in return for increased payment – but rather the Union's entrenched position on employment guarantees. It had particular issues over the future of the Training Academy as part of the wider connection it sought to enshrine between the use of records and the employment of musicians.[21] For the first time, a more fundamental debate had opened up as to whether the Union had any legitimate interest in needletime.

This had been accentuated by the eventual publication, in March 1977, of the Annan Report, which questioned the BBC's ability to support the existing levels of orchestral employment. If this put the Union on the defensive, Morton, invoking performers' rights, had a robust defence. His view was that the recognition of such rights in the Rome Convention of 1961 (to which the UK was a signatory) meant that legislation legally to enact the Convention's provisions was overdue in the UK. Therefore, he argued at a tripartite meeting on 29 July 1977, if the BBC and PPL were to reject the musicians' interest in the use of recordings then the MU would 'have to press for legislation giving formal status to the performers' interest'. This was a plausible threat that meant the BBC had to take seriously Morton's claim that 'there should be a formal link between the level of the guarantee [of employment] and the needletime agreement' (WAC, R104/195/1).

These external considerations clouded discussions and Morton recalls that talks at the BBC took on a different tone. 'Gradually it moved to a harder style of management, but not necessarily a better type of management' (*2014*). This partly reflected changing personnel, but also an awareness that the Corporation's financial position left it unable to meet demands around guaranteed employment. Despite this, a new needletime agreement was reached in 1978. This was

20 Despite its restrictions Radio 1 had become a primary vehicle for successful pop records.

21 After being set up in 1966 as a consequence of the needletime agreement of 1964, the Training Orchestra was downsized and renamed the Training Academy in 1971. The BBC's commitment to the Academy was only until 1977 and it was soon clear that it had no intention of extending this. Subsequently the Union was one of a number of parties involved in setting up the successor, National Centre for Orchestral Studies (see Tschaikov 2009: 258–9).

implemented, but never formally signed, as PPL was being taken to the PRT by the AIRC and was worried that signing might have legal implications. The headline term was an additional fifteen hours per week for Radio 1 and Radio 2,[22] but of more interest was the BBC's stance on the conceptual issues surrounding the Union's interests in the matter. A letter from the BBC's legal adviser to Morton in February 1978 stated that the BBC 'cannot marry the entirely different concepts of needletime and the employment of permanent staff by the BBC', but for agreement to be reached, he was forced in subsequent correspondence to agree a 'guaranteed level for employment of musicians to be calculated on the base line of £4,257,000 at 31 March 1977' (WAC, R104/203/1).

This appeared to be a triumph for the Union. The BBC had been forced not only to recognise its legitimate interest in needletime, but also to agree to provide the type of employment guarantees it had been resisting just a few months earlier. Unfortunately this proved to be merely a sticking plaster before the Annan Report, the referral of the independent radio agreements to the PRT, and the election of another Conservative Government combined over the next two years to weaken the Union's position. By the end of the 1970s, the theoretical underpinning and practical implementation of needletime were under considerable political pressure; the Union's leadership understood the importance of maintaining a stout defence of the system and spent the following decade doing so.

Annan's Report

Since the late 1960s it had been apparent that the BBC viewed the twelve staff orchestras (which by 1976 employed 589 musicians) as a luxury it could not afford when under difficult financial constraints. Matters here concerned wider issues around the BBC's role as a patron of music, its funding, a more aggressive style of management, a more parsimonious Government, and wider economic circumstances.

Questions about who should fund the BBC's orchestras had reappeared at various points. In 1976 Howard Newby, the Managing Director of BBC Radio, gave a lecture at which he noted that the BBC's commitment to the orchestras was 'greater than required for the need of broadcasting', and argued for sharing their costs with other interested parties on the grounds that 'the orchestras represent a national as well as a broadcasting interest' (*The Times*, 16 January 1976: 2).

22 This allowed the stations to separate their previously shared output and Radio 2 to broadcast for twenty-four hours a day.

A similar theme was picked up in the Annan Report, which although not specifically tasked with reviewing the BBC orchestras had to address the Corporation's finances. Despite representations from the MU and others[23] that the BBC should be a patron of the arts, the Committee was ambivalent. It supported previous views (e.g. Redcliffe-Maud 1976) that there were too many London orchestras and made suggestions that the rigid structures of the BBC orchestras should be broken up. More fundamentally, Annan argued that the BBC 'cannot become Fairy Godmother to the long line of Cinderellas in the arts' (Annan Committee 1977: 333). In response Morton declared the report to be 'disastrous as well as ... breathtakingly arrogant' (*Musician*, April 1977: 2). In accepting the need to disband the Training Academy and in advocating restructuring and new forms of finance for the BBC orchestras, Morton claimed that Annan had 'swallowed the current BBC nonsense hook, line and sinker' and warned of a 'formidable struggle' (*Musician*, April 1977: 2) in the coming years.

A strike at the BBC

Matters came to a head in early 1980 when the BBC finally addressed the £130 million of cuts it had been forced to make (largely as a consequence of its licence fee income not keeping up with rising inflation).[24] Though the majority of savings were to be achieved from cuts to programmes and staffing, the issue of the orchestras was again broached. Cuts were initially outlined to staff in a letter from the Director-General, Ian Trethowan, dated 28 February and reported more widely the following day (Gosling 1980a). The Union's major concern was the proposed disbandment of five of the BBC's orchestras (the Scottish Symphony, Northern Irish, Northern Radio, and Midland Radio Orchestras as well as the London Studio Players[25]), with the potential loss of 153 full-time and 19 part-time jobs. It responded immediately by threatening a boycott of all BBC music, while the BBC announced a period of discussion during which they expressed the hope of finding some external funding for the orchestras.[26] When none was forthcoming, the orchestral cuts were confirmed at a meeting of the BBC's Board of Governors on 17 April.

The delay in implementation had allowed the Union time to ascertain that there was considerable anger across the music profession, other trade unions,

23 Including PRS, the Arts Council, and the Society of Authors.

24 The Government refused to allow an increase in the (colour) television licence to £40 as requested by the Corporation. Instead, it went up to £34 in 1980.

25 A group of regularly used freelance musicians based in London.

26 Some initiatives were subsequently taken in Scotland and Northern Ireland, but these were not to lead to long-term solutions (Gosling 1980b).

and the wider public about the BBC's proposals. For example, the letters pages of *The Times* included general pleas to reverse the cuts from Simon Rattle and Yehudi Menuhin while, as the largest and most politically sensitive of the orchestras under threat, the BBCSSO garnered particularly strong support. Adrian Boult and Peter Pears were among those associated with the Royal Scottish Academy of Music and Drama (RSAMD) who put their names to a letter in its support, arguing that the orchestra was 'a fundamental part of the of the fabric of Scotland' (*The Times*, 7 March 1980: 17). The orchestra's conductor, Karl Anton Rickenbacher, called the proposals an 'act of barbarism' (*The Times*, 15 March 1980: 4) and a campaign to save the BBCSSO was set up by David Lumsden, Principal of the RSAMD.[27]

The ability to mobilise such support and the trenchant position of BBC management emboldened the Union, and it duly began planning what was to become the largest and most significant musicians' strike in its history. After a ballot among the BBC orchestras had voted 419 to 81 in favour of strike action, the Union announced that, from 1 June, all MU members would refuse BBC engagements and the orchestras would go on strike. Initially, the BBC downplayed the likely impact on its programmes, claiming to have a plentiful supply in reserve. But perhaps the Union's greatest weapon was the threat to the Proms, the annual series of concerts organised by the BBC that was due to begin on 18 July.

Reflecting on the strike, Morton remembered the difficulty of calling the orchestras out, but believes that the inflexibility of BBC management left the MU with no other option. He recalled: 'One of the advantages of being active in Unions and being on strike myself in the printing trade was I know what it is like to try and live on strike. And so it was the most heart-rending decision I've ever had to make' (*2014*). As the strike began, there was no sign of the BBC compromising, despite support for the Union from other orchestras (who performed benefit concerts for the strike fund), other trade unions, MPs of both major parties in a parliamentary debate, celebrities (even the Union's old adversary, Kenny Everett, briefly joined a picket line), and the press (including the notoriously anti-union *Financial Times* and *Daily Telegraph*).

A lack of dialogue was Morton's major frustration with Aubrey Singer, the BBC's Managing Director of Radio, who embodied what Morton saw as the new BBC management style. He described meetings with the BBC in the run up to the strike as 'useless ... no amount of argument, discussion or threats would make them say "oh we might modify this a bit", or perhaps "we might do this instead"' (*Morton 2014*). Having taken some orchestral members

[27] For an account of the strike in Scotland see Purser (1987: 45–8).

along to the final meetings before the strike, Morton explained to them what he saw as the importance of the action – the precedent it would set. He told them: 'In my view, the position is this, that if we accede to this … our position afterwards would be hopeless. We know that the BBC has much longer-term objectives about the replacement of live music with record performances and so on' (*2014*).

Once on strike, the musicians made a conspicuous impact with demonstrations and pickets (see Figures 15 and 16) of BBC buildings across the UK (including frequent musical interludes from striking musicians). The overall impression of the MU's picket lines given by those present was one of mischievous fun. Richard Watson, who was in the BBC Concert Orchestra and organised pickets at Television Centre, described how 'we had loads of support, but it often came in strange ways' (*Watson 2012*). As well as from expected sources (other unions and musicians), he cites the generosity of spirit of delivery drivers, the public, and some of the police, who did not enforce the laws on picketing as strictly as some BBC security staff wished.

The pickets gave a very visible public face to the strike while attempts were made to instigate discussions. The wide support for the dispute meant that it was not financially ruinous for either the Union or individual members. The strike fund raised a total of £84,857, with the majority coming from other

Figure 15 MU members protest against plans to close five BBC orchestras, 1980 (MU, 5/1).

Figure 16 An MU picket outside the BBC during the 1980 strike (MU, 5/1).

orchestras or special concerts arranged by the Union or on its behalf. For example, the members of the LSO donated their fees from a performance at the Royal Festival Hall, and, when the First Night of the Proms was cancelled for the first time in eighty-five years, the Union organised an unofficial Prom at Wembley Conference Centre featuring some of the striking orchestras. Singer – at least publicly – remained defiant, saying that 'we are not going to do the Proms at the sacrifice of not going through with our intentions' (Huckerby 1980).

The Union was initially equally non-conciliatory. Schlesinger (1980) reported that it 'evidently wants a return to the status quo before reopening negotiations' and had 'offered no thought-out alternative'. After six weeks, there were no signs of a breakthrough, despite its having been discussed in Parliament, Cabinet, and meetings at the Advisory Conciliation and Arbitration Service (ACAS). The BBC budged first with an offer to form a new Scottish Symphonia[28] and some sweeteners in the form of redundancy payments and offers of freelance work for those made redundant. This was rejected by the Union's Executive, and there were signs of the strike escalating with Equity threatening to become more involved. A familiar figure was then drafted in to mediate between the two sides at ACAS.

Lord Goodman's involvement brought a swift resolution in the seventh week of the strike. After three days of talks, between 21 and 23 July, a solution was found, subject to approval by the Union's Executive and BBC management. The headlines centred on the reprieve for three of the orchestras threatened with closure. The BBCSSO was to remain with sixty-two instead of sixty-nine members; the BBC Northern Ireland Orchestra was to continue with a view to the eventual creation of a new Ulster Orchestra partially funded by the BBC; and the London Studio Players ensemble was to be reorganised, but with guaranteed funding. However, all of these apparent concessions by the BBC were at the cost of the Scottish, Northern, and Midland Radio Orchestras. These were to be disbanded, with members offered two-thirds of their salaries for five years and some guarantees of freelance work. The wider settlement included guarantees that the BBC would look immediately at orchestral and freelance salaries and would seek to increase the size of the orchestras should the licence fee be increased.

The terms were agreed by the EC on 25 July, subject to a members' ballot. The following day Morton sent a ballot paper to all the musicians affected, telling them that 'they represent the best overall package that can be achieved at the present stage of the strike and very substantial improvement on the BBC's original intentions' (MU, 3/2/3/5). In the subsequent ballot, 83 per cent of the BBC musicians voted to end the strike, with any opposition coming largely from Scotland, where the decision to sacrifice the SRO – which had not originally been under threat – was to be a source of lingering resentment. The strike officially ended on 1 August and the Proms resumed on 7 August.

The strike had mixed outcomes for the contending parties. For the BBC, it had inflicted serious reputational damage (especially surrounding the Proms) but had allowed it to challenge many of the assumptions that had underpinned relations with the MU since the end of the war – most notably the connection between needletime and employment levels. For the Union, the strike had at

28 This would have employed fifty-four of the existing BBCSSO musicians, but would also have meant the end of BBC funding for the SRO – although it would have been allowed to continue with external funding.

least mitigated or postponed some job losses and shown it to be a united and effective campaigning organisation, capable of gaining widespread media and public support. Morton reflected the mixed feelings at the end of the strike, writing that 'no one will claim the final settlement is perfect, but it only has to be compared to the BBC's original proposals to see the effort was worthwhile' (*Musician*, autumn 1980: 7). Over thirty years later, his view remained the same, and he remarked that: 'No strike is ever a success. The fact that there had been a strike was a failure, but if you are asking me "were things better after the strike than they would have been if we hadn't had the strike?" then I have to say they were. That is the best I can say for it' (2011).

The return of the PRT

If the strike represented the Union's battle to preserve the principles underpinning the use of records on radio and the preservation of employment, then this overlapped with what was to be a greater challenge from the commercial broadcasters. By referring its agreements with PPL to the PRT in 1978, the AIRC was nominally seeking a review of the charges imposed by PPL. However, Morton viewed this as a more direct challenge to the whole needletime system. While the hearing would not technically involve the Union, Morton ensured that it was listed as an interested party and able to give evidence during the Tribunal hearing.

This ran for seventy-seven days from 19 November 1979 until 13 May 1980 and revealed much about the approach (and finances) of the three parties involved. Both the AIRC and PPL hired expensive legal representation,[29] while Morton single-handedly represented the MU. The AIRC's case for a reduction in the cost of its PPL licences was based on comparisons with similar radio stations worldwide, and on their belief that they paid more than the BBC and that the payment was less important – and should therefore be charged at a lower rate – than the equivalent ones levied by PRS.

Bert Gilbert of PPL argued that 'the AIRC claim is rather like a bald-headed man who goes to a hat manufacturer and says I have no hair, so I need a hat, but since while wearing it I will be publicising your hat, I should be given it for free' (cited in Robertshaw 1980). It was a cause of much resentment among the record companies that while their profits were sagging in hard economic times, those of businesses that used their records (the broadcasters and dance halls/discos) were still seemingly successful.

[29] This was estimated to have cost PPL £500,000 by January 1980 (WAC, R104/184/1).

Morton's contribution provided PPL's position with considerable underpinning. Significantly, Morton remembers that PPL 'were there in their traditional role. No record industry executives came along to the Tribunal. Bert [Gilbert] was there and he got his Counsel and Learned Counsel and Junior Counsel – they spent a bloody fortune' (*2014*). He also highlighted the mixed messages being sent out by the recording industry. On the one hand, they were paying an army of pluggers to get their records played on radio, while PPL – owned by the same companies – was backing the MU in trying to limit the opportunities for this to happen. But Morton had more pressing concerns. He recalls that 'The issue was not really how much [they had to pay]. That was the ostensible issue, because for the AIRC, the was the only way they could get into the debate was to make it about the amount to be paid. But the real issue they were getting at was whether they should be constrained at all' (*2014*). The eventual ruling of the Tribunal came, in the midst of the BBC dispute, on 15 July 1980 and was something of a relief to both PPL and the Union. It rejected all the major arguments put forward by the AIRC, and made only relatively minor changes to the royalty scales, largely to accommodate the prevailing high rates of inflation. Stoller describes the outcome as a 'body blow' for the AIRC and quotes their lawyers as admitting that they had 'sustained defeat on virtually all significant matters of principle' (2010a: 189). The other side of this coin was Morton's view that 'the outcome of the Tribunal did what I had hoped we could get it to do, which was to confirm that the arrangement [between PPL and the MU] was (a) legal, (b) moral and (c) equitable all round' (*2014*).

However, the reality was that this was the start of a challenge rather than the end of one. For the remainder of the decade, it remained close to the surface and, to the Union's detriment, both the political context and economic conditions changed substantially in the interim. Having been backed into a corner by the ruling, the AIRC felt obliged to appeal. It did this in October 1980, setting off a chain of challenges through the courts that were to span a further six years. When the appeal was finally heard in 1986, its outcome was still not to the AIRC's liking. While it was recognised that the original Tribunal 'had erred in law on certain points' (PRT 1986: 2), apart from some modest decreases in the rates payable to PPL in certain circumstances, it 'reasserted its principle that the original rate of 7% [of net advertising revenue] across the board should continue' (Stoller 2010a: 191).

Although this may have seemed like a decisive victory for PPL and the Union, the time lag between the original decision and the appeal meant that the agreement was susceptible to other forms of attack. These ultimately led to the unravelling of the MU and PPL agreements barely two years later. A number of factors were in play here, including the Conservative Government's attitude to trade unions and their developing policies on copyright and broadcasting. Lamenting the lack of change in independent radio over the 1980s, Stoller argues that the transition from the 'public service model of independent radio endorsed by the Annan Committee's report in March 1977, to an emerging system of commercial radio outlined by Peacock, was halting and uneven' (2010b: 1).[30]

This represented an important demarcation that had bubbled under debates about radio in the early 1970s. Chataway was keen to avoid the new stations being branded 'commercial radio' and, partly as a fob to the BBC and the MU, retained a large number of public service commitments within the franchises. Sensing that the approach of the second Thatcher Government was more conducive to their aim of less regulation over the sector, the AIRC, under the leadership of Jimmy Gordon,[31] was strengthened by the growth in the number of ILR stations during the 1980s and became a formidable lobbyist.[32] Dissatisfied by the outcomes of their attempts to alter copyright legislation, the stations made a series of demands at a specially convened meeting in 1984 (known as the Heathrow Conference), which gained some traction with Government ministers – notably the Home Secretary, Leon Brittan. Among other things, the AIRC sought deregulation, a reduction in fees payable to the rights organisations, and less interference from the IBA.

Initially the independent radio stations had found that Government rhetoric was often far removed from the reality of running their businesses, which were still bogged down by various restraints. Policy on copyright and broadcasting was often formed via a succession of committees and Green and White Papers. Both the AIRC and the Union were to be frustrated by the proposed contents of the eventual copyright legislation (the Copyright Designs and Patents Act 1988). This gave 'no ground to the radio companies' aspirations' (Stoller 2010b: 7) and again failed fully to recognise the rights of the performer in UK law. Indeed, it took until the Broadcasting Act of 1990 before the independent radio sector was able to move towards the free market its advocates had always desired.[33] This created a new Radio Authority, which was to award franchises to both the three new national commercial stations and a plethora of local and community-based stations, all to be awarded to the highest bidders. Of more immediate interest to the Union and PPL was

30 Peacock produced yet another report, this time on the financing of the BBC, in 1986. Among other things it recommended the privatisation of Radios 1 and 2, while retaining the licence fee system.

31 Gordon was Managing Director of Radio Clyde during the 1970s and 1980s.

32 There were thirty-eight stations by 1983 and seventy-nine by 1990.

33 The Act enshrined statutory licence provisions.

the placing of the final nail in the coffin of needletime restrictions. This meant that PPL was no longer able to refuse a licence to any radio station to play records, so long as the two had reached an agreement on the cost of such uses.[34] As a result needletime remained in name only, as a means of measuring the amount of music used, for which PPL had to be remunerated.

Trade union reform and a Commission

If progress in realigning broadcasting was slow, the Thatcher Government was quicker to implement trade union reform. Coming to power at the end of a series of strikes during the so-called 'Winter of Discontent', they formed part of what David Metcalf calls 'a period of relentless, sustained corrosion of British unionisation' (2005: 4), By 1990, six pieces of legislation had been passed that, among other things, curtailed the right to strike and to take strike action in solidarity with other workers, and made the pre-entry closed shop illegal.[35] In addition, the 1982 Employment Act restored trade unions' liability for damages caused as a result of strikes. These not only limited unions' power, but also had an effect on their membership levels and, consequently, finances. The peak of British trade union membership (13.2 million) was in 1979, but its subsequent erosion left it at 6.5 million in 2012 (DBIS 2013: 5).

At first the reforms had little impact on the MU. As a relatively small craft union, it was not the target of the initial tranche of legislation aimed at larger industrial unions, and was rarely involved in large-scale strikes or secondary picketing. Its leadership was also careful to deny the existence of a closed shop, although the rule that prevented members playing with non-members went some way to creating the same effect. Membership of the MU was steady throughout the 1980s, reaching a peak of 41,657 in 1981, before dropping to around the 39,000 mark for the remainder of the decade – a level to which it would never return.

The Government's interest in the power of trade unions gradually turned to the media unions,[36] and the practices of the entertainment unions were increasingly on the radar of senior politicians. Their device for change was the MMC. In March 1988, an inquiry was launched into what were labelled restrictive or uncompetitive practices in the film and television industries, and within a matter of weeks a further investigation was set up into the operation

34 The 'statutory licence' system imposed meant that stations could start broadcasting without agreement and refer the matter to the Copyright Tribunal to decide the appropriate fees.

35 The Employment Acts of 1980, 1982, 1988, 1989, and 1990, and the Trade Union Act of 1984.

36 Most notably as a result of the disputes with the print unions at Warrington and Wapping.

of collective licensing in the music industries. This was to have huge implications for the MU.

When the Secretary of State for Trade and Industry, Lord Young, requested that the MMC 'report on practices relating to the collective licensing of sound recordings for broadcasting and public performance' (MMC 1988: 1), it was widely assumed that the report would extend across all the copyright organisations.[37] But a more detailed examination of the terms of reference revealed that, given the specific focus on the licensing of sound recordings, only PPL fell within them (MMC 1988: 31).

Under pressure from the commercial radio stations, the inquiry was clearly designed to focus on the workings of PPL and, inevitably, this involved examining its relationship with the MU. Along with other interested parties, the Union gave both written and oral evidence. However, it feared that the outcome was something of a foregone conclusion.[38] Morton claimed that the outcomes had been rushed under Government pressure, saying that 'if any sort of investigation body is under this sort of pressure, it raises eyebrows and does not allow a competent and thorough enquiry' (*Stage and Television Today*, 8 December 1988: 1). He still maintains that the whole investigation was 'an outrageous affair, because what they were looking at was outside their terms of reference altogether' (*Morton 2014*).

The investigation placed considerable focus on three areas of PPL activity that were of particular importance to the MU – needletime, the conditions within public performance licences requiring venues to employ musicians, and the distribution of PPL's income via the 'phonographic funds'. The wider context was PPL's growing revenues from both broadcasting and public performances. In the three years prior to the investigation, PPL's annual income had risen from £11.5 million in 1985 to £15.1 million in 1987, with the MU's share rising from £1.1 million to £1.3 million over the same period (MMC 1988: 8). The report also noted that the MU's Special Fund had reserves of £5.1 million at the end of 1987. Clearly, the stakes were high for both sides.

The report outlined the prevailing PPL arrangements with both the BBC and ILR and suggested that while the restrictions placed on the BBC and ITV had not been too onerous, those imposed on the ILR stations had had 'adverse effects on the companies' management of their businesses' (MMC 1988: 8). It was reported by PPL that it was willing to licence the ILRs, for any use, subject only to fees, while the MU said that while it would expect

37 Also including PRS and the Mechanical-Copyright Protection Society (MCPS).

38 However, the broadcasting unions were cleared of restrictive working practices in the report into the film and TV industries published by the MMC in April 1989. See Evans and Jones (1989).

PPL to discuss any proposed changes in needletime 'it did not contemplate industrial action against PPL in support of (its) retention'. The MU agreed too that abandoning needletime 'could be of financial benefit to the MU' (because it would lead to more PPL income), but also gave the impression that it wanted it to be maintained (MMC 1988: 8).

Unsurprisingly, the evidence given to the Commission was described as 'polarised' (MMC 1988: 23) between that of licensors and the music users. The Union and PPL argued – with support from individual record companies and their trade organisations (BPI and IFPI) – for the maintenance of the status quo. The MU's submission claimed that the collective licensing agreements were part of the 'industrial relations structure' of the recording industry and that their disruption would not be in the public interest (MMC 1988: 28). Furthermore, it noted that needletime affected employment and justified the system under which it received 12.5 per cent of PPL's licensing revenue as a voluntary agreement that had been reached in the absence of performers having a statutory right to equitable remuneration in UK law. This notion stemmed from Article 12 of the Rome Convention, which stated that 'if a phonogram published for commercial purposes, or a reproduction of such phonogram, is used directly for broadcasting or for any communication to the public, a single equitable remuneration shall be paid by the user to the performers, or to the producers of the phonograms, or to both' (WIPO 1961).[39] More importantly, the Convention stated that, in the absence of agreement between the interested parties, 'domestic law may lay down the conditions as to the sharing of this remuneration' (WIPO 1961). In the absence of such provision in UK law, the MU and PPL were able to argue that their agreement filled this void but were also vulnerable to legislative interference.

The evidence of PPL to the MMC immodestly proposed that 'collective licensing was the only practicable mechanism that could be adopted for the protection and the use of such a large body of copyright material' and that its practices were 'beneficial to British culture, to the record industry, to the wider music industry, to broadcasting and to all who wish to listen to recorded music'. Perhaps the most interesting part of their submission was the contention that 'needletime was not a significant issue' and that it would be willing to 'remove all constraints if agreement could be reached on rates' (MMC 1988: 23).

39 Significantly, the split in the existing arrangement between PPL and the MU was not equitable and involved an intermediary (the Union) rather than a direct payment to performers.

Complaints about the operation of the agreement between the MU and PPL, in each of the three areas of operation, were manifold. The Music Users' Council (MUC)[40] particularly deplored the requirements to employ live musicians in discos and nightclubs (MMC 1988: 26),[41] especially in a context where demand for live music was negligible compared to that of dancing to records. The broadcasters used rhetoric designed to spark concern within the MMC to condemn the parts of the agreements that impacted on their operations. The AIRC complained of PPL's 'cartel', describing the needletime system as 'an indefensible use of monopoly power', while the BBC 'considered the PPL monopoly to be an uncompetitive practice not in the public interest' (MMC 1988: 25).

For the MU, the most important concern surrounded how the Commission viewed its use of the 12.5 per cent of PPL's net revenue 'in respect of the services of unidentified session musicians' (MMC 1988: 9). Here particular attention was paid to the way in which the Union required all members entering into a contract with non-BPI members or ILRs to use standard forms that required the station or company to assign copyright to PPL, seeing this as a restraint of trade (38). It noted that though the system allowed the *possibility* of performers receiving direct payment, none of the disbursements from the Union's Special Fund had 'been made specifically to the MU members whose work had generated the income from PPL' (38). It was also clear from the report's findings that while it was accepted that the Union had been well intentioned in its actions, there was sufficient evidence of what could be regarded as restrictive practices or monopolistic behaviour to justify substantial changes to the system. Inevitably, this was not to the Union's liking and its ire focused on the fact that what was ostensibly an investigation of the record-company-owned PPL had resulted in far greater consequences for the Union than for the record companies.

Ultimately, PPL came out of the investigation relatively unscathed. It was accepted that collective licensing was 'the best available mechanism for licensing sound recordings' and that 'PPL, as the price of its monopoly, should be obliged to permit the use of its repertoire in return for equitable remuneration' (MMC 1988: 41). In addition, the existing rates and mechanisms for disputes were to be settled by the Copyright Committee (the renamed PRT). By way of contrast, while stating that 'we do not criticize the MU for … [the

40 The MUC included the British Entertainment and Dancing Association, which represented clubs and discothèques.

41 This was covered by PPL licences for 'specially featured entertainment'. In venues where average attendance was over 150, PPL imposed conditions within such licences requiring the venues to employ live musicians.

existing] state of affairs' (38) and noting that it was 'doing no more than its duty to its members in seeking to preserve such employment opportunities as there are' (41), the MMC made a number of recommendations that were drastically to reduce the Union's power. It found that both needletime and the connected employment constraints were 'anti-competitive practices which ... should be abandoned' and, disastrously for the Union, that 'performers should be given equitable remuneration from the royalty income received by PPL, in substitution for the existing unsatisfactory arrangements' (41).

On the report's publication, Lord Young accepted its findings and sought to implement them through a mixture of voluntary arrangements among the parties and legislation. He reported to Parliament that AIRC and PPL had already reached an agreement to remove needletime constraints for a trial period (7 December 1988) and the following year the BBC reached a new agreement with PPL that 'agreed hourly rates, but made no reference to permitted hours of use' (Briggs 1995: 510). In effect the report's implementation signalled an end to two types of musical employment and a key source of revenue. For over twenty years the Union had been able to link needletime directly with levels of musician employment across both the BBC and the independent broadcasters, but this was now ended. Similarly, large venues with PPL 'specially featured entertainment' licences were no longer obliged to provide employment opportunities. Thus what had previously been forms of guaranteed employment were now left to the whims of the market, with the 'phonographic funds' – which had yielded the Union over £12 million since 1951 – also at an end. Reflecting on the consequences of the MMC report, Morton's successor as GS, Dennis Scard, told the Union's 1991 Conference that its 'influence went right down the pan' (Scard 1991: 9). Henceforth it would be survival – not influence – that would be at stake.

Conclusion

When Morton announced his impending retirement in 1989,[42] it brought to an end almost two decades in which he had presided over a substantial revitalisation of the Union and delayed some serious external threats to both musicians' employment (at the BBC) and ithe MU's continued power over broadcasting and public performance. However, by the time Scard was elected to replace him at the end of 1989,[43] the implications of the MMC report were

42 He officially left at the start of 1990 after a three-month handover period.

43 Previously Chair of the Central London Branch and a full-time Branch official since 1985, Scard defeated Stan Martin by 1,500 votes in the second ballot of the 1989 election.

beginning to become clear and the momentum of the Thatcher Government's reforms to trade unions and broadcasting was irreversible.

In his final article for the *Musician* as GS, Morton reflected on his time in office and focused on what he called 'a sense of déjà vu about many current events' (March 1990: 18). Specifically, he compared the Broadcasting and Employment Bills placed before Parliament in 1990 with similar ones in 1971 that had been designed to 'radically change British broadcasting' and 'further limit trade union rights'. He also reflected on the closure of another BBC orchestra (the BBC Radio Orchestra), as well as 'continuing economic difficulties' and technological changes, as typical of the problems that 'although they manifest themselves in slightly different forms – are still around' (*Musician*, March 1990: 18).

If the external threats to the Union were similar and constant throughout his tenure, they also served as a distraction from more radical internal change. Although the Union was far better equipped to deal with the music industries (and musicians outside the orchestras and big bands) than it had been in 1971, the change proved to be a gradual process fraught with difficulties – mostly concerning the essentially freelance and disorganised nature of the workforce. Despite Morton's more open-minded approach and the efforts of some key officials, the Union was institutionally slow in adapting to changes around it. Perhaps significantly, the organisational structure that was being criticised at conferences in the late 1960s remained, for the most part, unchanged.

Nevertheless, Morton was the Union's most impressive leader since Williams. He greatly enhanced its stature among the organisations it dealt with, both nationally and internationally. A skilled negotiator, his command of legal matters and international reputation ensured that he remained a compelling presence after his departure as GS. He accepted the EC's offer of a consultancy role with the Union,[44] remained President of FIM, and was particularly involved in matters surrounding the performers' rights (and wider copyright issues) after his retirement.

44 Despite an offer from PPL to take on a similar role.

8

Disharmony: 1991–2002

The Union's impact has waxed and waned throughout its history and it has been more influential during times when both the economic and political circumstances were in its favour (especially during the post-war era). However, the previous chapter illustrated the beginning of the end of this situation. Although John Morton played a sizeable role in ensuring the retention of its influence, this was achieved with the odds increasingly loaded against him. When the Government accepted the findings of the MMC report it was clear that this, combined with the Broadcasting Act (1990), would not only reduce the Union's influence, but present considerable organisational problems as it adapted to its changed position in the political and industrial landscape. The remainder of the book examines both the problems this caused and how the Union had adapted to them.

None of this came as a surprise to Dennis Scard when he was elected GS. Indeed, his campaign material was prescient, listing 'changes in employment legislation, cuts in public arts subsidy, the "freeing of the airwaves" under the Broadcasting Bill, [and] the changing nature of the "Gig" scene' as being just some of the challenges the winner would face. He was equally aware of the desperate need to refresh the Union's internal mechanisms and stood for election on five key policies, promising to 'modernise our administrative structure for greater efficiency; improve our public image to attract new members; broaden our advice and information services; increase our financial and legal services and expand our education workshops' (Scard, personal communication).

Each of these was typical of the challenges facing all trade unions at the start of the 1990s.[1] Here we concentrate on those unique to the MU. This requires returning to some of the connected themes picked out in previous

[1] See Heery (2005); and Martinez-Inigo *et al.* (2012).

chapters. At the start of the decade, the American exchanges that began in the 1950s were consigned to the past.[2] Closer to home, the Keep Music Live campaign and the work of the Music Promotion Committee (MPC) were first substantially curtailed and later discontinued.

We examine what we regard as the most substantial areas of change during Scard's period in office, before assessing their disruptive impact on the Union's workings. We start with the outcomes of the MMC report and then outline developments in the profession, specifically among the orchestras. We then turn to Scard's attempts to reform the Union internally. We conclude by considering the protracted and divisive sequence of events spanning 1999–2002 that were a consequence of each of the aforementioned changes and constituted the biggest crisis facing the MU since the 1930s.

A report's fallout

The most pressing issue facing Scard was dealing with the implications of the MMC ruling. This was a multifaceted problem and one over which the Union had only limited influence. Not only was it no longer able to allocate the 'phonographic funds' across the music profession as a whole, it was initially suggested that responsibility for distributing the funds to individual musicians be taken away from the Union, as the report recommended that 'all performers should receive equitable remuneration, directly paid by PPL, specific to each recording's use in broadcasting or public performance' (MMC 1988: 39).

However, the Union retained its commitment to wider distribution, and its 1991 Conference reaffirmed its policy that the PPL-derived income should be 'used in ways that serve the general interests of the profession [and] be partly applied to the interests of those musicians who make the recordings and those whose employment prospects are influenced by the increasingly widespread use of recorded music' (MU, 1/7/1991). Of longer-term importance, and more immediate practical concern, was the Union's claim that it was best placed to distribute the funds collected for non-featured performers.[3] The Conference resolved that the Union should administer any future PPL funds and further agreed that the EC should 'vigorously pursue a revised agreement under which the Union will administer, through the expanded Collection and Distribution system, both the individual distribution and the collective use of the performers' share of this revenue' (MU, 1/7/1991). It also agreed that the Union would continue its longstanding pursuit of legislative changes that

[2] Their last mention appears in the EC report to the 1991 Conference (MU, 1/7/1991).

[3] Those performers who were session musicians and played on records but were not signed directly to the recording companies.

would change the basis of the performers' remuneration from a voluntary agreement to a legal entitlement.

Resolving this issue came to occupy the Union for the first part of the decade, before reaching a culmination of sorts in 1996. Despite its good intentions, the Union's desire to distribute the PPL money was to create administrative problems and fuel discontent among its session musician members. Following much discussion among the Union, PPL, and the Department of Trade and Industry, it was finally agreed that the MU would indeed be responsible for making the payments to musicians. This was complicated by the amounts involved – which had grown with the end of needletime and the expansion of ILR – and the time taken to determine the method of distribution. Scard (*2013*) recalled receiving a cheque for £8 million in 1994,[4] which the Union had to allocate according to its own records of who had performed on the recordings that had generated income during the period spanning 1989–94.

This proved to be extremely difficult. There was virtually no record of which session musicians played on recordings made in the 1970s and 1980s. Union consent forms for sessions had been introduced in the early 1980s (*Sandys 2014*), meaning that the MU's record of who merited payment was more accurate than that of any other organisation. However, it was still far from definitive. The Union's distributed payments were based on a mixture of known facts, claims from individual musicians. and informed guesswork. This had a number of predictable consequences, as stories emerged of unexpected windfalls, inequities, and grievances. More problematically, it raised questions among some members about how PPL funds had been used prior to 1989. Emboldened by the individualistic ethos of the MMC's findings and the possibility of unexpected personal enrichment, such disgruntled elements ensured that the Union had a serious fight on its hands.

With anecdotal evidence being backed up by press articles (e.g. Wroe 1995) and even on investigative television programmes,[5] it was easy to see why a sense of grievance remained among some members. Among the most vocal was Vic Flick, a renowned session guitarist, who wrote extensively at the time and later in his autobiography (2008) about the perceived misappropriation by the Union of funds to which a sizeable number of session and orchestral musicians believed they were entitled. Although the Union did its best to allocate the funds from the post-1989 period fairly, Flick claimed that 'there is

[4] Covering 12.5 per cent of PPL's income for 1989–92. The MU was to continue to distribute PPL monies on behalf of non-featured performers until the formation of PAMRA and AURA in 1996.

[5] Scard was interviewed on ITV's *Thames Reports* on 18 June 1991 and the BBC's *Here and Now* on 4 December 1996.

factual proof of significant payments being made to musicians who had only been in studios one or two times' (175) and discontent about the previous use of the funds grew.

Another member, Freddie Staff, took to the courts to pursue his case that the Union was holding PPL funds that should have been distributed directly to individual musicians. His lengthy legal battle for access to financial records was finally resolved in 2002, and though the Union was cleared of any wrongdoing it generated more bad publicity (Lebrecht 2001; Sweeting 2001), adding to an atmosphere of suspicion and discord.

Against this backdrop, Union officials had to make increasingly robust defences of their both their present and past decisions. As AGS Media, Stan Martin used the *Musician* to defend the Union's actions and reiterated the position that it had taken in 1946 about the collective good of all musicians being greater than the individual needs of those making recordings. Martin argued that 'the money received by the Union from PPL prior to 1989 was on the basis that this money should be used for collective purposes' and had been 'used to provide services and to fund employment opportunities for members' (1996: 16). The Union's hierarchy clearly viewed its use of the funds as having been in the spirit of the original agreement with PPL. Martin also pointed out that these decisions had been subject to scrutiny and discussion both internally (via conferences) and externally (via PRT and MMC investigations) and had received a clean bill of health. Nevertheless, in the aftermath of the MMC's 1988 intervention it was somewhat inevitable that decisions, made in a different era and context, were going to be subject to further scrutiny.

While the aftermath of the MMC report dragged on for a few more years, two major, connected, developments in 1996 ultimately made life easier for the Union. The first came when the right of performers to equitable remuneration when their recordings were played or broadcast finally became a statutory right (rather than a voluntary agreement) on 1 December 1996 as the UK Government implemented European Directive 92/100. Such reform would have been impossible without the representations of the performers' unions, which dated back to when the MU (and FIM) began lobbying copyright bodies in the run-up to the Rome Convention in 1961.

A second development was an immediate outcome of this as the system for distributing monies collected on behalf of performers changed. Along with Equity, the MU formed the Performing Artists' Media Rights' Association (PAMRA) to act as a distribution agency for performers' monies collected by PPL. This removed a sizeable administrative burden from the MU, but the transition was complicated by the emergence of a rival organisation, the Association of United Recording Artists (AURA), which was instigated by the International Managers' Forum (IMF), who sought a higher percentage of the performers' allocation for featured performers. The two organisations competed for members and – despite the usual squabbling about distributions – these arrangements, underpinned by legal changes, went some way towards professionalising the collection and distribution of monies for recording artists.[6]

Events during 1996 also went a long way to reformulating the relationship between the Union and the recording industry following the MMC report. Performers' rights were now enshrined in law and, though flawed, a mechanism was in place for paying them for use of their work. From the Union's perspective the main casualty was the collective ethos that underpinned the work it conducted under the banner of the MPC. The MU now had to look on from afar as PPL's revenues increased without benefit to the Union. It also had to try to maintain and develop the services expected by its members while also losing a key source of funding.

Orchestral strife

The MU's salaried members in orchestras also found themselves with a problem during the 1990s that the Union had to confront: the perennial threat to their jobs. Since the end of the 1960s, the Union's industrial-relations role around orchestras had shifted from focusing on increasing both pay and levels of employment to one orientated towards maintaining existing employment levels. Although for many years press and other commentators has suggested the UK had more orchestras than it needed, the Union had fought – with considerable success – any attempts to reduce their number.

Such a stance was understandable. The orchestras remained the most unionised part of the music profession and were of vital importance to the Union. Under ever-increasing pressure from proposed Arts Council budget cuts and the turmoil inflicted within the BBC by the introduction of the internal market and producer choice, the MU's pragmatism did much to avert, delay, and prevent further major cuts to orchestras during the 1990s.

In January 1990, the portents were not good. The BBC announced an economy drive to reduce its budget by £75 million a year and immediately thoughts turned to the burdensome costs of musicians (Press Association 1990). The Arts Council similarly found its finances squeezed and had to trim £5 million from its annual budget (Witts 1998: 214). Pressure was also

[6] This was short-lived. By 2006, AURA and PAMRA had merged with PPL and payments to performers are now made directly from PPL, where the MU has two places on its Performer Board.

being applied on the orchestras to embrace a more market-orientated and commercial approach, seeking business sponsors and new sources of revenue while relying less on public subsidy. The issue of competition from foreign musicians also reared its head again. In 1992 VOCA disbanded, having found that its recommendations on visas for visiting orchestras were no longer listened to. Not only were the UK orchestras losing recording work to those in Central and Eastern Europe (Alberge 1999); the same competition was an increasingly attractive proposition for UK promoters (Miller 1994).

This combination of decreasing funds and increasing competition was to test the MU's resolve and flexibility throughout the 1990s, but remarkably the decade was to end with all the major British symphony orchestras still in place. While this was partly down to public support and the political difficulties that surround axing an orchestra, the MU can take considerable credit for the role it played in ensuring their continuance. We now examine its role in three places that saw their orchestras threatened: Scotland, London, and the BBC.

As with the rest of the UK, the reorganisation of Scotland's orchestras had long been on the political agenda. Writing in 1995, Robert Dawson Scott noted that it was widely agreed that 'there are, in simple terms, too many orchestras in Scotland. Or there are too few classical music concert-goers. Or there is not enough public money to fill the gap between what the orchestras manage to earn and what it costs to run them' (1995). However, he also noted widespread disagreement amongst the interested parties about remedying the problem.

By 1995 the Scottish orchestras had been subject to two inquiries within three years. These stemmed from an extraordinary intervention from the Scottish Arts Council when, along with the BBC and Scottish Opera, they held a news conference in December 1992 announcing the merger of the BBCSSO and Scottish Opera's orchestra in to a new National Orchestra of Scotland with the loss of twenty-two jobs (Tumelty 1992). With no consultations or detailed proposals apparent, the MU inevitably became involved after the musicians in both orchestras unanimously rejected the proposed merger and Union officials joined in subsequent discussions with the three bodies. Two years later a report by Helen Liddell concluded that the plan had been hatched without 'due regard to consultation', and the MU's Scottish Organiser, Ian Smith, told the press that 'The National Orchestra of Scotland is now dead' (cited in Bruce 1994). Liddell's report highlighted the difficult financial position of both orchestras, and yet another report – this time by Sir Lewis Robertson – further muddied the waters. It agreed that Scotland had excess orchestral provision but this time suggested that Scottish Opera disband its orchestra and use musicians from the other Scottish orchestras instead. This too was met with disapproval from the musicians, the Union and – in something of an about-turn – Scottish Opera itself.

The costs of Scotland's national companies remained on the agenda for the remainder of the decade[7] and beyond and, perhaps inevitably, one of the first acts of Scotland's newly devolved Government was to set up another inquiry into Scottish Opera and the other national companies in 1999 (BBC News 1999). Partly because of the Union's involvement, each of these further delayed any job losses in Scottish orchestras and, despite the mid-1990s consensus that Scotland was over-served by orchestral musicians, the orchestras remain in place and have avoided substantial job losses.[8]

The difficulty of implementing meaningful orchestral reform was even more evident in London, where attempts to reduce the number of orchestras had been debated since the middle of the twentieth century. Witts notes that there had been 'nineteen key reports' (1998: 188) commissioned on orchestral provision in the UK between 1949 and 1999, of which eleven focused on London. Again, the widespread view was that London had a surplus of orchestras, but each of the four major London orchestras that were subject to threats to their existence in the 1960s remained thirty years later.

This matter surfaced again when, faced with a new round of budget cuts, the Arts Council decided in 1993 to set up an Advisory Committee on London Orchestras under the auspices of Lord Justice Hoffman with a view to reducing its funding commitments.[9] At its outset the Committee detailed a plan to continue funding the LSO, and whichever of the other three orchestras submitted the best artistic plan to it. Witts describes how this beauty contest was given 'a walloping press profile so potent even the tabloids gave it space' (1998: 214), meaning that Hoffman reported he was 'unable to offer the Arts Council the clear advice for which it asked' (cited in Witts 1998: 216).

In this case, the MU could justifiably lay claim to playing a part in the inquiry's failure to produce the savings its instigators were seeking. Scard reflected that the Union was able to capitalise on Hoffman's ambivalence towards the task in hand. 'His first remark to me', he recalls, 'was that 'I don't want to do this job' and we were able to capitalise on that' (*2013*). At the MU's 1995 Conference, John Patrick claimed that 'it was the Union's tactics that finally derailed this review and forced the resignations of the [Arts Council's] Director of Music, Kenneth Baird, and the Secretary-General,

7 See Tumelty (1996).

8 The Orchestra of Scottish Opera was subsequently forced to go part-time in 2010 (Service 2010).

9 Hoffman had been Goodman's aide on the 1965 inquiry.

Anthony Everitt' (Scard, personal communication). This may overstate the Union's role, but it had undoubtedly played a part in preventing Hoffman reaching the conclusions the Arts Council wanted or expected. As with Scotland, London retains all its orchestras to this day.

The 1980 BBC strike had witnessed the first weakening of the Union's negotiating position when, for the first time, it was forced to recognise that the BBC simply did not have the money to maintain its previous levels of musical employment. Even so, it managed to retain the vast majority of BBC musicians' jobs on terms that had been negotiated years previously when the Union was more powerful and the BBC more compliant. But by the time Scard replaced Morton, both parties had been weakened: the MU by legislation, the BBC by budget cuts. In addition, a new managerial culture within the BBC (Born 2004) presented far greater challenges to the Union than those Morton had encountered. These radically changed circumstances meant that the Union had to be more pragmatic in its dealings with the Corporation and accept a pace of change unthinkable ten years earlier.

Such change manifested itself in a number of ways and prospects looked ominous in 1990 when plans were announced for the abolition of the BBC Radio Orchestra[10] at a cost of fifty-six jobs and a reported saving of £1 million per year (Press Association 1990). By this time the orchestra was arguably an under-utilised product of a different era and the MU's response was markedly more resigned than when BBC jobs had previously been threatened. Its priority was to retain the five BBC symphony orchestras and to ensure that those musicians facing redundancy left on the best terms, with a combination of pay-offs and guaranteed freelance work. Patrick again defended the Union's achievements, telling the 1995 Conference that the Union had 'managed to curb the worst excesses of the BBC's demands' and had also secured 'a commitment from the BBC to safeguard the future of the five existing orchestras' (Scard, personal communication).

This was achieved over a series of protracted negotiations, which stemmed from fundamental questions being asked within the BBC about whether it needed any orchestras at all and, if it did, on what basis. The Union was painfully aware that this time the BBC's management would not be coming from the same, largely sympathetic, perspective as their predecessors. Noted music critic Norman Lebrecht[11] explained the BBC's predicament, telling us that: 'The BBC was saying, "We need savings here. We don't need five orchestras. Why are we doing this? There are independent

10 Also known as the BBC Big Band.

11 Lebrecht has worked for *The Times*, the *Daily Telegraph*, and Radio 4. He currently blogs at http://slippedisc.com.

orchestras out there and we are under pressure from Parliament and the public not to compete with independent institutions, why are we maintaining these orchestras?"'. Lebrecht noted that at one point 'There were eleven BBC orchestras. There was a Radio Orchestra. Radio didn't need that many orchestras frankly. It probably didn't need any orchestras at all' (*2014*).

Another issue was the cost to the BBC of using its own orchestras. In many instances this was prohibitive and stemmed from agreements with the Union dating back to the days when it was opposed to almost any use of recorded music that might prevent a live performance. Central to this was the payment of 'residuals', a system whereby every time the BBC recorded one of its orchestras and the recording was repeated on air the musicians were paid again. When Roger Wright was appointed Head of Classical Music at the BBC in 1997,[12] he described a situation where the broadcaster 'had to jump through contractual hoops in order to put a camera in front of its own Symphony orchestra' and in which 'its Natural History unit found it cheaper to go to Munich or Prague to record a soundtrack than to book the BBC Concert Orchestra' (cited in Morrison 1999).

Telling the Union that such a situation was no longer tenable, Wright completed negotiations that resulted in a new agreement between the BBC and the MU described by Lebrecht as 'revolutionary in British terms' (*2014*). Put simply, the trade-off agreed was that, in return for the retention of the orchestras, from 1 July 1998 all rights for the use of their performances would be bought out at the point of contract. For Lebrecht, this represented 'an absolute breakthrough' not just for the BBC, but also for the other British orchestras who also benefited from the end of the residuals system – something he claims 'probably saved the orchestral economy in this country' (*2014*).

A frequent critic of the Union, Lebrecht now reflects that this was a 'moment of enlightenment ... which took a bit of vision on both parts, on Roger Wright's and Dennis Scard's' (*2014*). Thereby it provided further evidence of the Union's ability to change from an organisation that was often intransigent and obstinate to one that was pragmatic and flexible. Thus, it may have lost its stranglehold over orchestral music in the UK, but this sacrifice helped to preserve all of the major UK orchestras at a time when they were under serious threat and orchestras were closing across Europe.

[12] He became Head of Radio 3 a year later.

Restructuring

Scard's other priority on taking office had been to change the Union's internal workings. Like Morton, he was assisted in this regard by some high-level changes. The retirement of Jack Stoddart and Stan Hibbert meant that between the 1989 and 1991 Conferences, the Union's GS and two AGS positions had all changed hands. Ken Cordingley took over Stoddart's duties in live music and Stan Martin assumed Hibbert's responsibilities for media and administration. However, changing personnel in the top posts and a wider desire to reform did not ensure a smooth period of transition. Instead, change was gradual and contested at every juncture.

Understanding the scale of the task requires recognising that at the start of the 1990s the Union was organised in almost exactly the same way as it was at its inception, with an EC, district, and local branch structure. The MU was slow to respond to the type of technological and organisational change that had permeated many other unions. In addition, the intervening years had decreased the relevance of local branches to the many professional musicians whose work was often national and international.

Resistance to reform is largely attributable to the importance of the Branch Secretaries and the reluctance of the EC (which from the 1960s to 1980s was dominated by them[13]) to effect change. In 1989 there were still 114 branches, and their Secretaries' main tasks were to collect cash subscriptions and stamp members' cards. In addition, many of the branches were effectively dormant with tiny memberships.

Recalling this in his farewell speech to the Union's EC in 2000, Scard noted that on 1 January 1990 'the Union had 40,527 members and four subscription rates ranging from £37.44 to £114.40 with an average subscription collected of only £31 per member' (Scard, personal communication).[14] The reason for the low average subscription was largely down to the inflexibility of the system and the large number of members (estimated to be around a third) who were seriously behind with payments. Taken alongside the 25 per cent commission paid to the Branch Secretaries and the further 25 per cent that went to individual branch funds, it is clear that the Union had a slow, inefficient, and expensive membership system.

Scard realised that internal restructuring had to be done gradually and sensitively, and began by commissioning a report on the Union's operation by accountancy firm Pannell Kerr Foster (PKF) in 1991. Responding to the

13 For example, in 1985, there were eleven Branch Secretaries (and one Branch Chairman on the EC); in 1999 only three remained (MU, 2/1/34).

14 Rates were based on a member's annual income from music.

negativity this received in some quarters within the Union, John Patrick told the 1991 Conference that 'You can be assured that any changes to the way in which the Union operates will be considered very carefully and implemented only if they are in the best interests of the Union and its members' (Scard, personal communication). The report was important for two reasons: it was the first time that the Union's operation had been subject to extensive external scrutiny and it offered Scard a means of achieving some necessary, but potentially unpopular, reforms while remaining slightly removed from them.

Pannell Kerr Forster conducted a members' survey and visited a number of branches, focusing on the administration of subscriptions and collection methods as well as wider organisational structures. The key findings identified a split between the needs and perceptions of part-time and full-time musicians and noted that 'the current levels of membership subscription are considered to be inappropriate and potentially subject to abuse' (PKF 1991: 1). The Union's organisational structure was seen as 'too fragmented and the lines of reporting unclear' (1) and the weaknesses of the subscription collection system was laid bare. The main recommendations were a centralisation of membership services and improvement of the Union's technology to implement new means of registering members and collecting their subscriptions. In addition, it suggested relieving Branch Secretaries of the responsibility for collecting and accounting membership subscriptions, redirecting their roles towards 'recruitment, promotion of the Union, and greater interactive involvement with the membership at a local level' (1). More controversially, it recommended that 'remuneration of Branch Secretaries should be based on this new emphasis' (2).

Much of the remainder of the decade was spent trying to implement such reforms. Bill Sweeney, then an EC member, recalled the suspicion about the Report, especially in the wake of an earlier internal review of the branch structure. He told us that 'because the previous review was internal it was almost never going to come up with anything very radical. As PKF was external they did come up with something very radical. I remember one of the EC members saying he was going to vote against having this review because they'll come up with things we don't want to do' (*2013*).

Despite this, the 1991 Conference passed a motion noting that the Central London Branch had begun using a direct debit system for the collection of subscriptions and calling for this to be extended 'throughout the Union' (MU, 1/7/1991). Rule changes that facilitated moves towards this and some of the other PKF recommendations were passed by a membership vote in 1992, and by the mid-1990s a more centralised and efficient model for collecting subscriptions emerged. Scard later reflected on the problems associated with the centralised system, noting that 'a number of members were lost from our books, but frankly, the vast majority of these had not paid their subs for up to two years' (1998: 5). So, while membership had declined to 31,000 by 1998, '35% of our members pay by direct debit and virtually all our members are up-to-date with their subscriptions' (5). This was the first time in the Union's history that such a claim could be made and it represented a considerable step forward in its modernisation.

Andy Knight, a former Branch Secretary with background in technology, was appointed as an AGS at the start of 1997 with responsibility for the Union's administration[15] and he set about completing the Union's transition to a computerised system. He recalls opposition to almost all the changes, including ones offering discounts to members paying by direct debit or credit card (*2013*). For Scard, this was a battle about necessary modernisation. He suggested that 'there were two factions, the Luddites and the progressives. The progressives were always just about in the ascendancy. And we did lobby those members that we thought we could take with us' (*2013*).

Reforming the branch system and the role of the Branch Secretaries proved far more rancorous. Since his appointment, Scard had been working with various district committees to try and reduce the number of branches, sometimes seeking mergers of the smaller ones. By the end of his period in office they had shrunk from 114 to 73, resulting in accusations that he had single-handedly pursued a branch-closing agenda. From his perspective, this was obvious and represented consensual change. As he told the EC in 2000: 'We have agreed to close Branches mainly where we couldn't get a secretary elected. When a Branch has been closed or amalgamated, every Branch member has been given a say. Every District Council has endorsed the closure, as has the Executive Committee' (Scard, personal communication).

While Scard also recalls some of the proposed mergers 'going down like a bag of sick' (*2013*), Knight sensed a willingness amongst members to embrace change: 'I travelled round the country a lot and most of the membership thought it was inevitable ... but the Branch Secretaries, they did resist, right until the end. Unfortunately, some of the EC were equally resistant to change' (*2013*). Scard remembers the changes in the Union as having been incremental and achieved through 'good old trade union stuff. You just wear people down if you do it in bite-sized chunks' (*2013*).

Problems around reforming the Branch Secretaries' role stemmed from its anachronistic nature, the frequently loose interpretation of duties and

15 In 1997, the two previous AGSs, Cordingley and Martin, retired. Knight's was a new position, with Bob Wearn replacing Cordingley and John Smith replacing Martin.

responsibilities, the size and demographics of individual branches, and the nature of the payments and bonuses to the Secretaries. The level of diligence and time applied to the job varied from those where local publications and social/musical events were organised on a regular basis, to those that were, in Scard's words, 'moribund' (personal communication). John Smith, who became a full-time Union official in 1994 and GS in 2002, reported that during his campaign to become leader he discovered that one Branch Secretary had long been in a residential nursing home (*2014*). Such was the fragile nature of local democracy in the Union that some Branch Secretaries remained *in situ* for decades because of either the creation of a fiefdom or, more often, members' apathy.

Almost seven years passed from the PKF report until Scard announced the outcome of EC decisions on the future structure of the branch system and the role of the Branch Secretaries. In an article headlined 'Organise or fossilise' in the *Musician*, he announced EC decisions that 'branches should not comprise fewer than a hundred members' and that payment for Branch Secretaries would be reduced (1998). Previously, 25 per cent of subscriptions went to Branch Secretaries, 25 per cent to branches, and only 50 per cent to the National Office. From 1999, the remaining Branch Secretaries were to be paid 10 per cent of subscriptions from their branch, with incentives of an additional 5 per cent if membership levels in their area were sustained and a further 5 per cent if they 'communicated regularly with branch members' and visited 'venues and workplaces to fly the MU flag' (1998).

Branch reform, with the revised role of the Branch Secretaries and the resultant reductions in costs, constituted the most important and overdue restructuring in the Union's recent history (its need having been discussed at Conferences as early as 1969). Looked at holistically, Scard is entitled to be proud of the reforms he implemented through the 1990s, gradually fulfilling many of the PKF recommendations. Despite a decrease in membership and the end of the PPL income, the Union's assets were valued at £10.5 million in 1989 and £10.6 million in 2000 (MU, 2/2/5). In addition, financial reporting and accounting were generally more transparent and punctual than previously.[16]

Moreover, under Scard's leadership there was considerable evidence that the Union was beginning to widen its membership base, become more engaged and influential across the music industries, and offer a wider range of services to members. For example, during the 1990s it dropped the joining fee[17]

[16] However, decreases in the value of some investments caused substantial losses in 2001 and 2002.

[17] Historically, members had initially paid to join the Union as well as paying an ongoing subscription.

and introduced discounted membership rates for young people and those on the New Deal for Musicians (NDfM).[18] Scard became a founder member of the Music Industry Forum, a cross-industry advisory body set up by Culture Minister Chris Smith in 1998, and there was also an expansion of both the Union's insurance and its legal services.[19]

Thus began a shift in the core activities of the Union from primarily being centred on industrial relations to placing a greater emphasis on lobbying and service provision. The extension of these activities is covered in the next chapter, but requires contextualisation. Faced with falling membership and severe limitations on their activities engendered by the legislation of the previous two decades, McIlroy describes how in many instances 'industrial relations and trade unions were no longer adversarial' (2009: 50). Bacon and Storey note that by the mid-1990s, many unions were relying 'less on the collective context for Union activity and more on services that can be provided to individual members' (1996: 56). Having been in partnership with some of the major musical employers for almost half a century, this perhaps represented less of a sea change for the MU than it did for some industrial unions, but it was not uncontroversial.

Electoral problems

Despite the considerable organisational reforms achieved under his leadership, some of the restructuring Scard initiated had alienated a significant number of members. He was ultimately to pay for this with his job. In retrospect, the events leading up to and following his removal as GS, which played out between 1999–2002, were the result of a perfect storm, caused by changes in the music profession and music industries, coupled with trade union legislation and discontent within the MU. Scard's failure to secure re-election as General Secretary in 2000 was both a complicated and unprecedented saga and engendered the most serious internal crisis the Union had faced since the advent of the talkies some seventy years earlier.

This chain of events was triggered by what, for the MU, was normally a procedural issue. Under its rules, an election for the GS post had to be held every five years, though previously no incumbent had been opposed. Members were informed of the forthcoming election via the *Bulletin to Branches* and potential candidates were invited to gather the ten nominations

18 A scheme instigated for young unemployed musicians under the 1997 Labour Government.

19 The Union offered members public liability insurance as well as discounted car and instrument insurance rates. The contractual advice scheme was outsourced when Mark Melton left in 1994.

from branches necessary to secure a place on the ballot paper. In both 1994 and 1999 Scard was elected unopposed and, despite rumblings of discontent around the distribution of the PPL monies and the reframing of the Branch Secretaries' roles, looked set to remain leader until at least 2004. However, the 1999 election was challenged by Brian Johnson who, along with two other members, complained to the Trade Union Certification Officer (TUCO) that it had been conducted in contravention of the Trade Unions and Labour Relations (Consolidation) Act 1992. Their complaints alleged insufficient notification of the election,[20] a lack of time for potential opponents to gather nominations,[21] and a lack of an independent scrutineer. With some of the complaints upheld by the TUCO, the Union was forced to rerun the election in November 2000.[22]

The publicity surrounding this allowed for a more sustained challenge to Scard – this time by Derek Kay, a member of the East London Branch, who comfortably gathered sufficient nominations from branches to secure his candidature. Kay's campaign was both controversial and effective – harnessing the various issues that had festered over previous years (notably over the use of the PPL funds, the Union's financial position, its conduct of elections to the EC and London District Committee, and the treatment of individual Branch Secretaries).[23] Through a mixture of direct engagement with branches and a website that published correspondence and complaints, Kay gathered considerable support. However, and perhaps because of the unprecedented nature of the election, his candidacy was not widely viewed as a significant threat to the incumbent. Retrospectively, Scard admitted that he did not take the challenge sufficiently seriously:

> I didn't worry about it to be frank. I thought it would be all right. Then I started to see what he was writing about me and the Union, which was just wrong. He said that we were bankrupt and that I had got rid of people, malcontents, whatever. Plus you have got a job to do. I didn't have all day to sit around worrying about my re-election. (*2013*)

Although Andy Knight admits now that 'in hindsight, I also think that we didn't believe Dennis would lose' (*2013*), others had warned Scard of

[20] Although it had been advertised in the Bulletin to branches, they argued that this did not go to all members of the Union, and that there had been no mention of the election in the Musician, the one publication that did.

[21] At the time of the original election date Johnson had gathered nine of the ten required nominations.

[22] The full ruling is at www.gov.uk/government/uploads/system/uploads/attachment_data/file/332390/79246639-fa93-4820-ad37-04ac315c993c.pdf.

[23] The most prominent case was that of the longstanding Oxford Branch Secretary, Roger Woodby, who took the Union to an employment tribunal and lost.

the dangers posed by Kay's campaign. Both Richard Watson and Horace Trubridge reported attempts to intervene, the latter admitting that 'Nigel McCune[24] and I became aware that Derek Kay was a real threat because up until then nobody had taken him too seriously. We went and saw Dennis and we said "Dennis, we are really worried that you are going to lose this election. We are prepared to run a little campaign to let people know that Derek Kay would not be a suitable GS"' (*2014*). Watson, who was running Scard's campaign, also spoke to the incumbent: 'I told him "Look Dennis, this chap is getting a lot of support for all the wrong reasons, there's a risk. You need to do something about this"' (*2012*).

For various reasons Scard declined to fight dirty. He told us that he had not wished to challenge some of Kay's more serious allegations directly as this would have involved going to the High Court for an injunction, with all the potential reputational and financial damage to the Union this might entail. Unbeknown to his colleagues, he had also been recently diagnosed with cancer. 'I'd been in hospital and had an operation and was having radiotherapy, so I wasn't at my best' (*2013*).

Announced on 13 November, the result of the election was, nevertheless, unprecedented. Scard lost by eight votes (4,024 to 4,016), setting off a chain of events that were to have far-reaching consequences. The nature of the campaign and the unprecedented circumstances – for which the Union's rules (and Executive) were completely unprepared – meant that there was little possibility of a smooth transition of power. Kay's scheduled assumption of office on 2 January 2001 was cast into doubt when, on the day after the election, Scard put six complaints against him to the London District Disciplinary Committee. Kay disputed Scard's right to do this[25] and the bad feeling between the two was further evidenced when Kay visited the Union office shortly after the election. 'I didn't let him in', Scard told us, 'and I said to him "Until such time as the EC has endorsed the result of the election, you are not the GS"' (*2013*).

Both men now found themselves in limbo. Scard was involved in ongoing negotiations with the EC to smooth his departure and Kay had to wait until the looming disciplinary hearing to be sure he would be permitted to assume office. What followed was two years of legal battles between the Union and Kay and his supporters before the situation was resolved. Meanwhile, the Union faced an unrelenting stream of negative reports in the press, internal disputes, referrals to the TUCO, and appearances in the High Court.

24 Then the MU's Music Business Adviser.

25 It was unclear whether Scard was legally entitled to sign the referral as GS and whether the Union was able to take disciplinary action against a GS.

Kay's disciplinary hearing took place on 20 December, two days before Scard's last day in office. The hearing upheld three of the six complaints against Kay, most notably that of bringing the Union into disrepute in relation to statements made during the campaign about its finances. This did not, however, settle matters, as the committee delayed announcing the sanctions to be imposed against him until 12 January, meaning that Kay could take office as planned on 2 January.

His time in office did not last long. The Disciplinary Committee suspended him from membership of the Union for nine months and prevented him from holding office within the Union for five years. Kay fought the decision, attempting to get an interim injunction from the High Court (he failed) and appealing to the Executive. In the interim, the EC and the three AGSs (Knight, Smith, and Wearn) were running the Union on a day-to-day basis while Kay was placed on gardening leave until his appeal was heard. This reduced Kay's suspensions to six months (from the Union) and two years (from holding office), but merely created further ructions and did not resolve the leadership issue. Kay threatened to take matters to an Employment Tribunal and a complaint was raised against the Chair of the EC, John Patrick, for exceeding his authority. Gerry Saunders, one of Kay's supporters on the EC, resigned in protest.

A hastily convened press conference at Ronnie Scott's on 1 March served only to draw attention to the divisions and problems. *Music Week* reported that the Union had 'lurched from one crisis to another' (10 March 2001: 1). This continued into April, when Saunders and Tony Richards set up the Concerned Musicians' Group (CMG), whose suspicions were further roused when details of proposed payments to Scard were leaked from within the EC. By now, despite Knight's dismissal of the CMG as 'bullshit and bluster' (cited in Ashton 2001a), the problems were considerable. Besides the two High Court challenges to Kay's suspension, the success of Johnson's complaint to the TUCO established this as a useful mechanism for disgruntled members and further complaints followed.

While these were to have mixed outcomes for the complainants, the uncertainty they caused made future planning difficult for those trying to lead the Union. Hamstrung by the time and cost of fighting the challenges, the EC's next move was ultimately to resolve the situation. Their decision to hold a membership ballot on whether Kay's suspension should stand was a means of legitimising the previous rulings of the EC and the London District, as any vote in favour would seriously undermine Kay's position. Kay described this as 'the most dishonourable thing the EC have done' (cited in Ashton 2001b) and again unsuccessfully applied for an injunction, before the ballot took place at the end of September. The outcome was a victory for the EC (4,319 votes to 2,437). *Music Week* was premature in announcing that 'the long, bitter and expensive battle between the MU and its suspended General Secretary is finally over' (Ashton 2001c), but shortly after the ballot, and prior to Kay's High Court appeal against his suspension, it was announced that an agreement between the two parties had been reached.

Andy Knight, who had been promoted to the post of Deputy General Secretary (DGS) partially to fulfil the GS functions,[26] met Kay at the TUC's headquarters to finalise an agreement. The details remain confidential, but Knight diplomatically described the outcome as an 'amicable agreement' and Ashton reported that 'the MU has paid Kay some compensation for legal fees incurred and the loss of his job' (2001c). In addition, he was asked to relinquish any claim to the post. While our interviewees offered differing accounts of the settlement, the detail is less significant than the consequences. The Union had incurred substantial costs in its efforts to resolve the situation and its priority was now to clear the way for a new election. Such had been the turmoil that this would also prove difficult. While a settlement had been reached with Kay, his supporters' grievances had not vanished.

Before the EC could meet to revise the rules for the next election to avoid a repeat of the previous debacle, John Patrick stood down from his position as Chair of the EC, a position he had held since 1968. The means of his election had also been taken to the TUCO,[27] but before its ruling on 12 October that Patrick had to leave the post, he quit. He told us that 'I saw the writing on the wall. I think if I wanted to stay on I would have been reasonably confident of being elected in 2002, but ... I was seventy and I was starting to feel that I had had enough' (*2014*). Patrick's lengthy service as Chair was recognised by Richard Watson in the *Musician* (December 2001). Thus another significant (and, like Scard, now divisive) figure in the Union's history had been a casualty of the election fallout.

If 2001 was the Union's *annus horribilis*, then 2002 was little better, with the move towards another election beset by both financial and legal problems. The Union continued to be leaderless and stagnant, unable to progress while fighting internal battles. The year started with a membership ballot over the new rules for the election of a GS, but these too were challenged at TUCO on a procedural technicality. Although each of the changes was approved with a large majority,[28] Knight realised in the course of the process that the branches

26 This was the first and last time the Union had filled such a post.

27 This was found to be in breach of the Trade Union and Labour Relations (Consolidation) Act of 1992: www.gov.uk/government/uploads/system/uploads/attachment_data/file/331225/Decisions_D-88–90.01_October_2001.pdf.

28 5,430 votes were returned; the majorities for the changes varied from 2,857 to 5,174.

had not been properly circulated prior to the ballot, prompting another complaint by Saunders. While the Union accepted its mistake, it unsuccessfully argued that the cost of another ballot (estimated at around £15,000) and the size of the majorities meant a repeat ballot was unnecessary. When the ruling was published in 2002 it declared the Union's new rules 'void and ineffective' and ordered a return to its previous rules.[29] This not only delayed a future GS election, but also rendered the election of Watson, Sweeney, and Phil Garnham to the EC under the new rules invalid.

This was resolved by another ballot, conducted under the old rules, but caused further embarrassment for the Union and pre-empted Knight's departure as DGS in September. Attempts to restore a degree of normality ensued with the establishment of a Strategic Review Group and the eventual advertisement of the GS position. The former was designed primarily to tackle the Union's increasing financial problems, which were blamed on a combination of poorly performing investments, low membership income, and the costs of the previous years' legal actions, while the latter at last allowed the possibility of a new leader. Four candidates stood for election – the two remaining AGSs (Smith and Wearn) as well as Chris Hodgkins and Kay, who attempted to regain his position. He was unsuccessful in the first ballot, with Smith and Hodgkins moving to a second ballot after no candidate received 50 per cent of the vote. When the results were announced on 13 December, Smith secured the GS position by 4,606 votes to 3,335. With a new GS the Union saw some prospect of stability for the first time in over three years.

Smith set out his objectives as 'rebuilding a cohesive Senior Officials team at National Office' and to 'work on a Strategic Review of all our operations and draw up a new rule book' (MU press release, 13 December 2002). He planned to have these in place by the following summer's conference, and while his election did not end the dissent within the Union, it was to mark the end of Kay and his supporters as a significant force within it.

Conclusion

It is easy to view Smith's election in the light of the battles against Staff, as well as those Kay and his various supporters conducted over the previous three years. However, its real significance lies in a much a wider context, involving a longstanding need for the Union to reform internally and to respond to legislative changes that had impacted on it. Such issues can be traced back to the

29 www.gov.uk/government/uploads/system/uploads/attachment_data/file/331347/D23.02.pdf (11).

start of John Morton's period as GS, and while he successfully delayed and mitigated the worst effects of cuts in public expenditure on the arts, the commercialisation of radio, and the curbing of trade union powers, the combination of these was an irresistible force by the time Scard took office in 1990.

Faced with the outcomes of the MMC report, perennial threats to orchestral employment, and the legislative restrictions placed on trade unions, Scard was no longer able to apply the same leverage or power over employers that his post-war predecessors had enjoyed. However, a large part of the membership found this difficult to accept, and were inherently hostile to structural change within the Union. Others embraced the individualistic, entrepreneurial traits encouraged by the Thatcher and Major Governments, and these assorted tensions provided the backdrop to the unprecedented events that concluded with Smith's election.

The period between 1999 and 2002 showed how a relatively small number of what Scard calls 'malcontents' (*2013*)[30] could disrupt the MU's present operations and shape its future direction. In common with other unions (Clegg 1980), the MU suffered from a low level of engagement and participation by members in its activities and ballots. However, it was the very specific circumstances within the MU during the 1990s that created a unique situation, whereby some members used the Union's democratic structures in conjunction with trade union legislation to effect change. In doing so, they were able to remove both the GS and the Chair of the EC from their posts, while forming a loose coalition in opposition to reform.

In some circumstances this could be viewed as a triumph of both internal democracy and legislation designed to make unions more accountable and transparent. In this instance, it is not as clear-cut. The short-term outcomes, and the personal toll on those who lost their jobs, were disastrous. They plunged the Union into a crisis that arguably threatened its very existence and certainly questioned its continued relevance. Nevertheless, Kay and his supporters also raised important and fundamental questions as to what a trade union representing musicians should look like in the twenty-first century. There is little evidence that they had the answers, but their intervention made the completion of radical reform of personnel, structure, and methods all the more imperative. To boot, Kay's emphatic defeat in the 2002 election effectively ended the influence of his supporters within the Union and allowed his successor (Smith) the kind of unobstructed run at implementing reform that had been denied to Scard.

30 The 4,024 votes Kay received represented about 13 per cent of the Union's membership.

9

Beginning again: the MU in the twenty-first century

This chapter brings matters firmly into the contemporary era. It examines the MU's internal reorganisation, its lobbying and campaigns, and its attempts to deal with equalities issues. Lastly, it considers the Union's present structure and activities. We draw on a number of interviews conducted during our research and argue that the current GS, John Smith, has been successful both in modernising the Union and in relocating it more centrally within the music industries.

Reorganising

The 'Derek Kay affair' illustrated the need for fundamental changes in how the Union operated. This was clearly another watershed moment, producing a clear consensus that without action the Union's future was in jeopardy. According to Smith (*2014*) the EC 'were saying "we can't go on like this. This has been such a *nightmare*"' (original emphasis). In retrospect the events provided an ideal opportunity for reform. This subsequently took place on two overlapping levels, the practical and the ideological.

Smith told us that his first job was picking the Union up off the floor, as 'it really was a demoralised organisation' (*2014*). He immediately began fulfilling his promises to appoint a new senior team and establish a Strategic Review. The former was made easier by the departures of Knight and Wearn, who were replaced by David Ashley and Horace Trubridge. The review was wide-ranging, but focused on solving the Union's financial problems, reforming the branch system, and rewriting the rule book. Reforming the branch system was of particular concern. The Union still had seventy-two branches across nine districts. This structure remained expensive to run, out of sync with modern music-making, and frequently a hindrance to effecting change. It was no longer fit for purpose.

A first test of whether Smith's plans would carry the support of the members came at the 2003 Conference. The Conference Chair, Bill Sweeney, conducted a straw poll of those present over a number of potential changes to the Union's rules and structure. Although this was breaking with convention, it showed the extent of the appetite for reform, even among some Branch Secretaries – who, as Richard Watson put it, were effectively 'turkeys voting for Christmas' (*2012*).

Formal implementation of the proposed new rules and structure came after a series of consultative meetings and a membership ballot in 2004. Smith wrote in the *Musician* that the EC's intention was 'to relaunch the Union as an organisation that is equipped and ready to face the challenges of the 21st century music industry', arguing that 'we have to leave behind our 19th century structure. This is one of the most important issues that the Union has faced in its 110 year history' (Smith 2003b).

Members were given a choice of two new structures, with one expressly backed by the EC. There was a 92 per cent vote in favour of the latter, in a 22 per cent turn out.[1] The new structure replaced the branches and districts with six regions,[2] each with its own full-time organiser and support staff. For David Ashley, this marked a 'move away from willing amateurs to professionals', while Smith noted that the new system would 'provide clearer and faster lines of communication' and allow the Union to 'concentrate on the industry' (both cited in Ashton 2004: 4).

Although there was an unsuccessful legal challenge to the restructuring, and some sentimental attachment to the local branches among older members, the structure remains in place today and there appears to be little appetite for further change. Regional officials were previously responsible for the functioning of branches within their locale, and abolishing the branches meant that officials could potentially spend more time dealing with members' individual concerns. Overall, it appears that the Union is now more 'professional' in campaigning, recruiting officials, and dealing with members. These reforms have had the general support of the membership, with Smith successfully standing unopposed for re-election in both 2007 and 2012. His reflection that 'I'm a dogged moderniser and that must be my legacy' (*Smith 2014*) appears to carry some weight.

The Union's ideological reorganisation centred on Smith's vision for the Union – 'to make sure we're a music industry organisation' (*Smith 2014*) – a process that he acknowledged had begun under Morton and developed under

1 6,201 to 509, with nine spoilt papers (*Musician*, June 2004: 5).

2 Scotland and Northern Ireland, North of England, Midlands, Wales and South-West England, London, East and South-East England.

Scard. For Horace Trubridge (*2014*) Smith's leadership had seen the Union 'better established in the music industry now than it has ever been'.

It is important to place this in the wider context of the music industries during the same period. Each of the major music industries (publishing, live, and especially recording) attempted to get closer to Government as they increasingly sought policies that, they hoped, would help them shore up their business models. Meanwhile, some politicians saw potential benefit in being associated with the music industries (Cloonan 2007), and the Blair Government had encouraged the representations of the industries in ways that previous Governments had not. In this regard the MU's leadership clearly saw a need to be part of a broad coalition seeking benefit for the music industries, and John Smith (*2014*) has commented that he was 'pleased we're at the table'. The Union's current relationship with the music industries can be illustrated by a study of some of the major issues on which it has worked in recent years.

Campaigning: live music and copyright

As a trade union the MU is constantly campaigning and lobbying for reform in various areas germane to its members and the wider music profession. Recent examples of this have included the Work Not Play campaign. Music Supported Here[3] – an anti-piracy initiative – and the Lost Arts campaign[4] aimed at countering cuts to Government support for the arts. The Union is also engaged in ongoing campaigning in areas such as music education (including the rights of members who teach) and in lobbying airlines to treat musical instruments with due care. To an extent such issues are routine and, by their nature, somewhat long-term. Their success can also be hard to measure. However, campaigns that produce legislative change can be viewed as successful, even if the result is not always entirely what was hoped for.

Here we examine two legislative changes for which the Union campaigned: live music regulation and copyright reform. Our argument is that while both campaigns can be viewed as successes for the Union, they were built not on traditional trade union industrial muscle, but around partnerships that can be seen as exemplifying the collaborative approach Smith has fostered.

One pressing issue when he became GS was how the Union should respond to proposed changes to the regulation of live music venues in England and Wales. These were contained in the Licensing Act 2003, the aim of which was

3 www.musicsupportedhere.com.
4 www.lost-arts.org.

to reform these countries' somewhat archaic (alcohol) licensing laws. In April 2000 the Government published a White Paper, *Time for Reform* (Home Office 2000), with a Licensing Bill following in November 2002. This aimed to bring somewhat disparate pieces of licensing legislation together into a coherent whole. One of its four types of licensable activity concerned the provision of regulated entertainment, including live music. The Bill became a key concern for the Union and was described by John Smith as a 'massive, massive, issue' (*2014*).

In England and Wales the system for licensing the provision of live music can be divided into those regulations affecting London and those pertaining to other areas.[5] Prior to the 2003 Act the prevailing system was that venues outside London applied for licences for permission to stage live music via a public entertainment licence (PEL) under the 1964 Licensing Act. Within London, the 1964 Local Government (Miscellaneous Provisions) Act empowered the capital's local authorities to issue, and charge for, PELs – a system that was extended to the rest of the country in 1982. In both cases PELs were additional to the licence needed to sell alcohol and the new Act proposed replacing the need for a separate PEL with a single licence covering both alcohol sales and the provision of live entertainment. The 1964 legislation stipulated that entertainment licences were not needed for events featuring up to two musicians under what became known as the 'two in a bar' provision. However, the new Bill proposed that, with the exception of up to twelve Temporary Events per annum, the provision of *any* live music would require a licence (Ward 2011: 11–12). The Government claimed that abolishing the 'two in a bar' regulation and bringing together the licences for music and alcohol would cut red tape (Ward 2011: 4) and facilitate a 'boom' in the provision of live music.[6]

The MU had long questioned the need for live music to require a licence at all in venues – such as bars and restaurants – where the provision of entertainment is secondary to their main business (Perkins 2003). It was to the fore in voicing concern that the new regulations would deter people from promoting live music (Wearn 2001). Its protests included getting groups of musicians to visit pubs and ask to be allowed to play, only to be refused (Wearn 2001), an Early Day Motion in Parliament, and getting the UK Parliament's All Party Music group to tape over their mouths at a Whitehall protest (Anon. 2002; Kennedy 2002). The Bill suffered several reversals during its passage through Parliament, including a defeat in the House of Lords where an MU-backed

[5] Northern Ireland and Scotland have separate regulatory regimes.

[6] See Live Music Forum (2007: 30) for examples of such claims.

amendment that would have exempted gigs of up to 200 people and finishing before 11.30 p.m. was accepted (Hall 2003).[7]

Despite such opposition the Act was passed on 8 July 2003 and came into force on 24 November 2005.[8] Faced with this reality, the Union could now only campaign for reform. In an effort to placate critics the Government had agreed to monitor the Act's impact, and to facilitate this the Department of Culture, Media and Sport (DCMS) established a Live Music Forum (LMF) comprising various stakeholders within live music.[9] The Forum aimed to 'take forward the Ministerial commitment to maximize the take-up of reforms in the Licensing Act 2003 relating to the performance of live music; promote the performance of live music generally; and monitor and evaluate the impact of the Licensing Act 2003 on the performance of live music' (cited in Cloonan 2007: 54). The MU praised this as 'the biggest commitment made by any government to live music' (Allison 2004).

The Forum met thirteen times and issued a number of reports on the state of the live sector, perhaps the most important of which came in July 2007. This reported on the Act's results, arguing that its impact on live music had been 'broadly neutral' and had 'not led to the promised increase in live music', despite numerous claims by Ministers that it would result in a 'vast increase' or 'explosion' (LMF 2007: 10). Overall, it suggested, serious issues remained (10), and whether live music even needed a licence remained questionable (11). The Government responded by accepting a number of suggested changes to the Guidance to the Act and committed itself to examining whether smaller gigs could be exempt from the need for a licence (DCMS 2007: 5). By this point, MU opposition to the Act had softened a little and rather than campaigning for its repeal, it concentrated on trying to ensure the fulfilment of ministerial promises to help live music.

In July 2008 the UK Parliament's cross-party Culture, Media and Sport Committee launched an inquiry into the Act including its impact on live music. This included hearing evidence from the MU, Equity, and LMF Chair Feargal Sharkey. The MU supplied written evidence that supported exemptions for small venues and further suggested tax breaks for venues that hosted more than fifty live music events each year. It also reiterated the Union's view that live entertainment should not have been included in the Act (Culture, Media and Sport Committee 2009: Ev88–91). During his evidence before the

7 The Act did not include this amendment.

8 For reflections on the MU's initial campaign see Blain (2003) and Smith (2003b).

9 Including the British Beer and Pub Association, the Arts Council for England, the National Foundation for Youth Music, the National Music Council, and the National Assembly for Wales.

Committee John Smith argued for a fast-track system for variations to live music licences (Ev95). The Committee found that the Act had not been the success the Government hoped for, cited research suggesting that the amount of live music in small venues might even have *fallen* by 5 per cent (28), and supported the MU's call for exemptions for venues of up to 200 people (30).

The Government response denied any link between audience size and the potential for disorder (Secretary of State for Culture, Media and Sport 2009: 9). But in October 2009 it announced that it was contemplating exempting gigs of up to 100 people from requiring licences. The DCMS carried out an impact assessment of this proposal (2009a), a consultation paper was issued (DCMS 2009b), and the possibility of the limit being raised to 200 was mooted (Ward 2011: 17). Progress was disrupted when, in May 2010, the Labour Government was voted out. The new Conservative/Liberal Democrat Coalition Government promptly announced another consultation, on plans to exempt audiences of up to 5,000 from the need for a licence (DCMS 2011: 21). Following this, in 2012 a Live Music Act was passed that allowed for amplified gigs of up to 200 people taking place between the hours of 8 a.m. and 11 p.m. to be exempt from the need for a licence.[10] Unamplified gigs of any capacity are were also exempted.

Smith hailed this as a 'very, very rare political victory' (Smirke 2012), and certainly this long-term campaign was ultimately successful. However, what is less clear is the extent to which this success can be attributed to the Union's affiliation to the Labour Party, which had introduced and implemented the 2003 Act and then failed to listen to reformers, including the LMF. When reform *did* come it was via a Liberal Democrat Lord, Tim Clement-Jones, who – having failed in previous attempts to reform the Act – eventually introduced the Live Music Act via a Private Member's Bill in the House of Lords.[11] This received Government support and its passing eased the restrictions on staging live music. It was an undoubted victory for the MU's position, but was not achieved as a result of its affiliation to Labour. Rather it was due to the work of individual campaigners and the MU's association with a range of industries' bodies.

A second major cross-industrial campaigning issue for the Union in the last decade has been that of copyright. As has been shown, the MU's relationship with copyright and its associated organisations has been an important feature of its history. It is therefore unsurprising that the Union became part of a broad consensus amongst music industries' organisations that one solution

10 See www.livemusicforum.co.uk/circulars.html.

11 See Ward (2011) for more on Clement-Jones' campaign (16) and the Bill's provisions (19).

to the problems facing the music economy was strengthened copyright legislation. The result was that it found common interest with, and campaigned alongside, many organisations that employed or sub-contracted its members in a campaign that also helped to bring to fruition Smith's vision of the Union being at the heart of the music industries.

Once again, the context here was technological change and the effects it was having on both the record industry and its workers. Of particular concern were internet-based file-sharing platforms that allowed consumers to upload – and share – their music collections online without any payment being made to rightsholders. The story of the evolution of peer-to-peer (P2P) exchange websites and in particular the rise of Napster is a familiar one,[12] but its main importance here is that it facilitated a crisis in the recording sector as revenues declined at the same time as file-sharing grew.[13] While the recording industry made various responses to the crisis the most important for the MU was its focus on reforming copyright legislation via extending the period for which sound recordings remained in copyright.

Within UK copyright legislation there are rights in the composition, recording, and performances of music, and it was the two latter elements that became the focus of attention for both PPL and the MU. As noted earlier, under the 1911 Copyright Act the period for which recordings remained in copyright was fifty years. In the context of declining sales of recorded music representatives from the recording industry came to see extending this term as a vital goal. The labels had the potential to benefit from being able to sell recordings for longer, while – depending on their contractual arrangements with the label – performers could also potentially benefit from an extended period during which any public use of their recordings would result in payments to PPL.

The ability of organisations from different parts of the British music industries to work together on copyright matters can be traced to the formation of British Music Rights (BMR) in 1996 by the British Academy of Songwriters, Composers and Authors (BASCA), the Music Publishers' Association (MPA), the Mechanical-Copyright Protection Society (MCPS), and the PRS. British Music Rights expanded its interests with the formation of the Music Business Forum (MBF) in 2002, where it joined with organisations whose primary interest was in the copyright on the recordings and the performances – notably the Association of Independent Music (AIM), the British Association of

12 For a record industry insider account see Silver (2013). For academic accounts see David (2010), Dolata (2011), and Wikström (2013).

13 This is not to imply causality.

Record Dealers (BARD), the Music Managers' Forum (MMF), the MU, the National Music Council, and PPL.

The MBF duly became the primary vehicle for music industries' representations around copyright as leading figures pressed for an extension of the fifty-year term. Inevitably, PPL was at the forefront of this campaign, as it was the record companies who were being hit hardest by the combination of falling CD prices and their loss of control over distribution. In short, they had the most to gain from term extension. In some ways this was history repeating itself, as it was falling income and a concomitant desire to expand existing revenue streams that had led the record companies to take the Carwardine case in 1933. Seventy years later and record companies again sought to expand their rights and revenues, this time via term extension. However, while in 1934 the MU had for the most part been an onlooker with little interest in copyright, it was now an active participant and joined the campaign for term extension. Though any potential benefits in a change in the law to its non-featured performer members would be substantially less than those accruing to the record companies and some featured artists, this was still a campaign behind which the Union could legitimately claim a shared interest with the record companies. It held out the possibility of more income for many of its members – something it would have been foolish to oppose.[14]

A further motivating factor for advocates of term extension was that many recordings from the 'golden age' of British popular music (*c.* 1962–69) were about to fall out of copyright. For the record labels this meant a loss of control; for the MU it meant that members who made such recordings faced losing a regular source of income. There was thus a common interest, and when BMR mutated into UK Music in 2008, the MU remained a member.

Debates around term extension had intensified in December 2005 when the Government announced the establishment of an Independent Review of Intellectual Property under the Chairmanship of former *Financial Times* editor Andrew Gowers. The Review concluded that 'the arguments in favour of term extension [are] unconvincing' (Gowers 2006: 56) and, much to the chagrin of some within the music industries, recommended retaining the fifty-year term. This resulted in outrage in the trade publication *Music Week*.[15] The MU criticised his rejection of term extension, his allowance of format-to-format copying for private use without fair remuneration for rightsholders, and his acceptance of exemptions on the grounds of parody and pastiche (*Musician*, spring 2007: 12).

14 Any such benefits would apply to those making recordings, with the actual amounts determined by whatever contractual arrangement the musicians had.

15 See Williamson *et al.* (2011: 466–9).

The lobbyists' attention now increasingly turned towards the European Parliament discussions that were taking place simultaneously. Further intensive campaigning by industries' bodies in Europe for term extension culminated in September 2011 when the European Parliament issued Directive 2011/77/EU. This extended protection to seventy years[16] and passed into UK law on 1 November 2013.[17]

The MU claimed to have 'played a key role in persuading the UK government to back term extension' (*Musician*, winter 2011: 6). Two things are worthy of note here. The first is that the battle was fought and won in the European Commission, thus illustrating the importance of international lobbying.[18] The second is that the MU had joined a range of music industries' organisations lobbying for term extension. Here, it was unity with the major employers, not its allies in the labour movement, that brought success.

Importantly, neither of the successes outlined here was a consequence of the Union's labour movement affiliations. One came via the EU and the other via a Liberal Democrat Lord following years of a Labour Government declining to move in the Union's direction. Working alongside industries' organisations – many of whom directly or indirectly employed musicians – might be seen a quite a change from 1893, when the formative AMU sought to impose *its* view of the music profession on employers. However, both positions encompass a concern for musicians' income. If in 1893 the battle was for waged musicians working in theatres and music halls, by 2011 it was a concern to increase the income of freelance musicians working in myriad areas. While one involved direct negotiation, the other involved protracted lobbying alongside employers. In both cases the Union sought to maximise income for as many musicians as possible. The seeds of this approach were sown in earlier years but flourished as part of the Union's 'modernisation'. This process also embraced wider concerns.

Equalities

The previous chapters have noted the absence of women and ethnic minorities in both the music profession generally, but also among the MU's membership and officials. We return to matters of equalities now in the context of the modernisation of the Union to illustrate how on matters of both gender and race the MU has progressed in more recent times.

16 http://ec.europa.eu/internal_market/copyright/term-protection/index_en.htm.

17 www.gov.uk/government/news/musicians-benefit-from-extended-copyright-term-for-sound-recordings.

18 Smith (*2014*) suggested that lobbying via FIM was one key aspect to the campaign's success.

The position of women in the music profession – and their representation – remains a problem, and a 2015 survey of equalities in the classical music sector found 'a relative lack of women in positions of authority and prestige' while people from minority ethnic and working-class backgrounds remained under-represented within the profession (Scharff 2015: 5). Within the MU (as across British society generally) issues of equality have risen up the agenda in recent times, but these remain a concern for many Union activists, and require placing within a wider historical overview. To do this we draw on feminist accounts of the music industries, the MU archive, and interviews with current officials.

It is telling that few feminist accounts of the UK's music industries make reference to the Union. Steward and Garratt's pioneering study (1984) ignores it, as do O'Brien (1995) and Leonard (2007), while Reddington (2007) only mentions it in passing. Bayton (1998) notes the low percentage of women active in music, but credits the Union with attempting to counter discrimination and forward equalities by things such as supporting Women in Music and the Women's Music Festival (202).

Similarly, trawling the Union's archive for references to women prior to the 1970s is an unrewarding task, and the casual observer could be forgiven for thinking there were no female members at all. Indeed, they were often only on the Union's radar when they were seen to be depressing wages by taking lower-paid jobs (for example during the First World War), and there has still to be a woman holding a position in the Union's Secretariat. The vast majority of Branch Secretaries were men, and it was 1990 before Barbara White became just the second woman to be elected to the EC. A 1971 staff list (MU, 1/7/ 1971) for the Union's National Office showed that Mike Evans' claim (*2013*) that 'all the officials were men and all the secretaries were women' when he joined six years later accurately reflects the Union at the time.

It was during the intervening period that things began to change, thanks largely to a small number of London-based activists. One of them, Liz Hambleton, noted that 'only 15% of the Central London Branch membership of the Musicians' Union and yet more than 50% of all music students are women' (1974: 44), and by the end of the 1970s only 12 per cent of the Union's entire membership was female (Morris and Price 1986: 40). This partly reflected the sizeable disadvantages women had in entering the music profession and the ingrained and prejudicial attitudes towards their ability.[19]

[19] For example, in 1975, the harpist was the only female member of the LSO; the LPO had 7 female members (out of 89), and the BBCSO 16 out of 105.

Hambleton's *Spare Rib* article, which was later reprinted in the *Musician* (see Figure 17), came in the lead-up to UNESCO's International Women's Year (1975) and the Sex Discrimination Act of the same year, with both raising the profile of issues of gender equality, including within the MU. Hambleton was one of the founders of a Women's Sub-Committee of the Central London

Figure 17 The *Musician* highlights International Women's Year in 1975 (MU, 1/5).

Branch, and argued for women to become more involved in Union affairs and for the setting up of 'a system of fair auditions for orchestras involving concealment of identity until the decision is made' (Hambleton 1974). She also called for the introduction of maternity leave ('almost non-existent') and job-sharing in orchestras, all radical ideas at the time but ones that have gradually become incorporated into mainstream thinking. In particular, moves towards 'blind' auditions for orchestral musicians – something the MU had supported (*Scard 2013*) – have, according to Lebrecht (*2014*), transformed the orchestral world.

Along with that of others such as Maggie Nicols, Lindsay Cooper, and Jinny Fisher, Hambleton's work both encouraged women to get involved in the Union and raised awareness of the issues they faced as working musicians. In response, the Union supported a 1975 conference on women's issues in the profession, which revealed 'areas of common oppression among women from all fields of music' (Fudger 1975: 44). Some monies from the PPL funds were also diverted towards projects that specifically involved women.

Subsequently, the proportions of women in orchestras and in the Union have both slowly increased. Women like Jan Ford and Marilyn Stoddart began to change the gender balance among MU officials during the 1980s and 1990s, paving the way for a larger representation of women at National Office level and among regional officials.[20] Concurrently, more women were elected to the EC,[21] and the Union now has an Equalities Committee – which seeks representation from women; lesbian, gay, bisexual, transgender, and queer (plus other sexual and gender orientations); disabled; and minority ethnic musicians – as well as boasting a full-time equalities official.[22]

Questions to interviewees about the absence of women in key Union positions tended to elicit acknowledgement and/or references to seemingly isolated individuals. Tschaikov (*2014*) recalled his experience of male orchestral musicians in the 1950s being opposed to having more women in orchestras on the grounds that they represented competition. The MU's longest-serving employee, Shirley Sandys (*2014*),[23] argued that the Union was a good employer that had never discriminated against female employees, but Regional Official Sheena MacDonald (*2013*) noted that the Union was still operating within music industries that remained 'pretty misogynistic'.

A number of interviewees also emphasised that equalities issues had moved up the Union's agenda in recent years. Part of this has been the recruitment

[20] In 2014, there were five women in organiser/official positions at National Office and two of the six regional organisers were women.

[21] With six women members out of twenty-one in 2013.

[22] This post has been held by Bindu Paul since 2013.

[23] Sandys began work at the MU in 1971 and is still working there in 2015.

of new officials since 2003, with such staff being drawn from a greater range of backgrounds in terms of gender, ethnicity, and previous career (more non-musicians are now employed) than previously. The MU's staff profile is much more diverse than it was in 1993, let alone 1893, and its officials seemingly more reflective of its membership than at any previous point.

A landmark was reached in 2013 when longstanding activist Kathy Dyson was elected as the EC's first female Chair. Reflecting on this, she argued that while it was 'quite shocking' that it had taken so long to happen it was 'really good' that it had (*2014*). For her, another reason for the lack of women previously involved in the Union was not so much direct opposition to their presence as certain cultural aspects. Here she noted that the Union had sometimes had a hard drinking culture that did not always sit well with women. This was something also highlighted by other interviewees, although with some sense that this was now largely in the past (*Lebrecht 2014*).

Dyson's election to a senior position is evidence that progress is being made, albeit from what might be seen as a low base. The brief picture offered here can only provide a glimpse into some of the issues, but it is clear that the modernisation process has refreshed the composition of the Union's workforce and its activists. This can also be seen in contextualising its approach to matters concerning racial discrimination.

Though it took until the 1970s for the Union to address issues surrounding gender inequality, its stance on race relations had a much longer gestation. With the attempts to limit entry of foreign workers leading to some suggestions of racist motives, the Union's position undoubtedly became more progressive in the post-war years. McKay says of the 'ban' on American musicians from 1935 to 1955 that 'it was difficult not to see a colour bar functioning' (2005: 147), but accepts that there were a number of mitigating factors – not least the retaliatory nature of the 'ban'.

What is clear is that in the post-war era, the Union began to develop a more progressive approach towards race relations, with any lingering racism being restricted to individual members. Something of a statement of intent was made at the 1947 Conference where it was unanimously decided that 'it should be the policy of the Union to oppose any attempt at discrimination amongst Union members on the grounds of race, creed, colour or sex' (MU, 2/1/7/1949). This was accompanied by instructions to branches and district councils to enforce such rules, although a further ten years passed before there was concrete evidence of the Union acting on the policy. When it did, it acted both nationally (in its opposition to colour bars in British venues) and internationally (in its opposition to the apartheid regime in South Africa).

Domestically, the Union's policies against racial discrimination were tested by the existence of 'colour bars'[24] in various venues that engaged MU members. John Morton (*2014*) stressed that the context here was that 'race discrimination was neither illegal nor generally objected to' in the UK at the time, thus making the MU's stance all the more laudable. Matters came to a head with the opening of the Scala Ballroom in Wolverhampton in 1958 and its imposition of a colour bar, an event that was to be one of Morton's first major campaigns within the Union.[25]

Morton then became involved, meeting the owner, Michael Wade, and challenging the bar. Wade, a solicitor, reassured the Union that he had and would employ black musicians[26] and suggested that the door policy was not the MU's business. Nevertheless, the Union instructed members not to accept engagements at the venue, a position that was challenged on two fronts: legally by Wade, who sought an injunction against the Union, and practically by some members, who ignored the command, resulting in three bandleaders being expelled (*Melody Maker* 23 August 1958: 11). Crucially, Wade's injunction failed at the Appeal Court and he dropped the case.[27]

Similar issues were to reappear periodically, most notably in a dispute between the Union and Eric Morley of Mecca over a colour bar at the Bradford Lyceum in 1961 (*Guardian*, 15 December 1961: 20).[28] Wolverhampton was significant, though, for establishing the Union's position and setting a legal precedent. Speaking after the failure of the injunction, Harry Francis claimed that the Union's position had been 'morally justified' (*Melody Maker*, 2 August 1958: 16) and Morton later spoke of the Union's stance on race as appealing to 'the innate senses of the members' (*2014*).

Around the same time the black American singer Paul Robeson both appeared on the cover of the *Musician* (see Figure 18) and as a speaker at the Union's 1959 Conference,[29] but it was the Union's stance on apartheid in South Africa that was to be the most visible manifestation of their campaigns against racial discrimination. This had a similar moral justification to its stance on the domestic colour bars, and notably was a policy formulated

24 Policies that prevented the admission of non-whites at some entertainment premises.

25 He was Wolverhampton Branch Secretary at the time.

26 Ray Ellington had already performed there.

27 *Scala Ballroom (Wolverhampton)* v *Ratcliffe and others* 1958.

28 Some of the affected MU members formed the breakaway British Federation of Musicians (Thompson 2008: 34).

29 The Union's association with Robeson was given added potency as he had been previously prevented from leaving the States by the US State Department on account of his political views.

Figure 18 The *Musician* cover on racial discrimination from December 1958 featuring Paul Robeson, who spoke at the Union's conference the following year.

before wider cultural boycotts of the country.[30] It began with a resolution at the 1957 Conference expressing 'concern at the apartheid policy of the South African government' (MU, 2/1/7/1959), while a follow-up instruction from the EC barred Union members from taking engagements there. In the wake of the Sharpeville Massacre in 1960, orchestras – which had previously been excluded from the ban[31] – were also forbidden from touring. However, this did not prevent various attempts to circumnavigate the Union's rules.

An initial complication was that other Unions were slow to operate similar policies and, with the VAF imposing no such restrictions, British singers continued to perform in South Africa – often accompanied by MU members. Famously, Adam Faith and Dusty Springfield abandoned South African tours in 1964 when promises that they would be playing to non-segregated audiences turned out to be untrue.[32] This gave further prominence to the MU's stand and, by 1965, it reported that it had succeeded in maintaining the policy 'despite pressure from interested organisations to abandon it',[33] and told members that 'a very imposing number of important bands, orchestras, beat groups, chamber music ensembles and conductors, acting upon Union instructions, refused offers of engagements' (MU, 1/7/1965).

The ban remained in place but was most famously challenged when Queen accepted a lucrative offer to play Sun City[34] in 1984. As they had blatantly broken the Union's embargo, John Morton asked Richard Watson, a member of the EC and Vice-Chairman of the Central London Branch Committee,[35] to charge them with conduct detrimental to the Union. This offered the possibility of the four band members being expelled from the Union or fined, and after a hearing (and subsequent appeal), it was agreed that each band member's fine of £500 would be paid to the Soweto School for the Deaf, a charity the band supported. Although the amounts paled in comparison with the fees accumulated by the band, it resulted in substantial criticism of their actions and sent a signal that the Union was not willing to stand idly by while the embargo was broken. Until the end of the apartheid regime,[36] the MU was a regular donor to Anti-Apartheid causes and earned praise for its efforts from

30 The Anti-Apartheid Movement formed in 1960 and advocated a cultural boycott from 1962. The United Nations did not request members to curtail cultural, educational, and sporting links with South Africa until 1968.

31 This had been permitted because they could play to mixed audiences.

32 Faith cancelled before leaving; Springfield went but returned early.

33 This alluded to Equity, which allowed its members to perform to segregated audiences provided a percentage of the overall performances were for 'non-European' audiences (Watkins 1965).

34 An entertainment complex in Bophuthatswana, South Africa.

35 By the time the case came to be heard Watson had become Chair of the Committee.

36 Apartheid ended through a series of negotiations, leading to the elections in 1994 that were won by the African National Congress with Nelson Mandela becoming President.

Archbishop Trevor Huddlestone[37] when it finally lifted the embargo towards the end of the regime in 1992 (*Musician*, June 1992: 5).

A more representative and accommodating Union is one facet of the reforms that have taken place over several decades but accelerated in recent years. We close this final chapter by painting a picture of the Union as it stands today.

The modern(ised) MU

A snapshot of the MU around the time of its 120th birthday gives some idea of the constants and the changes in its history, offers some clues to its future direction, and serves as a reminder of at least some of the issues that have dominated it since 1893. We briefly examine these in terms of the Union's membership, finances, internal structure, main external relationships, and current functions. At the end of 2013, the Union had 30,718 members,[38] a level almost the same as it was in 1970. This remains its single biggest achievement: at a time when other trade unions have either merged or shrunk in size, the MU remains the largest musicians' organisation in the UK and, even after the legislation of the Thatcher and Major Governments, continues to represent a significant proportion of the country's working musicians. The demographics of the membership continue to reflect the biases that have been present since the Union's formation: 71 per cent of members are male, and just over a third are in London (MU 2013a).

Though the majority of the Union's income comes from subscriptions, it has two other main sources: collective rights management and investments. The events detailed earlier removed the Union's responsibility for distributing the PPL funds, but it continues to manage a number of other collective arrangements, notably involving the BBC, IBA, and Educational Recording Agency. Some of these monies are reunited with the musicians whose performances generated the income, while others are used to provide services for members. The Union also has a number of long-term stock market investments. Combined, these mean that it remains a solvent and viable proposition with reasonable reserves, though Horace Trubridge recognises the potential threat to collective income in the future, explaining that 'we have to, and we are, contemplating a union that will need to survive on subscription income alone, and that is a very different union' (*2014*).

The structural and organisational changes we outlined above may prove to be a precursor of further changes in the light of a slowly declining membership and possible cuts to income. In 2013, the Union had, in addition to the

37 A veteran anti-apartheid campaigner.

38 Including around 1,300 student members who pay a reduced rate membership and around 1,800 retired members who do not pay.

Secretariat, twenty-seven members of full-time staff at National Office and twenty-five staff in its six regional offices. Staff costs remain the biggest single item of expenditure for the Union, with salaries amounting to £2.95 million (MU 2013a). In addition, it has a number of committees (to which members have to be nominated) and sections, which any member can join. The latter are currently organised by type of work[39] (having previously been arranged by musical genre). The MU's current functions can be loosely grouped under a number of headings: employer relations and negotiations, benefits and service provision, political alliances, and specific campaigns. In broad terms, these are all areas in which the Union has always operated. Only the scale, nature, and specifics of each have changed.

A large proportion of the MU's work still involves negotiating rates of pay for musicians in an ever-increasing number of contexts. It negotiates with employers for eighteen of the UK's twenty-two full-time orchestras.[40] Some are negotiated collectively (the BBC orchestras), while others are negotiated individually between the Union's orchestras' official, Bill Kerr, and the relevant orchestra's management.[41] In addition, freelance rates and conditions are set and agreed with not only the major orchestras and employers but also organisations like the ABO, UK Theatre/SOLT, and BPI, covering a wide range of circumstances in which musicians may be employed. Although these do not, by any stretch, cover all musical employment in the UK, the Union still plays a major part in negotiating the pay of most *professional* musicians.

Benevolence functions that underpinned the Union on its formation are also still evident, alongside a range of services that have been formulated to help musicians deal with particular aspects of the profession. As well as a benevolent fund, the Union provides medical aid for members (via the British Association of Performing Arts Medicine) and a pension scheme specifically aimed at freelance workers. Its other main services are legal advice[42] and insurance,[43] with some of these included in the cost of subscription and others offered at a discounted rate.

Further afield, the Union's external connections show a mixture of political affiliations and alliances based around the labour movement as well working with employers and other interests across the music industries. In the former category, the MU is still affiliated to the Labour Party, TUC, Scottish TUC, and Welsh TUC. It also remains part of both the Performers' Alliance

[39] Live Performance, Music Writers, Orchestras, Recording and Broadcasting, Teachers, and Theatres. Members can join more than one section.

[40] The four self-governing London orchestras set their own rates of pay.

[41] These comprise the various regional orchestras and those associated with opera and ballet companies.

[42] The CAS continues to operate through Paul Russell and Co.

[43] The Union offers public liability, car, instrument, personal accident, and income protection insurance.

and Federation of Entertainment Unions and is a member of the General Federation of Trade Unions. Internationally it remains the largest and most influential member of FIM. Relations with music industries' employers and collective rights organisations are evident in the MU's membership of UK Music and the British Copyright Council and its active support for the work of the BPI's anti-piracy unit, while it is represented on PPL's Performer Board[44] and works with the PRS for Music Foundation on its British Music Abroad scheme.

Meanwhile, the Union has continued to run its own campaigns, often focusing on issues that have been at the heart of its activity for some time. For example, Work Not Play was launched at the 2012 TUC Congress and came in the light of stories of musicians being asked to play for free at the London Olympics (Hewett 2012; Lindvall 2012). It brought the Union almost full-circle back to Williams' issues with semi-professional musicians undercutting those seeking to make a full-time living as a musician, an issue that has reappeared throughout this history.

Work Not Play seems set to raise awareness but not to solve the underlying problem – one that is as old as the music profession itself. It does, however, highlight the Union's importance as the only organisation that will at least reject and publicise the widespread acceptance of undercutting among some employers and musicians. Nevertheless, it returns to the issues implied in the title of this book that have underpinned the story of the MU: what it is to be a musician, and where, when, and by whom this is considered to be work. For the Union itself, this raises the question of how an organisation whose membership is largely freelance, part-time and/or semi-professional can represent all parts of its constituency. These are problems that it has been dealing with for 120 years and that seem unlikely to disappear. Notwithstanding this, it was Williams' vision – to make the Union inclusive and open to *all* paid musical workers and not merely those in permanent or salaried employment – that has been the basis of its longevity. It may not look much like it did it 1893, but many of the MU's concerns remain the same.

[44] In 2015, John Smith and sessions official Pete Thoms occupied these positions. The same year it was announced that John Smith would become chair of PPL in 2016.

Conclusion

In 1990 Simon Frith wrote that 'The Musicians' Union remains scandalously neglected as an object of popular music research' (1990: 257). We hope that the previous pages have at least lessened this scandal. As researchers located within popular music studies, we have endeavoured to illustrate the importance of the Union for *all* those working in music over the past 120 years. The campaigns and negotiations the Union has undertaken illustrate that its interactions with the music profession and the music industries have shaped the destinies of the contending parties. The Union has tales to tell that can enrich the understanding of Britain's musical life.

From its origins in 1893 the Union has sought to improve the working lives of musicians. If initially the concentration was on local employers, then as the profession and its allied industries changed, so the issues – and the Union's modus operandi – became increasingly first national and then international. The AMU–NOUPM merger helped broaden its field of operations but was almost immediately hamstrung by the catastrophe engendered by the arrival of the talkies, which threatened the Union's very survival. That it endured was due to the particular way the British music profession and its attendant industries developed.

By now the reader will have noted that our concentration has been on the period between 1934 and 1970. While we still believe that each of our chapters might easily have filled a book (and one of our headaches has been what to omit), we feel that this period represents the time in which the Union was most powerful and most able to impose its worldview on the music industries and the music profession. From the end of the talkies crisis to the end of the beat group era the Union was, as Lebrecht told us, 'the power in the land' (*2014*).

That it achieved this position was down to some astuteness and a great deal of good fortune. The MU was a beneficiary of a Britain in which the public sector came to play an increasingly important role. The rise of the BBC and publicly funded orchestras put the Union in a powerful position to influence terms of employment across the profession. Meanwhile PPL's initial nervousness about the legal underpinning of its business model ensured that it felt obliged to make *ex gratia* payments to performers whose main representative body was the MU.

In both cases a mixture of business sense and *noblesse oblige* combined fortuitously with the MU's own activities to leave it in a position of power that Williams would surely have envied. All this came together in the 1946 agreement the Union struck with PPL. This was an agreement with the private sector that had profound implications for the public-sector BBC. Here the Union was able to exploit both the Corporation's monopoly position and its sense of obligation to the British music profession to great effect. That it did so via the private-sector PPL is perhaps one of the great ironies of Britain's musical history and something that has been overlooked by previous writers.

The 1960s, which witnessed such a flourishing of UK popular music, also saw the beginnings of the end of the Union's power. In retrospect the first signs of this can be seen in the rise of pirate radio in the mid-1960s. Here was a response to a market problem – the demand for pop music – that both the BBC and the MU had failed to solve. The moves to make the pirates illegal merely delayed the introduction of commercial radio based on recorded music – both of which the MU vehemently opposed. The pirates let the genie out of the bottle and from the introduction of ILR in 1973 the story became one of the MU trying to put it back in. Ultimately a Union that had prospered in the post-war consensus struggled to maintain its influence in a world where traditional thinking and ways of working were increasingly questioned.

As the public sector fell into crisis in the 1970s and was increasingly dismantled and reorganised from the 1980s on, so organisations – such as the MU – with a vested interest in the public provision of services such as broadcasting and culture also struggled. The Morton era can be seen as representing the last vestiges of the MU's post-war power-base. In common with other trade unions the MU was to suffer in the Thatcher years, but also faced specific problems of its own. The 1988 MMC report sounded the death knell of its own golden era and the 1946 agreement. Added to this was a crisis precipitated by its own initial failure to reorganise structurally in ways that reflected the changing composition of both the music profession and the wider music industries. In many ways Derek Kay's ascendancy encapsulated this crisis and forced the Union into radical reform.

Following Kay, the moves to realign the Union with more of the private sector accelerated. The provision of services and products, which formed part of the modernisation process, were accompanied by moves to position the Union firmly as a music industries' organisation more than a workers' one. It remains both. If our focus is on musicians as workers, then in recognising this the Union also recognises the diversity of its membership. In modernising, the MU has sought to maintain its provision to workers but has conducted fewer negotiations on their behalf.

However, it is important to see 'modernisation' in its historic context, and doing this requires some consideration of the themes with which we began. The fate of the MU and its members has been intertwined with the fate of the music profession, with the state of competition within it, with musical tastes, and – perhaps above all – with the state of technology (with which the Union has had a more nuanced relationship than many previous accounts have allowed). All this has, of course, been mediated by musicians' gender.

We hope to have been balanced in our account. We write as trade unionists and music fans interested in the political economy of the music industries. We came neither to praise the Union, nor to bury it. We hope to have given insight into the factors that have shaped its history and in doing so to have provided new ways of thinking about the UK's musical history. The history we have written suggests that it is possible to imagine a future without the MU, but also that this would make the world an even more perilous place for working musicians.

Appendix: list of interviews

Citations to interviews in the text are given in *italics* to distinguish them from references to publications.

Barber, C. 2013. 26 July, Edinburgh. Chris Barber is a jazz musician.

Blain, B. 2012. 18 December, London. Brian Blain is a retired MU official who had responsibility for the Keep Music Live campaign.

Dyson, K. 2014. 16 May, Manchester. Kathy Dyson was the first woman to be elected Chair of the MU's EC.

Evans, M. 2013. 12 September, London. Mike Evans served as the MU's Rock Organiser for seven years.

Hyde, G. 2012. 19 December, London. Gary Hyde was a long-serving branch secretary and union official.

Kerr, W. 2014. 16 May, Manchester. Bill Kerr is the MU's National Organiser – Orchestras.

Knight, A. 2013. 23 April, Eastbourne. Andy Knight is a former AGS of the MU.

Lebrecht, N. 2014. 9 January, London. Norman Lebrecht is a commentator on classical music.

Lucas, T. 2013. 16 May, Manchester. Tony Lucas was formerly the MU's North-West District Organiser.

MacDonald, S. 2013. 9 May, Glasgow. Sheena MacDonald is the MU's Regional Official for Scotland and Northern Ireland.

Melton, M. 2012. 19 December, London. Mark Melton is a former MU music industry adviser.

Morton, J. 2014. 20 January, Dartford. John Morton was GS of the MU between 1970 and 1990.

Patrick, J. 2014. 19 February, Birmingham. John Patrick served forty-one years on the MU's EC, thirty-two as its Chair.

Prince, T. 2012. 20 December, Maidenhead. Tony Prince is a DJ and entrepreneur.

Reed, J. 2013. 11 April, Wokingham. John Reed formerly worked for various major record companies after working as a musician.

Sandys, S. 2014. 21 May, London. Shirley Sandys has worked in a number of roles for the MU since 1971.

Scard, D. 2013. 23 April, Eastbourne. Dennis Scard served as MU GS between 1990 and 2000.

Smith, D. 2013. 24 April, London. Don Smith was the MU's Session Organiser.

Smith, J. 2014. 20 May, London. John Smith is the current GS of the MU.

Stoddart, J. 2015. 25 September, Dartford. Jack Stoddart is a former AGS of the MU.

Sweeney, W. 2013. 11 April, Glasgow. Bill Sweeney is a composer and MU activist. He is a former EC member.

Trubridge, H. 2014. 21 May, London. Horace Trubridge is currently AGS of the MU.

Tschaikov, B. 2014. 14 April, Norwich. Nick Tschaikov is a retired musician and MU activist.

Watson, R. 2012. 19 December, London. Richard Watson is a long-serving MU activist and EC member.

Notes

Dennis Scard and Andy Knight were interviewed simultaneously.
All interviews were conducted by the authors.

References

Alberge, D. 1999. 'Orchestras losing the score on film themes', *The Times*, 26 July, 4.

Allison, R. 2004. 'Music union strikes accord on new act'. *Guardian*, 6 April, 5.

Anderson, T. 2004. 'Buried under the fecundity of his own creations: Reconsidering the recording bans of the American Federation of Musicians, 1942–1944 and 1948', *American Music*, 22:2, 231–69.

Annan Committee. 1977. *Report on the Future of Broadcasting*. London: HMSO.

Anon. 1892. 'The Musical Graduates' Union', *Musical Times*, 33:597, 654–5.

Anon. 2002. 'Campaign moves up a gear', *Musician*, September, 26–7.

Anon. 2007. 'MU confirms position on the impact of the Licensing Act', *Musician*, Summer, 4.

Arthur, B. 1997. 'Ban the talkies! Sound film and the Musicians' Union of Australia 1927–1932', *Context: Journal of Music Research*, 13, winter, 47–56.

Arthur, B. 2003. 'Industrial relations', in J. Whiteoak and A. Scott-Maxwell (eds), *Currency Companion to Music and Dance in Australia*. Strawberry Hills: Currency Press, p. 348.

Ashton, R. 2001a. 'Kay organises rebel group as pressure from MU intensifies', *Music Week*, 28 April, 3.

Ashton, R. 2001b. 'MU steps up battle to remove Kay', *Music Week*, 14 July, 1.

Ashton, R. 2001c. 'Musicians' Union vs. Kay: Out-of-court deal settles row', *Music Week*, 20 October, 3.

Ashton, R. 2004. 'Reform strengthens MU's industry status', *Music Week*, 30 October, 4.

Attali, J. 1985. *Noise: The Political Economy of Music*. Minneapolis: University of Minnesota Press.

Baade, C. 2012. *Victory through Harmony: The BBC and Popular Music in World War II*. New York: Oxford University Press.

Baade, C., Fast, S., and Grenier, L. 2014. 'Musicians as workers: Sites of struggle and resistance', *MusiCultures*, 41:1, 1–9.

Bacon, N. and Storey, J. 1996. *Individualism, Collectivism and the Changing Role of Trade Unions*. London: Routledge.

Barfe, L. 2004. *Where Have All the Good Times Gone?* London: Atlantic.

Batstone, E. 1988. 'The frontier of control', in D. Gallie (ed.), *Employment in Britain*. Oxford: Blackwell, pp. 218–47.

Batten, W. 1929. 'Ministers of Labour and alien musicians', *Musicians' Journal*, July, 31.

Batten, W. 1930. 'The alien menace', *Musicians' Journal*, January, 30.

Bayton, M. 1998. *Frock Rock: Women Performing Popular Music*. Oxford: Oxford University Press.

BBC. 1969. *Broadcasting in the Seventies*. London: BBC.

BBC News. 1999. 'MSPs launch Scottish Opera inquiry', http://news.bbc.co.uk/1/hi/scotland/503468.stm.

Beckett, F. 1995. *Enemy Within: The Rise and Fall of the British Communist Party*. London: Merlin Press.

Blain, B. 1967. 'Pirate radio', *Musician*, January 1967, 14–15.

Blain, B. 2003. 'A well fought campaign', *Musician*, June 2003, 19.

Bohm. C. and Mitchell, A. 1937. 'Art Workers' Union', *Musicians' Union Monthly Report*, May, 7–8.

Born, G. 2004. *Uncertain Vision: Birt, Dyke and the Reinvention of the BBC*. London: Secker and Warburg.

Brewster, B. and Broughton, F. 2012. *The Record Players*. London: Ebury.

Briggs, A. 1979. *The History of Broadcasting in the United Kingdom*, Vol. IV: *Sound and Vision*. Oxford: Oxford University Press.

Briggs, A. 1995. *The History of Broadcasting in the United Kingdom*, Vol. V: *Competition*. Oxford: Oxford University Press.

British Music Rights. 2008. *Submission to Ofcom's Second Public Services Broadcasting Review*. London: British Music Rights.

Bruce, K. 1994. 'Fatal review for national orchestra', *Glasgow Herald*, 7 January, 3.

Burnham, A. 2008. 'A moral case for extending copyright', *Financial Times*, 15 December, 8.

Chapman, R. 1992. *Selling the Sixties*. London: Routledge.

Clegg, H. 1980. *The Changing System of Industrial Relations in Great Britain*. Oxford: Blackwell.

Clegg, H., Fox, A., and Thompson, A. 1964. *A History of British Trade Unions 1889–1910*. Oxford: Clarendon Press.

Cloonan, M. 2007. *Popular Music and the State*. Aldershot: Ashgate.

Cloonan, M. 2012. 'Trying to stop George from having a night out', www.muhistory.com/from-the-archive-3-trying-to-stop-george-from-having-a-night-out/.

Cloonan, M. 2013. 'Hang the DJ! The Musicians' Union and the early days of Radio 1', www.muhistory.com/hang-the-dj-the-musicians-union-and-the-early-days-of-radio-1/.

Cloonan, M. and Brennan, M. 2013. 'Alien invasion: The British Musicians' Union and foreign musicians', *Popular Music*, 32:2, 279–97.

Coase, R. H. 1950. *British Broadcasting: A Study in Monopoly*. Cambridge, MA: Harvard University Press.

Cohen, S. 1991. *Rock Culture in Liverpool*. Oxford: Oxford University Press.

Cohn, N. 2004. *Awopbop-Aloopbop Alopbam-Boom: Pop from the Beginning*. London: Pimlico.

Cole, G. and Postgate, R. 1948. *The Common People 1746–1946*. London: Methuen.

Copyright Committee. 1952. *Report*. London: Board of Trade.

Cottrell, S. 2004. *Professional Music-Making in London*. Aldershot: Ashgate.

Countryman, V. 1948. 'The Organized Musicians', *University of Chicago Law Review*, 16:1, 56–85.

Croft, A. (ed.). 1998. *A Weapon in the Struggle*. London: Pluto.

Culture, Media and Sport Committee. 2009. *The Licensing Act, Sixth Report of Session 2008–09*. London: House of Commons.

Curran, C. 1970. *Music and the BBC*. London: BBC.

Dambman, F. 1929. 'Musicians and the Trades Union Congress', *Musicians' Journal*, October, 14–15.

Dambman, F. 1939. 'Outbreak of war', *Musicians' Union Report*, October, 1.

David, M. 2010. *Peer to Peer and the Music Industry: The Criminalization of Sharing*. London: Sage.

David-Guillou, A. 2009. 'Early musicians' unions in Britain, France, and the United States: On the possibilities and impossibilities of transnational militant transfers in an international industry', *Labour History Review*, 74:3, 288–304.

Davies, G. 2012. *The Show Must Go On: On Tour with the LSO in 1912 and 2012*. London: Elliott and Thompson.

Davison, A. 2012. 'Workers' rights and performers' rights: Cinema music and musicians prior to synchronised sound', in J. Brown, and A. Davison (eds), *The Sound of the Silents in Britain*. New York: Oxford University Press, pp. 243–62.

Davison, L. 1988. 'Musicians' Union prices members out of work', *Sunday Times*, 20 March, 17.

Dawber, J. 1882. 'The Society of Professional Musicians', *Musical Times*, 23:474, 455.

Dawson Scott, R. 1995. 'Bands on the run: Scottish musicians are fighting for survival against each other', *Guardian*, 5 December, 12.

Dearlove, J. 1937. 'Wages, the cost of living and rearmament', *Musicians' Union Monthly Report*, 4.

Department of Business Innovation and Skills [DBIS]. 2013. *Trade Union Membership 2012*. London: DBIS.

Department of Culture, Media and Sport [DCMS]. 2007. *Government's Response to the Live Music Forum's Report*. London: DCMS.

Department of Culture, Media and Sport [DCMS]. 2009a. *Impact Assessment of Proposal* [to] *Exempt Small Live Music Events from the Licensing Act 2003*. London: DCMS.

Department of Culture, Media and Sport [DCMS]. 2009b. *Proposal to Exempt Live Music Events from the Licensing Act 2003*. London: DCMS.

Department of Culture, Media and Sport [DCMS]. 2011. *Regulated Entertainment: A Consultation to Examine the Deregulation of Schedule One of the Licensing Act 2003*. London: DCMS.

DeVeaux, S. 1988. 'Bebop and the recording industry: The 1942 AFM recording ban reconsidered', *Journal of the American Musicological Society*, 41:1, 126–65.

DHA Communications. 2012. *The Working Musician*. London: Musicians' Union.

Doctor, J. 1999. *The BBC and Ultra-Modern Music, 1922–1936: Shaping a Nation's Tastes*. Cambridge: Cambridge University Press.

Dolata, U. 2011.*The Music Industry and the Internet: A Decade of Disruptive and Uncontrolled Sectoral Change*. Stuttgart: University of Stuttgart.

Dreyfus, K. 2009. 'The foreigner, the Musicians' Union, and the State in 1920s Australia: A nexus of conflict', *Music and Politics*, 3:1, 1–17.

Ehrlich, C. 1985. *The Music Profession in Britain since the Eighteenth Century*. Oxford: Clarendon Press.

Ehrlich, C. 1989. *Harmonious Alliance*. London: Oxford University Press.

Evans, J. 1966. *The Conways: A History of Three Generations*. London: Museum Press.

Evans, R. and Jones, T. 1989. 'Broadcasting unions cleared of restrictive working practices', *The Times*, 14 April, 5.

Farmer, H. 1931. 'The Death of E. S. Teale', *Musicians' Journal*, April, 3.

Fiddick, P. 1969. 'BBC reforms by the book', *Guardian*, 17 October, 1.

Finnegan, R. 1989. *The Hidden Musicians: Music Making in an English Town* Cambridge: Cambridge University Press.

Flanders, A. 1968. *Trade Unions*. London: Hutchinson University Library.

Flick, V. 2008. *Guitarman*. Albany: Bear Manor Media.

Forster, J. 1948. *Report for Right Honourable Minister of Labour and National Service*. London: Ministry of Labour and National Service (WAC, R8/88/3).

Frame, P. 2007. *The Restless Generation*. London: Rogan House.

Francis, H. 1949. '100% organisation', *Musicians' Union Report*, May, 6.

Frith, S. 1978. *The Sociology of Rock*. London: Constable.

Frith, S. 1990. Review, *Popular Music*, 9:2, 255–7.

Fudger, M. 1975. 'The quota system and black shiny handbags', *Spare Rib*, June, 44–7.

Godbolt, J. 1976. *All This and 10%*. London: Robert Hale.

Godbolt, J. 1984. *A History of Jazz in Britain 1919–50*. London: Quartet.

Gorman, R. 1983. 'The recording musician and union power: A case study of the American Federation of Musicians', *Southwestern Law Journal*, 37, 697–784.

Gosling, K. 1980a. 'Five orchestras and 1,500 jobs to go in BBC's £130m cuts', *The Times*, 29 February, 1.

Gosling, K. 1980b. 'Four parties in talks found Ulster Orchestra', *The Times*, 28 May, 2.

Gowers, A. 2006. *Review of Intellectual Property*. London: The Stationery Office.

Green, G. 1937. 'Spanish sketch', *Musicians' Union Monthly Report*, October, 3.

Gronow, P. and Saunio, I. 1998. *An International History of the Recording Industry*. London: Cassell.

Hall, S. 2003. 'Tenth defeat for "draconian" licensing bill', *Guardian*, 20 June, 12.

Hambleton, L. 1974. 'Discrimination in orchestras: Women organise in the Musicians' Union', *Spare Rib*, June, 44–6.

Hanlon, R. and Waite, M. 1998. 'Notes from the left: Communism and British classical music', in A. Croft (ed.), *A Weapon in the Struggle*, London: Pluto, pp. 68–88.

Heery, E. 2005. 'Sources of change in trade unions', *Work, Employment and Society*, 19:1, 91–106.

Heery, E., Conley, H., Delbridge, R., and Stewart, P. 2004. 'Beyond the enterprise: Trade union representation of freelances in the UK', *Human Resource Management Journal*, 14:2, 20–35.

Hesmondhalgh, D. and Baker, S. 2010. '"A very complicated version of freedom": Conditions and experiences of creative labour in three cultural industries', *Poetics*, 38:1, 4–20.

Hesmondhalgh, D. and Baker, S. 2011a. *Creative Labour: Media Work in Three Cultural Industries*. New York: Routledge.

Hesmondhalgh, D. and Baker, S. 2011b. 'Toward a political economy of labour in the media industries', in J. Wasko, G. Murdock, and H. Sousa (eds), *The Handbook of Political Economy of Communications*. London: Wiley, pp. 381–400.

Hesmondhalgh, D. and Percival, N. 2014. 'Unpaid work in the UK television and film industries: Resistance and changing attitudes', *European Journal of Communication*, 29:2, 188–203.

Hewett, I. 2012. 'Is the London 2012 Olympics exploiting musicians?', *Daily Telegraph*, 10 July, www.telegraph.co.uk/culture/music/9382467/Is-the-London-2012-Olympics-exploiting-musicians.html.

Hewison, R. 1995. *Culture and Consensus*. London: Methuen.

Hobsbawm, E. 1949. 'General labour unions in Britain, 1889–1914', *Economic History Review*, 1:2, 123–42.

Hobsbawn, E. 1968. *Industry and Empire*. London: Penguin.

Home Office. 2000. *Time for Reform: Proposals for Modernisation of Our Licensing Laws*. London: The Stationery Office.

Hubbard, P. 1985. 'Synchronised sound and movie-house musicians 1926–9', *American Music*, 3, 429–41.

Huckerby, K. 1980. 'Promenade concerts may be sacrificed, BBC says', *The Times*, 18 June, 1.

Hyde, G, 2001. 'Fifty years of a branch newsletter', *Musician*, March 2001, 21.

Hyde, G. 2013. 'A view from the branches', www.muhistory.com/a-view-from-the-branches.

Jempson, M. 1993. *Always in Tune with the Times: The Musicians' Union 1893–1993*. London: Musicians' Union.

Johns, A. 2009. 'Piracy as a business force', *Culture Machine*, 10, 44–63.

Johns, A. 2011. *Death of a Pirate: British Radio and the Making of the Information Age*. New York: W. W. Norton.

Jones, M. 2012. *The Music Industries*. Basingstoke: Palgrave Macmillan.

Kennedy, M. 1960. *The Hallé Tradition*. Manchester: Manchester University Press.

Kennedy, M. 2002. 'MPs stifle their song in support of music', *Guardian*, 25 July 2002, 11.

Kenyon, N. 1981. *The BBC Symphony Orchestra 1930–1980*. London: BBC.

King-Smith, B. 1995. *Crescendo! 75 Years of the City of Birmingham Symphony Orchestra*. London: Methuen.

Kraft, J. 1996. *From Stage to Studio: Musicians and the Sound Revolution 1890–1950*. London: Johns Hopkins University Press.

Lebrecht, N. 2001. 'Time to take stock', *Daily Telegraph*, 31 January, www.telegraph.co.uk/culture/4721345/Time-to-take-stock.html.

Lee, D. 1997. 'In the mix', *Guardian*, 24 October, 20.

Leiter, R. 1953. *The Musicians and Petrillo*. New York: Bookman.

Leonard, M. 2007. *Gender in the Music Industry*. Aldershot: Ashgate.

Lindvall, H. 2012. 'Play at the Olympics! Just don't expect to be paid much', *Guardian*, 19 July, www.theguardian.com/music/musicblog/2012/jul/19/olympics-london-2012-musicians-pay.

Live Music Forum [LMF]. 2007. *Findings and Recommendations*. London: Live Music Forum.

Lockwood, D. 1958. *The Blackcoated Worker*. London: Unwin.

Loft, A. 1950. 'Musicians' Guild and Union: A Consideration of the Evolution of Protective Organisations among Musicians'. Unpublished Ph.D. thesis. New York: Columbia University.

London Orchestral Association [LOA]. 1962. *London Orchestral Association 1893–1962*. London: LOA.

Lunde, A. 1948. 'The American Federation of Musicians and the recording ban', *Public Opinion Quarterly*, 12:1, 45–56.

McCarthy, W. E. J. 1964. *The Closed Shop in Britain*. London: Basil Blackwell.

McDevitt, C. 1997. *Skiffle: The Definitive Inside Story*. London: Robson Books.

MacDonald, H. 2010. *BBC Scottish Symphony Orchestra: Celebrating 75 Years of Music Making*. Glasgow: BBCSSO. Available online at www.bbc.co.uk/orchestras/pdf/bbcsso_75brochure.pdf.

McFarlane, G. 1980. *Copyright: Performing Right*. Eastbourne: John Offord.

McIlroy, J. 2009. 'A brief history of British trade unions and neoliberalism: From the earliest days to the birth of New Labour', in G. Daniels and J. McIlroy (eds), *Trade Unions in a Neoliberal World*. London: Routledge, pp. 21–62.

McKay, G. 2005. *Circular Breathing*. London: Duke University Press.

Mackerness, E. 1964. *A Social History of English Music*. London: Routledge.

Martin, S. 1996. 'Exploding a myth', *Musician*, March, 16–17.

Martinez-Inigo, D., Crego, A., Garcia-Dauder, S., and Dominguez-Bilbao, R. 2012. 'Organisational culture as a source of change in trade unions'. *Employee Relations*, 34:4, 394–410.

Martland, P. 1997. *Since Records Began: EMI – The First 100 Years*. London: Amadeus Press.

Martland, P. 2013. *Recording History: The British Record Industry 1888–1931*. Lanham, MD: Scarecrow.

Melly, G. 1970. *Revolt into Style*. London: Penguin.

Mermey, M. 1929. 'The vanishing fiddler', *North American Review*, 227, 301–7.

Metcalf, D. 2005. *British Unions: Resurgence or Perdition?* London: The Work Foundation.

Michelson, G. 1997. 'Out of tune? Union amalgamations and the Musicians' Union of Australia', *Journal of Industrial Relations*, 39:3, 303–31.

Miller, M. 1994. 'As more and more orchestras and opera companies from outside the EC visit Britain, what are the implications for British musicians?', *Scotsman*, 24 October, 7.

Monopolies and Mergers Commission [MMC]. 1988. *Collective Licensing: A Report on Certain Practices in the Collective License of Public Performances and Broadcasting Rights in Sound Recordings*. London: Monopolies and Mergers Commission.

Moore, J. 2006. 'The sensitive matter of work permits', www.mgthomas.co.uk/dancebands/American%20Visitors/Pages/Work%20Permits.htm.

Morgan, K. 1998. 'King Street Blues: Jazz and the left in Britain in the 1930s–1940s', in A. Croft (ed.), *A Weapon in the Struggle*, London: Pluto, pp. 123–41.

Morris, M. 1969. 'Recording companies may support Musicians' Union', *Guardian*,15 July, 18.

Morris, S. and Price, K. 1986. 'Calling the tune', *Spare Rib*, April, 40–1.

Morrison, R. 1999. 'Live and lively at the new Radio 3', *The Times*, 3 February, 29.

Morrison, R. 2004. *Orchestra. The LSO: A Century of Triumph and Turbulence*. London: Faber and Faber.

Morton, J. 2011. Interview with Dave Laing. Sound recording, British Library.

Moynihan, M. 1960. 'Musicians say "It's pop or poverty"', *The Times*, 20 November, 11.

Mulder, C. 2009. *Unions and Class Transformation: The Case of the Broadway Musicians*. New York: Routledge.

Musicians' Union [MU]. 1962. *The Rules of the Musicians' Union*. London: MU.

Musicians' Union [MU]. 2007. *Licensing Act 2003: Statement of Policy*. London: MU.

Musicians' Union [MU]. 2013a. *Membership Statistics 1 January to 31 August 2013*. London: MU.

Musicians' Union [MU]. 2013b. *Annual Return*, https://www.gov.uk/government/publications/musicians-union-annual-returns.

Musicians' Union [MU]. 2015. *36th Delegate Conference: Executive Committee's Report and Agenda*. London: MU.

Negus, K. 1992. *Producing Pop*. London: Edward Arnold.

Newton Brooke, B. 1935. 'Confidence', *MU Report*, January, 7.

Nott, J. 2002. *Music for the People: Popular Music and Dance in Interwar Britain*. Oxford: Oxford University Press.

O'Brien, L. 1995. *She Bop*. London: Penguin.

Oliver, Paul (ed.). 1990. *Black Music in Britain*. Buckingham: Open University Press.

Osborne, R. 2014. 'I am a one in ten'. Unpublished paper presented at 'Studying music: An international conference in honour of Simon Frith', University of Edinburgh.

Pannell Kerr Forster. 1991. *Musicians' Union: Strategy and Organisation and Methods Study*. London: PKF.

Parsonage, C. 2005. *The Evolution of Jazz in Britain 1880–1935*. Aldershot: Ashgate.

Peacock, A. and Weir, R. 1975. *The Composer in the Market Place*. London: Faber.

Pelling, H. 1992. *A History of British Trade Unionism*. London: Penguin.

Perkins, A. 2003. 'Howells made to face the music', *Guardian*, 4 March, 12.

Peterson, R. 1990. 'Why 1955?', *Popular Music*, 9:1, 97–105.

Press Association. 1990. 'Job fears on BBC savings drive', 26 January.

Preston, K. 1992. *Music for Hire: A Study of Professional Musicians in Washington (1877–1900)*. Stuyvesant, NY: Pendragon Press.

Prout, E. 1893. 'The Amalgamated Musicians Union', *Monthly Musical Record*, 23:271, 145–7.

Performing Right Tribunal [PRT]. 1986. *AIRC* v *PPL*, 16 January. London: HMSO.

Purser, J. 1987. *Is the Red Light On? The Story of the BBC Scottish Symphony Orchestra*. Glasgow: BBC Scotland.

Rastall, R. 2009. 'The origin of the town waits, and the myth of the watchman-turned-musician', www.townwaits.org.uk/essays/waitsorigin.pdf.

Redcliffe-Maud, J. 1976. *Support for the Arts in England and Wales*. London: Calouste Gulbenkian Foundation.

Reddington, H. 2007. *The Lost Women of Rock: Female Musicians of the Punk Era*. Aldershot: Ashgate.

Reid, A. 2004. *United We Stand: A History of Britain's Trade Unions*. London: Allen Lane.

Roberts, M. 2010. 'A working class hero is something to be', *Popular Music*, 29:1, 1–16.

Roberts, M. 2014. *Tell Tchaikovsky the News: Rock 'n' Roll, the Labor Question, and the Musicians' Union, 1942–1968*. Durham, NC: Duke University Press.

Robertshaw, N. 1980. 'AIRC views over needletime', *Billboard*, 1 March, 50.

Russell, D. 1997. *Popular Music in England 1840–1940: A Social History*. Manchester: Manchester University Press.

Russell, T. 1945. *Philharmonic Decade*. London: Hutchinson.

Russell, T. 1952. *Philharmonic Project*. London: Hutchinson.

Russell, T. 1953. *Philharmonic*. London: Penguin.

Scard, D. 1991. 'The Union and the record industry', *Musician*, June, 8–9.

Scard, D. 1998. 'Organise or fossilise', *Musician*, November, 5.

Scharff, C. 2015. *Equality and Diversity in the Classical Music Profession*. London: King's College.

Schlesinger, P. 1980. 'The massacre of the musicians', *New Statesman*, 20 June, 941.

Secretary of State for Culture, Media and Sport. 2009. *Government Response to House of Commons Culture, Media and Sport Committee on the Licensing Act 2003 Session 2008–09*. London: HM Government.

Seltzer, G. 1989. *Music Matters: The Performer and the American Federation of Musicians*. Metuchen, NJ: Scarecrow Press.

Service, T. 2010. 'The band plays on – part-time – but Scottish Opera is sinking', *Guardian*, 17 September, www.theguardian.com/music/tomserviceblog/2010/sep/17/scottish-opera-orchestra.

Silver, J. 2013. *Digital Medieval*. London: Xstorical.

Smirke, R. 2012. 'British pubs to rock even harder: Why the UK Live Music Act Mattters', *Billboard Online*, 19 April, www.billboard.com/biz/articles/news/touring/1097809/british-pubs-to-rock-even-harder-why-the-uk-live-music-act-matters.

Smith, E. 2011. 'Are the kids united? The Communist Party of Great Britain, Rock Against Racism and the politics of youth culture', *Journal for the Study of Radicalisation*, 5:2, 85–117.

Smith, J. 2003a. 'Is the glass half empty or half full?', *Musician*, September 2003, 11.

Smith, J. 2003b. 'One year on', *Musician*, winter 2003–04, 5.

Southgate, T. 1893. 'Questionable orchestral organisations', *Musical News*, 4 November, 395.

Stahl, M. 2013. *Unfree Masters: Popular Music and the Politics of Work*. Durham, NC: Duke University Press.

Steward, S. and Garratt, S. 1984. *Signed, Sealed and Delivered: True Stories of Women in Pop*. London: Pluto Press.

Stoller, T. 2010a. *Sounds of Your Life*. London: John Libbey.

Stoller, T. 2010b. 'No such thing as society: Independent Local Radio in the eighties', www.nosuch-research.co.uk/pdfs/PaperILR.pdf.

Street, J. 1986. *Rebel Rock*. Oxford: Blackwell.

Sutherland, A. 1988. 'Screen and print: Time for studio orchestras to face the music', *Sunday Times*, 28 February.

Sweeting, A. 2001. 'Playing with fire: The Musicians' Union is accused of failing its members?', 6 February, www.guardian.co.uk/culture/2001/feb/06/artsfeatures2.

Taylor, S. 2006. *Musicians' Union: State of the Nation 2006*. London: Inputech.

Taylor, S. 2008. *Musicians' Union: State of the Nation 2008*. London: Inputech.

Teale, E. S. 1929a. 'The story of the Amalgamated Musicians' Union', *Musicians' Journal*, 1, 8–9.

Teale, E. S. 1929b. 'The story of the Amalgamated Musicians' Union' (continued), *Musicians' Journal*, 3, 27–8.

Thomson, R. 1989. 'Dance bands and dance halls in Greenock, 1945–55', *Popular Music*, 8:2, 143–55.

Thompson, E. P. 1963. *The Making of the English Working Class*. London: Victor Gollancz.

Thompson, G. 2008. *Please Please Me: Sixties British Pop Inside Out*. Oxford: Oxford University Press.

Thornton, S. 1990. 'Strategies for reconstructing the popular past', *Popular Music*, 9:1, 87–95.

Thornton, S. 1995. *Club Cultures*. Cambridge: Polity.

Trade Union Certification Officer. 2002. *Decision: Mr B. Johnson and Mr B. Daly vs. Musicians' Union*. London: Trade Union Certification Officer.

Tschaikov, B. 2009. *The Music Goes Round and Around*. London: Fastprint.

Tumelty, M. 1992. 'Musicians unanimously reject proposed merger of orchestras', *Glasgow Herald*, 18 December, 18.

Tumelty, M. 1996. 'Merger and Government funds are way to resolve the tawdry and dissonant saga of Scottish orchestras', *Glasgow Herald*, 18 July, 20.

Waksman, S. 2001. *Instruments of Desire: The Electric Guitar and the Shaping of Musical Experience*. Cambridge, MA: Harvard University Press.

Walford, R. G. 1971. *Radio's Bridle: A Plain Man's Guide to Needletime*. London: BBC (WAC, R101/191/1).

Walker, I. 1964. 'BBC seeking 94 hours' more music a week', *Sunday Telegraph*, 31 May, 7.

Ward, P. 2011. *Live Music in Small Venues*. London: House of Commons Library.

Watkins, R. 1965. 'British Equity and Foreign Office probe act tours of apartheid South Africa', *Variety*, 20 January, 1.

Wearn, B. 2001. 'Two in a bar: The campaign begins', *Musician*, September 2001, 20–1.

Webb, S. and Webb, B. 1920. *The History of Trade Unionism*. New York: Longmans, Green.

Wikström, P. 2013. *The Music Industry*. Cambridge: Polity.

Williamson, J. 2013. 'An everlasting love affair', www.muhistory.com/an-everlasting-love-affair/.

Williamson, J. 2014. 'Co-operation and conflict: The British Musicians' Union, musical labour and copyright', *Musicultures*, 41:1, 73–92.

Williamson, J. 2015. 'For the benefit of all musicians? The Musicians' Union and performers' rights in the UK', in A. Rahmatian (ed.), *Concepts of Music and Copyright*. London: Edward Elgar, 167–94.

Williamson, J. and Cloonan, M. 2007. 'Rethinking the music industry', *Popular Music*, 26:2, 305–22.

Williamson, J. and Cloonan, M. 2013. 'Contextualising the contemporary recording industry', in L. Marshall (ed.), *The International Recording Industries*. London: Routledge, pp. 11–29.

Williamson, J., Cloonan, M., and Frith, S. 2011. 'Having an impact? Academics, the music industries and the problem of knowledge', *International Journal of Cultural Policy*, 17:5, 459–74.

Wilson, P. 2001. 'Alderman musicians', RootsWeb.com, http://archiver.rootsweb.ancestry.com/th/read/LONDON-COMPANYS/2001–02/0981209118.

Winder, R. 2004. *Bloody Foreigners: The Story of Immigration to Britain*. London: Abacus.

Witts, R. 1998. *Artist Unknown*. London: Little, Brown.

Witts, R. 2012. 'Needle time: The BBC, the Musicians' Union, popular music, and the reform of radio in the 1960s', *Popular Music History*, 7:3, 241–62.

Woodfill, W. 1953. *Musicians in English Society*. Princeton: Princeton University Press.

Woollacott, M. 1969. 'Stay of execution for BBC orchestras', *Guardian*, 9 June, 16.

World Intellectual Property Organization [WIPO]. 1961. *International Convention for the Protection of Performers, Producers of Phonograms and Broadcasting Organizations: Done at Rome on October 26, 1961*, (www.wipo.int/treaties/en/text.jsp?file_id=289757#P117_10846).

Worshipful Company of Musicians. 1915. *Handbook*. London: Worshipful Company of Musicians.

Wrigley, C. 2002. *British Trade Unions since 1933*. Cambridge: Cambridge University Press.

Wroe, M. 1995. 'Riches drummed up for musicians', *Observer*, 17 December, 4.

Index